Global Ecology

D1470426

Global Ecology

A New Arena of Political Conflict

Edited by

WOLFGANG SACHS

ZED BOOKS
London & New Jersey

FERNWOOD PUBLISHING
Halifax, Nova Scotia

Global Ecology is published in Canada by Fernwood Publications Ltd,
P O Box 9409, Station A, Halifax, Nova Scotia, Canada B3K 5S3,
and in the rest of the world by Zed Books Ltd, 7 Cynthia Street,
London N1 9JF, UK, and 165 First Avenue, Atlantic Highlands,
New Jersey 07716, USA in 1993.

Second impression, 1995.

Cover designed by Andrew Corbett.
Typeset by EMS Photosetters, Rochford, Essex.
Printed and bound in the United Kingdom
by Biddles Ltd, Guildford and King's Lynn.

A catalogue record for this book is
available from the British Library.

US CIP data is available from the Library of Congress.

ISBN 1 85649 163 3 Cased
ISBN 1 85649 164 1 Limp

In Canada
ISBN 1 895686 29 6 Limp

Canadian Cataloguing-in-Publication Data

Global Ecology
        Includes bibliographical references and index.
        ISBN 1-895686-29-6
    1. Economic Development – Environmental aspects.
    2. Environmental policy.   3, Sustainable development.
    ed. Sachs, Wolfgang.
    HC79.E5G56 1993   333.7   C93–098667–9

Contents

Contributors

Hans Achterhuis is Professor of Eco-philosophy at the University of Twente, Netherlands. For a long time he has explored the conceptual foundations of the welfare and full employment state. In his latest book, *Het Rijk va de Schaarste* (The Reign of Scarcity), Baarn: Ambo, 1988, he exposed the idea of scarcity as the founding myth of modern social thought.

Anil Agarwal directs the Centre for Science and Environment in New Delhi. Under his leadership, the Centre broke new ground in the early eighties, when it published *The State of India's Environment*, a comprehensive report about the impact of Indian society on nature. In this context, he developed the notion of the Gross Nature Product to be opposed to the conventional Gross National Product. In 1991, he (and S. Narain) denounced a Western bias in the environmentalist wisdom on the greenhouse effect in their *Global Warming in an Unequal World: A Case of Environmental Colonialism*, New Delhi: CSE, 1991. He rose to be a prominent spokesperson for Third World environmentalism, as his Centre put forth the *Statement on Global Environmental Democracy*, New Delhi: CSE, 1992, providing a counter platform to UNCED.

Frédérique Apffel Marglin discovered anthropology while studying temple dance in Orissa, India. This experience is reflected in her *Wives of the God-King: The Rituals of the Devadasis of Puri*, New Delhi: Oxford University Press, 1985. More recently, she has formulated a critique of development as a particular system of knowledge and coedited with S. Marglin *Dominating Knowledge: Development, Culture and Resistance*, Oxford: Clarendon Press, 1990. She is presently Professor of Anthropology at Smith College in Massachusetts, USA.

Tariq Banuri is Executive Director of the Sustainable Development Policy Institute in Islamabad, Pakistan. He has been teaching economics at the University of Massachusetts at Amherst and at Harvard University. In 1989 he joined the World Institute for Development Economics Research (WIDER) in Helsinki as a Research Fellow. He is the editor of *Economic Liberalization: No Panacea – The Experiences of Latin America and Asia*, Oxford: Clarendon Press, 1990, and (with F. Apffel Marglin) of *Who Will Save the Forests?*, London: Zed Books, 1993.

Guy Beney has a doctorate in biology. Travelling across the borders of biology, philosophy and sociology, he is concerned with examining the moral and humanistic aspects of the life-sciences. As a former general secretary of the Groupe de Reflexion Inter- et Transdisciplinaire of the French Ministry of Research and Technology and editor of *de Lettre Science–Culture du GRIT*, he has contributed to many French journals, including *Futuribles*, *Terminal*, *Revue du MAUSS*, or *La Quinzaine Littéraire*. He lives in Paris.

Paul Ekins has inspired a number of initiatives that aim at a fundamental reform of economics, notably 'The Other Economic Summit' (TOES) or the Living Economy Network, and was Research Director of the Right Livelihood Award until the end of 1992. He has edited *The Living Economy: A New Economics in the Making*, London: Routledge, 1986; *A New World Order: Grassroots Movements for Global Change*, London: Routledge, 1992; *Wealth Beyond Measure: An Atlas of Green Economics*, London: Gaia Books, 1992 (with M. Hillman and R. Hutchinson); and *Real Life Economics: Understanding Wealth Creation*, London, Routledge, 1992 (with M. Max-Neef). He is currently Research Fellow at the Department of Economics, Birkbeck College, University of London.

Matthias Finger is Swiss and has been with the International Academy of the Environment, Geneva. Apart from teaching assignments in Fribourg, Geneva and Syracuse, he has edited *Eco-Currents* and the collection *The Green Movement Worldwide*, New York: JAI Press, 1992. His *A Social History of the Worldwide Green Movement*, London: Zed Books, is forthcoming. He is presently Professor of Adult Education at Columbia University, New York.

Eduardo Gudynas is researcher at the Latin American Centre of Social Ecology and professor at the Franciscan Multiversity of Latin America in Montevideo, Uruguay. While his training was in animal ecology, he has more recently made many contributions to a deeper understanding of the connection between social conflicts and environmental crisis in Latin America. He was coordinator of the first Latin American Congress on Ecology.

Nicholas Hildyard, as co-editor of *The Ecologist*, has for years kept the spotlight on the impact of large development agencies, like the World Bank, on the environment. He has published several books, including (with E. Goldsmith) *Green Britain or Industrial Wasteland?*, Cambridge: Polity Press, 1986; and (with E. Goldsmith) *The Social and Environmental Effects of Large Dams*, Wadebridge: Wadebridge Ecological Centre, 1986. Together with his colleagues, he wrote 'Whose Common Future?', a major critical statement on the politics of global ecology after UNCED (special issue of *The Ecologist*, July/August 1992). He lives and works in Dorset, UK.

Smitu Kothari has been among the founders of Lokayan ('Dialogue of the People'), a centre promoting exchanges among activists from non-party political organizations and concerned intellectuals in India. He is the editor of *Lokayan Bulletin*, a political organizer involved in environmental and human rights issues, and has recently been a guest lecturer at Cornell University. He has edited (with H. Sethi) *Rethinking Human Rights: Challenges for Theory and Action*, Delhi: Lokayan, 1991. He lives in New Delhi.

Larry Lohmann worked for several years in Thailand with non-governmental organizations concerned with rural struggles and, from England, maintains links with campaigning groups in the South. An American citizen, he taught in the US and in Thailand. He is an Associate Editor of *The Ecologist* and his articles have appeared in *Asian Survey*, *New Scientist*, *Bulletin of Concerned Asian Scholars*, and he co-edited with M. Colchester *The Struggle for Land and the Fate of the Forests*, London: World Rainforest Movement and Zed Books, 1992. He recently also co-authored 'Whose Common Future?', a manifesto of *The Ecologist* (special issue July/August 1992).

Klaus Michael Meyer-Abich is Professor of Philosophy of Nature and co-director of the Institute for Cultural Studies at Essen. For many years he has played a leading role in animating public debate on environmental reform in Germany. He is a former Minister for Science and Research of the City of Hamburg and, since 1987, a member of the Study Commission of the German Bundestag on Protection of the Earth's Atmosphere. His numerous publications include *Wege zum Frieden mit der Natur*, Munich: Hanser, 1984; *Wissenschaft für die Zukunft – Holistisches Denken in ökologischer und gesellschaftlicher Verantwortung*, Munich: Beck, 1988; and *Aufstand für die Natur*, Munich: Hanser, 1990.

Sunita Narain has been associated with the Centre for Science and Environment, New Delhi, of which she is currently the Deputy Director. Along with Anil Agarwal she has contributed a number of articles and publications, among them the *State of India's Environment 1981: A Citizens Report*, New Delhi: CSE, 1982, and the subsequent edition in 1985. She also collaborated in writing *Towards Green Villages: A Strategy for Environmentally Sound and Participatory Rural Development*, New Delhi: CSE, 1990, and the memorandum which was highly influential in the pre-UNCED discussions, *Global Warming in an Unequal World. A Case of Environmental Colonialism*, New Delhi: CSE, 1991.

Pramod Parajuli is Nepalese and teaches anthropology at Syracuse University in the State of New York. As an engaged intellectual, he combines practice at the grassroots with theoretical reflection. With regard to theory, his attention focuses on whether and how subordinate groups create their own autonomous space by contesting the dominant discourses on development, ecology and knowledge. As an activist, he is involved with several grassroots groups in South Asia which are reshaping these autonomous spaces by recovering as well as critiquing vernacular traditions of knowledge.

Wolfgang Sachs, who has been active in the German and Italian green movements, is particularly concerned with how ecology has changed in recent years from a knowledge of opposition into a knowledge of domination. He has been co-editor of the journal *Development* and visiting professor at Pennsylvania State University. He is the author of *For Love of the Automobile: Looking Back into the History of Our Desires*, Berkeley: University of California Press, 1992; and the editor of *The Development Dictionary: A Guide to Knowledge as Power*, London: Zed Books, 1992. He is currently a fellow at the Institute for Cultural Studies in Essen, Germany.

Vandana Shiva lives in Dehradun, India, at the foot of the Himalayas. As an activist and a scholar, she has been shaped by the experiences of the Chipko movement which grew in the seventies in defence of the forests. Having been trained as a physicist, she has elaborated critical studies of the praxis of forestry, agro-science and biotechnology. Moreover, she has gained recognition by forcefully combining feminist analysis with a recourse to non-Western knowledge, exposing the biased nature of modern science along with development. Her books include *Staying Alive: Women, Ecology and Development*, London: Zed Books, 1989; *The Violence of the Green Revolution: Third World Agriculture, Ecology and Politics*, Zed Books and Third World Network, 1991; and (with M. Mies) *Ecofeminism*, Zed Books and Kali, forthcoming.

Yash Tandon is a Ugandan who now lives in Zimbabwe. He studied at the London School of Economics and taught for many years at Makerere University, Uganda, and the University of Dar es Salaam, Tanzania. He presently runs a consultancy in rural development in Harare and works as a researcher with the Southern African Non-governmental Development Organizations Network (SANDON). He edits their *Sustainable Development Bulletin*, which sets itself the task to report on the struggle between two lines, the one to self-empower and survive, the other to dis-empower and subdue.

Christine von Weizsäcker, who has been trained as a biologist, presides over a large family and lives in Bonn, Germany. As a freelance author, she has become an original voice in the public debate on the less reputable implications of technology and economics. She is particularly impressed by the marginalization of the domestic sphere in industrial society and argues for a modern reinvention of the 'commons'. In a similar vein, she has criticized genetic engineering as an invasion of the common heritage of life, calling for respect in the face of the intricate richness of evolution.

Donald Worster is Professor of Environmental History at the University of Kansas. He has greatly contributed to the rise of environmental history, both as an academic field and as a depository of collective memory. His *Nature's Economy: A History of Ecological Ideas*, New York: Cambridge University Press, 1977, has been a landmark in the history of environmentalist thought, while his *Dust Bowl: The Southern Plains in the 1930s*, New York: Oxford University Press, 1979, and his *Rivers of Empire: Water, Aridity and the Growth of the American West*, New York: Pantheon, 1985, have been examples of a socio-economic history of nature. More recently, editing the collection *Ends of the Earth*, New York: Cambridge University Press, 1988, he widened his scope of attention and focused on the complexities of global ecology.

Introduction

Once, environmentalists called for new public virtues, now they call rather for better managerial strategies. Once, they advocated more democracy and local self-reliance, now they tend to support the global empowerment of governments, corporations and science. Once, they strove for cultural diversity, now they see little choice but to push for a worldwide rationalization of life-styles. Indeed, as ecological issues have moved to the top of the agenda of international politics, environmentalism appears in many cases to have lost the spirit of contention, limiting itself to the provision of survival strategies for the powers that be. As a result, in recent years a discourse on global ecology has developed that is largely devoid of any consideration of power relations, cultural authenticity and moral choice; instead, it rather promotes the aspirations of a rising eco-cracy to manage nature and regulate people worldwide. Ironically, a movement which once invited people to humility has produced experts who succumb to the temptation of hubris.

Different observers have different opinions about the 1992 UN Conference on Environment and Development (UNCED) in Rio de Janeiro. Very few consider it a success, many more maintain that it was at least a satisfying start for a long process to come, and some regard it as an outright failure. The novelty of Rio was certainly the fact that for the first time, the governments of the world jointly acknowledged the threat of the ecological crisis and moved to formulate common obligations for conducting politics in the future. But this success had its price. As governments, business and international agencies raise the banner of global ecology, environmentalism changes its face. In part, ecology – understood as the philosophy of a social movement – is about to transform itself from a knowledge of opposition to a knowledge of domination. In fact, ideas and concepts – like 'risk', 'eco-system', 'sustainability' or 'global' – which were once hurled from below to the élites at the top, begin now to bounce back from the commanding heights of society to the citizens at the grassroots. In the process, environmentalism doesn't remain the same; it becomes sanitized of its radical content and reshaped as neutral expert knowledge, until it can be wedded to the dominating world-view. This course of affairs is probably inevitable when popular concerns reach the corridors of power, yet it presents a challenge to the movements of opposition to recover their original message.

It is therefore time to make new distinctions. After nearly everybody – heads of states and heads of corporations, believers in technology and believers in growth – has turned environmentalist, the conflicts in the future will not centre on who is or who is not an environmentalist, but on who stands for what kind of environmentalism. For a long time it was sufficient to raise the critical voice denouncing politics as environmentally 'too little and too late', but now it is necessary to focus on the political, social and cultural implications involved in different environmentalist designs. Though it is a considerable step forward that in these years the discussion on global ecology has become institutionalized in ministries, agencies, research centres, conferences and newspaper columns, it is nevertheless overdue to probe critically the new language which is put forth by the rising breed of environmental professionals. Political conflicts and cultural contradictions loom large behind the official discourse on global ecology; the views expressed in this book intend to expose them for public scrutiny.

Part 1 of this collection attempts to survey the new landscape of conflicts on the international level which emerged during the 'Earth Summit' 1992 in Brazil. To put the outcome of UNCED in a nutshell: the governments at Rio came around to recognizing the decline of the environment, but insisted on relaunching development. As worn-out development talk prevailed, attention centred on the South and its natural treasures and not on the North and its industrial disorder. There were conventions on biodiversity, climate and forests, but no conventions on agri-business, automobiles or free trade. This indicates that UNCED attempted to secure the natural resources and waste sinks for economic growth in favour of the global middle class, rather than to embark upon a path towards industrial self-limitation and local regeneration.

Behind the media hype and the solemn expressions of concern at Rio lay a complex terrain of conceptual confusion, conflicts of interest and even philosophical dispute. The chapters in Part 2 try to dispel some of the fog which surrounds 'sustainability', the key concept of the global ecology debate. After all, the discussion on sustainability is full of contradictions and tends to blur rather than to clarify the fundamental choices. Thinking through the socio-economic implications would mean to opt for a shrinkage and restructuring of economies, at least in the North. But as the call for 'sustainability' becomes common currency, the concept becomes infected by the time-honoured certainties of the ruling economic world-view. With that focus, the environment is pictured as an aggregate of ever-scarce resources which have to be strictly managed. Gradually, the image of nature is shifting; even the unspoiled parts are no longer seen as 'commons' which nobody is allowed to cash in, or as a heritage endowed to all living beings, but as a commercial asset in danger. As a result, the widespread acclaim of 'sustainability' makes it harder to sustain an environmentalism which talks about earth ethics and aesthetics, rather than about resources and economics.

As with 'sustainability', the call for 'globalism' can also easily lead into quicksand. For many years, environmentalists have celebrated the satellite picture of the 'one earth' with the intention of illustrating the ultimate limit of all human action. However, as the contributions in Part 3 demonstrate, the invitation to think globally inadvertently paves the way for worldwide surveillance and management. In a time when, like a boomerang, the insidious consequences of Westernization come back to the industrialized countries, the North has a growing interest to influence the South in the name of risk prevention. This interest coincides nicely with the quest for globalism; the survival instinct of the North shapes its claim to save humanity. Some people therefore are more global than others; indeed, did Senegalese peasants ever pretend to have a say in Europe's energy consumption, or did the people of Amazonia ever rush to North America to protect the forests in Canada and the Pacific North West?

The eco-cratic view likes universalist ecological rules, just as the developmentalist view liked universalist economic rules. Both pass over the rights of local communities to be in charge of their resources and to build a meaningful society. Global ecology can easily be at odds with local ecologies, since global resource planning protects nature as environment around the economy, while local conservation efforts protect nature as environment around the home (Hildyard). Part 4 of this book tells about local communities in India and Africa which derive their livelihoods from the forests, fields and waters which surround them. In all these instances, the conservation of nature is intimately related to rights of communal ownership, traditional ways of knowing, cultural autonomy, religious rituals, and freedom from state-centred development. For these communities, resistance is the main form of sustainable development. Indeed, their experience reflects the more general truth that the debt to nature cannot be paid, as Barry Commoner once said, person by person, in recycled bottles or ecologically sound habits, but in the ancient coin of social justice.

I would like to thank Christoph Baker and Judithe Bizot for their help in translation and editing. I appreciate the support given by the Heinrich-Böll Foundation for convening the international consultation in June 1991, which marked the beginning of this book. And most of all, I am deeply grateful for the hospitality I enjoyed during these years at the Institute for Cultural Studies, Essen.

Wolfgang Sachs

Part I
In the Wake of Rio

1.   Global Ecology and the Shadow of 'Development'

Wolfgang Sachs

The walls in the Tokyo subway used to be plastered with advertising posters. The authorities, aware of Japan's shortage of wood-pulp, searched for ways to reduce this wastage of paper. They quickly found an 'environmental solution': they mounted video screens on the walls and these now continuously bombard passengers with commercials – paper problem solved.

This anecdote exemplifies an approach to the environmental crisis which was also very much on the minds of the delegates who descended upon Rio de Janeiro for the 'Earth Summit' (UNCED), to reconcile 'environment' and 'development'. To put the outcome of UNCED in a nutshell: the governments at Rio came round to recognizing the declining state of the environment, but insisted on the relaunching of development. Indeed, most controversies arose from some party's heated defence of its 'right to development'; in that respect, Malaysia's resistance to the forest declaration or Saudi Arabia's attempt to sabotage the climate convention trailed not far behind President Bush's cutting remark that the lifestyle of the US would not be up for discussion at Rio. It is probably no exaggeration to say that the rain dance around 'development' kept the conflicting parties together and offered a common ritual which comforted them for the one or other sacrifice made in favour of the environment. At the end, the Rio Declaration ceremoniously emphasized the sacredness of 'development' and invoked its significance throughout the document wherever possible. Only after 'the right to development' has been enshrined, does the document proceed to consider 'the developmental and environmental needs of present and future generations' (Principle 3). In fact, the UN Conference in Rio inaugurated environmentalism as the highest state of developmentalism.

Reaffirming the centrality of 'development' in the international discussion on the environment surely helps to secure the collaboration of the dominating actors in government, economy and science, but it prevents the rupture required to head off the multifaceted dangers for the future of mankind. It locks the perception of the ecological predicament into the very world-view which stimulates the pernicious dynamics, and hands the action over to those social forces – governments, agencies and corporations – which have largely been responsible for the present state of affairs. This may turn out to be self-defeating. After all, the development discourse is deeply imbued with Western certainties like progress, growth, market integration, consumption, and universal needs, all notions that are part of the problem, not of the solution. They cannot but distract attention from the urgency of public debate on our relationship with nature, for they preclude the search for societies which live graciously within their means, and for social changes which take their inspiration from indigenous ideas of the good and proper life. The incapacity to bid farewell to some of the certainties which have shaped the development era was the major shortcoming of Rio. The great divide between development enthusiasts and development dissenters will be at the root of future conflicts about global ecology.

Truman and what followed

Epochs rise slowly, but the development era opened at a certain date and hour. On 20 January 1949, it was President Harry Truman who, in his inauguration speech before Congress, drawing the attention of his audience to conditions in poorer countries, for the first time defined them as 'underdeveloped areas'.[1] Suddenly, a seemingly indelible concept was established, cramming the immeasurable diversity of the South into one single category – the underdeveloped. That Truman coined a new term was not a matter of accident but the precise expression of a world-view: for him all the peoples of the world were moving along the same track, some faster, some slower, but all in the same direction. The Northern countries, in particular the US, were running ahead, while he saw the rest of the world – with its absurdly low per capita income – lagging far behind. An image that the economic societies of the North had increasingly acquired about themselves was thus projected upon the rest of the world: the degree of civilization in a country is to be indicated by the level of its production. Starting from that premise, Truman conceived of the world as an economic arena where nations compete for a better position on the GNP scale. No matter what ideals inspired Kikuyus, Peruvians or Filipinos, Truman recognized them only as stragglers whose historical task was to participate in the development race and catch up with the lead runners. Consequently, it was the objective of development policy to bring all nations into the arena and enable them to run in the race.

Turning the South's societies into economic competitors not only required the injection of capital and transfer of technology, but a cultural transformation, for many 'old ways' of living turned out to be 'obstacles to development'. The ideals and mental habits, patterns of work and modes of knowing, webs of loyalties and rules of governance in which the South's people were steeped, were usually at odds with the ethos of an economic society. In the attempt to overcome these barriers to growth, the traditional social fabric was often dissected and reassembled according to the textbook models of macro-economics. To be sure, 'development' had many effects, but one of its most insidious was the dissolution of cultures which were not built around a frenzy of accumulation. The South was thus precipitated into a transformation which had long been going on in the North: the gradual subordination of ever more aspects of social life under the rule of the economy. In fact, whenever development experts set their sights on a country, they fell victim to a particular myopia: they did not see a society which *has* an economy but a society which *is* an economy. As a result, they ended up revamping all kinds of institutions, such as work, schools or the law, in the service of productivity, degrading the indigenous style of doing things in the process. But the shift to a predominantly economic society involves a considerable cost: it undermines a society's capacity to secure well-being without joining unconditionally the economic race. The fact that the unfettered hegemony of Western productivism has made it more and more impossible to take exit roads from the global racetrack dangerously limits the space of manoeuvre for countries in times of uncertainty. Also in that respect, the countries of the North provide an ambiguous example: they have been so highly trained in productivism that they are incapable of doing anything but running the economic race.

After 40 years of development, the state of affairs is dismal. The gap between front-runners and stragglers has not been bridged; on the contrary, it has widened to the extent that it has become inconceivable that it could ever be closed. The aspiration of catching-up has ended in a blunder of planetary proportions. The figures speak for themselves: during the 1980s, the contribution of developing countries (where two-thirds of humanity live) to the world's GNP shrank to 15%, while the share of the industrial countries, with 20% of the world population, rose to 80%. Admittedly, closer examination reveals that the picture is far from homogeneous, but neither the South-East Asian showcases nor the oil-producing countries change the result that the development race has ended in disarray. The truth of this is more sharply highlighted if the destiny of large majorities of people within most Southern countries is considered; they live today in greater hardship and misery than at the time of decolonialization. The best one can say is that development has created a global middle-class of individuals with cars, bank accounts, and career aspirations. It is made up of the majority in the North and small élites in the South and its size roughly equals that eight per cent of the world population which owns a car. The internal rivalries of that class make a lot of noise in world politics, condemning to silence the overwhelming majority of the people. At the end of development, the question of justice looms larger than ever.

A second result of the development era has come dramatically to the fore in recent years: it has become evident that the race track leads in the wrong direction. While Truman could still take for granted that the North was at the head of social evolution, this premise of superiority has today been fully and finally shattered by the ecological predicament. For instance, much of the glorious rise in productivity is fuelled by a gigantic throughput of fossil energy, which requires mining the earth on the one side and covering it with waste on the other. By now, however, the global economy has outgrown the earth's capacity to serve as mine and dumping ground. After all, the world economy increases every two years by about the size ($60 billion) it had reached by 1900, after centuries of growth. Although only a small part of the world's regions has experienced large-scale economic expansion, the world economy already weighs down nature to an extent that she has in part to give in. If all countries followed the industrial example, five or six planets would be needed to serve as 'sources' for the inputs and 'sinks' for the waste of economic progress. Therefore, a situation has emerged where the certainty which ruled two centuries of growth economy has been exposed as a life-lie: growth is by no means open-ended. Economic expansion has already come up against its bio-physical limits; recognizing the earth's finiteness is a fatal blow to the idea of development as envisaged by Truman.

Ambiguous claims for justice

The UNCED process unfolded against this background of 40 years of post-war history. As implied in the title of the Conference, any consideration of global ecology has to respond to both the crisis of justice and the crisis of nature. While the Northern countries' main concern was about nature, the South, in the run up to the Conference, managed to highlight the question of justice. In fact, during the debates leading up to UNCED, attentive spectators wondered if they had not seen it all before. Slogans, which had animated the 1970s discussions on the 'New International Economic Order', kept creeping back to the forefront. Suddenly, calls for better terms of trade, debt relief, entry to Northern markets, technology transfer and aid, aid, and more aid, drowned the environmentalist discussion. Indeed, it was difficult to overlook the regressive tendencies in the controversy which opened up. The South, deeply hurt by the breakdown of development illusions, launched demands for further rounds of development. Already, in the June 1991 Beijing Declaration of the Group of 77, the point was made clearly and bluntly:

Environmental problems cannot be dealt with separately; they must be linked to the development process, bringing the environmental concerns in line with the imperatives of economic growth and development. In this context, the right to development for the developing countries must be fully recognized.[2]

After the South's years of uneasiness in dealing with the environmental concerns raised by the North, the plot for Rio had finally thickened. Since the North expects environmentally good behaviour worldwide, the South, grasping this opportunity, discovered environmental concessions as diplomatic weapons. Consequently, the South reiterated the unfulfilled demands of the 1970s and opposed them to the North's ecological impositions.

If matters look bad with respect to the environment, according to Southern countries, they look worse with respect to development. It was along these lines that they succeeded, after the 'lost decade' of the 1980s, in putting back the North–South division squarely on the international agenda. The spotlight was thus largely focused on the North's willingness to come up with $125 billion of yearly assistance, to fulfil its long overdue promise of allocating 0.7% of its GNP to development aid, to provide clean technologies, or access to bio-industrial patents. On the diplomatic level, this was hardly surprising, for most of the Third World, trapped by the failure of the politics of catching-up, fears that the world will eternally be split between the North's super-economy and the South's wretched economies. But on a deeper level, the continuing commitment to run the development race leaves the Southern countries in an untenable position. In fact, the Rio documents make clear that the South has no intention of abandoning the Northern model of living as its implicit utopia. In using the language of development, the South continues to subscribe to the notion that the North shows the way for the rest of the world. As a consequence, however, the South is incapable of escaping the North's cultural hegemony; for development without hegemony is like a race without a direction. Apart from all the economic pressures, adherence to 'development' puts the South, culturally and politically, in a position of structural weakness, leading to the absurd situation in which the North can present itself as the benevolent provider of solutions to the ecological crisis.

Needless to say that this constellation plays into the hands of the Northern countries. With the blessing of 'development', the growth fatalists in the North are implicitly justified in rushing ahead on the economic race-track. The cultural helplessness of the industrial countries in responding adequately to the ecological predicament thus turns into a necessary virtue. After all, the main concern of the Northern élites is to get ahead in the competitive struggle between USA, Europe, and Japan, achieving an ecological modernization of their economies along the way. They are light-years away from the insight that peace with nature eventually requires peace in economic warfare; consequently, a country such as Germany, for instance, manages to pose as a shining example of environmentalism, while pushing ahead with such ecologically disastrous free-trade policies as the European common market and the reform of GATT. The fact that 'development', that race without a finishing line, remains uncontested, allows the North to continue the relentless pursuit of overdevelopment and economic power, since the idea of societies which settle for their accomplished stage of technical capacity becomes unthinkable. Indeed, such matters as limits to road-building, to high-speed transport, to economic concentration, to the production of chemicals, to large-scale cattle ranching, and so on, were not even pondered in Rio.

The unholy alliance between development enthusiasts in the South and growth fatalists in the North, however, works not only against the environment but also against greater justice in the world. For in most countries, while development has benefited rather small minorities, it has done so at the expense of large parts of the population. During the development era, growth was expected to abolish poverty. Instead, it led to social polarization. In many cases, communities which guaranteed sustenance have been torn apart in the attempt to build a modern economy. Southern élites, however, often justify their unmitigated pursuit of development by ritual reference to the persistence of poverty, cultivating the worn-out dogma that growth is the recipe against poverty. Locked in their interests of power and fixed on the life-style of the affluent, they fend off the insight that securing livelihoods requires a careful handling of growth. Yet the lesson to be drawn from 40 years of development can be stated bluntly: the issue of justice must be delinked from the perspective of 'development'. In fact, both ecology and poverty call for limits to development. Without such a change in perspective, the struggle for redistribution of power and resources between North and South, which is inevitably renewed in facing environmental constraints, can be only what it was in the 1970s: a quarrel within the global middle class on how to divide the cake.

Earth's finiteness as a management problem

'Development' is, above all, a way of thinking. It cannot, therefore, be easily identified with a particular strategy or programme, but ties many different practices and aspirations to a common set of assumptions. Whatever the theme on the agenda in the post-war era, the assumptions of 'development' – like the universal road, the superiority of economics, the mechanical feasibility of change – tacitly shaped the definition of the problem, highlighted certain solutions and consigned others to oblivion. Moreover, as knowledge is intimately related to power, development thinking inevitably featured certain social actors (for example, international agencies) and certain types of social transformation (for example, technology transfer), while marginalizing other social actors and degrading other kinds of change.[3]

Despite alarming signs of failure throughout its history, the development syndrome has survived until today, but at the price of increasing senility. When it became clear in the 1950s that investments were not enough, 'man-power development' was added to the aid package; as it became obvious in the 1960s that hardship continued, 'social development' was discovered; and in the 1990s, as the impoverishment of peasants could no longer be overlooked, 'rural development' was included in the arsenal of development strategies. And so it went on, with further creations like 'equitable development' and the 'basic needs approach'. Again and again, the same conceptual operation was repeated: degradation in the wake of development was redefined as a lack which called for yet another strategy of development. All along, the efficacy of 'development' remained impervious to any counter evidence, but showed remarkable staying power; the concept was repeatedly stretched until it included both the strategy which inflicted the injury and the strategy designed for therapy. This strength of the concept, however, is also the reason for its galloping exhaustion; it no longer manifests any reactions to changing historical conditions. The tragic greatness of 'development' consists in its monumental emptiness.

'Sustainable development', which UNCED enthroned as the reigning slogan of the 1990s, has inherited the fragility of 'development'. The concept emasculates the environmental challenge by absorbing it into the empty shell of 'development', and insinuates the continuing validity of developmentalist assumptions even when confronted with a drastically different historical situation. In Rachel Carson's *Silent Spring*, the book which gave rise to the environmental movement in 1962, development was understood to inflict injuries on people and nature. Since the 'World Conservation Strategy' in 1980 and later the Brundtland Report, development has come to be seen as the therapy for the injuries caused by development. What accounts for this shift?

Firstly, in the 1970s, under the impact of the oil crisis, governments began to realize that continued growth depended not only on capital formation or skilled manpower, but also on the long-term availability of natural resources. Foods for the insatiable growth machine, such as oil, timber, minerals, soils, genetic material, seemed on the decline; concern grew about the prospects of long-term growth. This was a decisive change in perspective: not the health of nature but the continuous health of development became the centre of concern. In 1992, the World Bank summed up the new consensus in a laconic phrase: 'What is sustainable? Sustainable development is development that lasts.'⁴ Of course, the task of development experts does not remain the same under this imperative, because the horizon of their decisions is now supposed to extend in time, taking into account also the welfare of future generations. But the frame stays the same: 'sustainable development' calls for the conservation of development, not for the conservation of nature.

Even bearing in mind a very loose definition of development, the anthropocentric bias of the statement springs to mind; it is not the preservation of nature's dignity which is on the international agenda, but to extend human-centred utilitarianism to posterity. Needless to say, the naturalist and bio-centric current of present-day environmentalism has been cut out by this conceptual operation. With 'development' back in the saddle, the view on nature changes. The question now becomes: which of nature's 'services' are to what extent indispensable for further development? Or the other way around: which 'services' of nature are dispensable or can be substituted by, for example, new materials or genetic engineering? In other words, nature turns into a variable, albeit a critical one, in sustaining development. It comes as no surprise, therefore, that 'nature capital' has already become a fashionable notion among ecological economists.⁵

Secondly, a new generation of post-industrial technologies suggested that growth was not invariably linked to the squandering of ever more resources, as in the time of smoke-stack economies, but could be pursued through less resource-intensive means. While in the past, innovations were largely aimed at increased productivity of labour, it now appeared possible that technical and organizational intelligence could concentrate on increasing the productivity of nature. In short, growth could be delinked from a rising consumption of energy and materials. In the eyes of developmentalists, the 'limits to growth' did not call for abandoning the race, but for changing the running technique. After 'no development without sustainability' had spread, 'no sustainability without development' also gained recognition.

Thirdly, environmental degradation has been discovered to be a worldwide condition of poverty. While formerly the developmentalist image of the 'poor' was characterized by lack of water, housing, health, and money, they are now seen to be suffering from lack of nature as well. Poverty is now exemplified by people who search desperately for firewood, find themselves trapped by encroaching deserts, are driven from their soils and forests, or are forced to endure dreadful sanitary conditions. Once the lack of nature is identified as a cause of poverty, it follows neatly that development agencies, since they are in the business of 'eliminating poverty', have to diversify into programmes for the environment. But people who are dependent on nature for their survival have no choice other than to pursue the last remaining fragments of its bounty. As the decline of nature is also a consequence of poverty, the poor of the world suddenly entered the stage as agents of environmental destruction. Whereas in the 1970s, the main threat to nature still appeared to be industrial man, in the 1980s environmentalists turned their eyes to the Third World and pointed to the vanishing forests, soils and animals there. With the shifting focus, environmentalism, in part, took on a different colour; the crisis of the environment is no longer perceived as the result of building affluence for the global middle class in North and South, but as the result of human presence on the globe in general. No matter if nature is consumed for luxury or survival, no matter if the powerful or the marginalized tap nature, it all becomes one for the rising tribe of ecocrats. And so it could be that, among other things, an 'Earth Summit' was called to reach decisions which should primarily have been the concern of the OECD – or even the G7.

The persistence of 'development', the newly-found potentials for less resource-intensive growth paths, and the discovery of humanity in general as the enemy of nature – these notions were the conceptual ingredients for the type of thinking which received its diplomatic blessings at UNCED: the world is to be saved by more and better managerialism. The message, which is ritually repeated by many politicians, industrialists and scientists who have recently decided to slip on a green coat, goes as follows: nothing should be (the dogmatic version) or can be (the fatalist version) done to change the direction the world's economies are taking; problems along the way can be solved, if the challenge for better and more sophisticated management is taken up. As a result, ecology, once a call for new public virtues, has now become a call for new executive skills. In fact, Agenda 21, for example, overflows with such formulas as 'integrated approach', 'rational use', 'sound management', 'internalizing costs', 'better information', 'increased co-ordination', 'long-term prediction', but by and large fails (except for some timid phrases in the hotly debated chapter 'Changing Consumption Patterns') to consider any reduction of material standards of living and any attempts to slow down the accumulation dynamics. In short, alternatives to development are black-balled, alternatives within development are welcome.

Nevertheless, it was an achievement for UNCED to have delivered the call for environmental tools from a global rostrum, an opening which will give a boost to environmental engineering worldwide. But the price for this achievement is the reduction of environmentalism to managerialism. For the task of global ecology can be understood in two ways: it is either a technocratic effort to keep development afloat against the drift of plunder and pollution; or it is a cultural effort to shake off the hegemony of ageing Western values and gradually retire from the development race. These two ways may not be exclusive in detail, but they differ deeply in perspective. In the first case, the paramount task becomes the management of the bio-physical limits to development. All powers of foresight have to be mustered in order to steer development along the edge of the abyss, continuously surveying, testing, and manoeuvring the bio-physical limits. In the second case, the challenge consists in designing cultural/political limits to development. Each society is called upon to search for indigenous models of prosperity, which allow society's course to stay at a comfortable distance from the edge of the abyss, living graciously within a stable or shrinking volume of production. It is analogous to driving a vehicle at high speed towards a canyon, either you equip it with radar, monitors and highly trained personnel, correct its course and drive it as hard as possible along the rim; or you slow down, turn away from the edge, and drive leisurely here and there without too much attention to precise controls. Too many global ecologists – implicitly or explicitly – favour the first choice.

Bargaining for the rest of nature

Until some decades ago, quite a few tracts of the biosphere still remained untouched by the effects of economic growth. It is basically over the last 30 years that the tentacles of productivism have closed on the last virgin areas, leaving now no part of the biosphere untouched. More often than not, the human impact grows into a full-scale attack, tearing up the intricate webs of life. Since time immemorial humanity defended itself against nature, now nature must be defended against humanity. In particular danger are the 'global commons', the Antarctic, ocean beds, tropical forests, with many species threatened by the voracious growth of demand for new inputs, while earth's atmosphere is overburdened with the residues growth leaves behind. For that reason, the 1980s saw the rise of a global environmental consciousness, expressed by many voices, all deploring the threats to the earth's biosphere and the offence to the generations to come. The collective duty to preserve the 'common heritage of mankind' was invoked, and 'Caring for the Earth'[6] became an imperative which agitated spirits worldwide. Respect for the integrity of nature, independently of its value for humans, as well as a proper regard for the rights of humanity demanded that the global commons be protected.

International environmental diplomacy, however, is about something else. The rhetoric, which ornaments conferences and conventions, ritually calls for a new global ethic but the reality at the negotiating tables suggests a different logic. There, for the most part, one sees diplomats engaged in the familiar game of accumulating advantages for their countries, eager to out-manoeuvre their opponents, shrewdly tailoring environmental concerns to the interests dictated by their nation's economic position. Their parameters of action are bounded by the need to extend their nation's space for 'development'; therefore in their hands environmental concerns turn into bargaining chips in the struggle of interests. In that respect, the thrust of UNCED's negotiations was no different from the thrust of previous negotiations about the Law of the Sea, the Antarctic, or the Montreal protocol on the reduction of CFCs; and upcoming negotiations on climate, animal protection or biodiversity are also hardly likely to be different.

The novelty of Rio, if there was one, lay not in commitments on the way to a collective stewardship of nature, but rather in international recognition of the scarcity of natural resources for development. The fragility of nature came into focus, because the services she offers as a 'source' and a 'sink' for economic growth have become inadequate; after centuries of availability, nature can no longer be counted upon as a silent collaborator in the process of 'technical civilization'. In other words, environmental diplomacy has recognized that nature is finite as a mine for resources and as a container for waste. Given that 'development' is intrinsically open-ended, the logic underlying international negotiations is pretty straightforward. First, limits are to be identified at a level that permits the maximum use of nature as mine and container, right up to the critical threshold beyond which ecological decline would rapidly accelerate. This is where scientists gain supremacy, since such limits can only be identified on the basis of 'scientific evidence'; endless quarrels about the state of knowledge are therefore part of the game. Once that hurdle has been overcome, the second step in the bargaining process is to define each country's proper share in the utilization of the 'source' or the 'sink' in question. Here diplomacy finds a new arena, and the old means of power, persuasion and bribery come in handy in order to maximize one's own country's share. And finally, mechanisms have to be designed to secure all parties' compliance with the norms stated by the treaty, an effort which calls for international monitoring and enforcement institutions. Far from 'protecting the earth', environmental diplomacy which works within a developmentalist frame cannot but concentrate its efforts on rationing what is left of nature. To normalize, not eliminate global overuse and pollution of nature will be its unintended effect.

Four major lines of conflict cut through the landscape of international environmental diplomacy, involving: rights to further exploitation of nature; rights to pollution; and rights to compensation; and overall, conflict over responsibility. In the UNCED discussions on the biodiversity convention, for example, the rights to further exploitation of nature held centre stage. Who is entitled to have access to the world's dwindling genetic resources? Can nation states exert their sovereignty over them or are they to be regarded as 'global commons'? Who is allowed to profit from the use of genetic diversity? Countries rich in biomass, but poor in industrial power were thus counterposed against countries rich in industrial power, but poor in biomass. Similar issues arise with respect to tropical timber, the mining of ocean beds, or to wild animals. Regarding the climate convention, on the other hand, diplomatic efforts were aimed at optimizing pollution rights over various periods of time. Oil-producing countries were not happy about any ceilings for CO_2 emissions, while small island states, understandably, hoped for the toughest limits possible. Moreover, the more economies are dependent on a cheap fuel base, the less the respective representatives were inclined to be strong on CO_2: the USA in the forefront, followed by the large newly industrialized countries, while Europe along with Japan could afford to urge stricter limits. In both cases, claims to compensation were voiced by an insistent chorus. How much compensation for retrospective development can the South demand? Who carries the losses incurred by a restrained exploitation of nature? Who should foot the bill for transferring clean technologies? Obviously, here, the South was on the offensive, led by countries with potentially large middle classes, while the North found itself on the defensive. In all these matters, however, the conflict over responsibilities loomed large; and again, the North was under pressure. After all, didn't the industrialized countries fell their own forests to feed development? Haven't they in the past used the entire world as the hinterland for their industrialization? With regard to greenhouse gases, is it appropriate or even justifiable to lump together methane emissions from India's rice fields with the CO_2 emissions from US car exhausts? In sum, a new class of conflicts has thrown into disarray the diplomatic routines: while in the 1970s particularly, multilateral conferences focused on how to achieve a broader participation of the South in the growth of world economy, in the 1990s these conferences are dealing with how to control the pollution produced by this growth. As the bio-physical limits to development become visible, the tide of the post-war era turns: multilateral negotiations no longer centre on the redistribution of riches but on the redistribution of risks.[7]

Efficiency and sufficiency

Twenty years ago, 'limits to growth' was the watchword of the environmental movement worldwide; today the buzzword of international ecology experts is 'global change'. The messages implied are clearly different.[8] 'Limits to growth' calls on *homo industrialis* to reconsider his project and to abide by nature's laws. 'Global change', however, puts mankind in the driver's seat and urges it to master nature's complexities with greater self-control. While the first formula sounds threatening, the second has an optimistic ring: it believes in a rebirth of *homo faber* and, on a more prosaic level, lends itself to the belief that the proven means of modern economy – product innovation, technological progress, market regulation, science-based planning – will show the way out of the ecological predicament.

The cure for all environmental ills is called 'efficiency revolution'. It focuses on reducing the throughput of energy and materials in the economic system by means of new technology and planning. Be it for the light-bulb or the car, for the design of power plants or transport systems, the aim is to come up with innovations that minimize the use of nature for each unit of output. Under this prescription, the economy will supposedly gain in fitness by keeping to a diet which eliminates the overweight in slag and dross. The efficiency scenario, however, seeks to make the circle square; it proposes a radical change through redirecting conventional means. It confronts modern society with the need to drastically reduce the utilization of nature as a mine for inputs and a deposit for waste, promising to eventually reduce the physical scale of the economy. Conversely, it holds out the prospect of achieving this transformation through the application of economic intelligence, including new products, technologies and management techniques; in fact, this scenario proposes the extension of the modern economic imperative, that is, to optimize the means–ends relationship,[9] from the calculation of money flows to the calculation of physical flows. 'More with less' is the motto for this new round in the old game. Optimizing input, not maximizing output, as in the post-war era, is the order of the day, and one already sees economists and engineers taking a renewed pleasure in their trade by puzzling out the minimum input for each unit of output. The hope which goes along with this strategic turnabout is again concisely stated by the World Bank: 'Efficiency reforms help reduce pollution while raising a country's economic output.'[10]

No doubt an efficiency revolution would have far-reaching effects. Since natural inputs were cheap and the deposition of waste mostly free of charge, economic development has for long been skewed towards squandering nature. Subsidies encouraged waste, technical progress was generally not designed to save on nature, and prices did not reflect environmental damages. There is a lot of space for correcting the course, and Agenda 21, for example, provides a number of signposts which indicate a new route. But the past course of economic history – in the East, West, and South – though with considerable variations – suggests that there is little room for efficiency strategies in earlier phases of growth, whereas they seem to work best – and are affordable – when applied after a certain level of growth has been attained. Since in the South the politics of selective growth would be a much more powerful way to limit the demand for resources, to transfer the 'efficiency revolution' there wholesale makes sense only if the South is expected to follow the North's path of development.

Even for the North scepticism is in order. Those who hail the rising information and service society as environment-friendly, often overlook the fact that these sectors can only grow on top of the industrial sector and in close symbiosis with it. The size of the service sector in relation to production has its limits, just as its dependence on resources can be considerable, for such sectors as tourism, hospitals, or data-processing.[11] Even commodities without any nature content, for example patents, blueprints, or money, derive their value from the command over a resource base which they provide. More specifically, gains in environmental efficiency often consist in substituting high-tech for energy/materials, a process which presupposes the presence of a resource-intensive economy. In short, the efficiency potential which lies in well-tuned engines, bio-technological processes, recycling technologies or systems thinking, is indigenous to the Northern economies. But the efficiency strategy obviously plays into the North's hands: this way, they can again offer the South a new selection of tools for economic progress, at a price which will be scarcely different from that paid in the decades of technology transfer.

Environmentalists who refer exclusively to efficient resource management concentrate social imagination on the revision of means, rather than on the revision of goals. Their ingenuity lies in advocating a strategy that emphasizes what business has always been best at, and their strength is to propose a perspective which is far from putting the growth imperative into question. But the magic words 'resource efficiency' have a shady side; staring at them for too long leads to blindness in one eye. Many environmentalists have already succumbed to this malady. In praising 'resource efficiency' alone, they obscure the fact that ecological reform must walk on two legs: scrutinizing means as well as moderating goals. This omission, however, backfires; it threatens the ecological project. An increase in resource efficiency alone leads to nothing, unless it goes hand-in-hand with an intelligent restraint of growth. Instead of asking how many supermarkets or how many bathrooms are enough, one focuses on how all these – and more – can be obtained with a lower input of resources. If, however, the dynamics of growth are not slowed down, the achievements of rationalization will soon be eaten up by the next round of growth. Consider the example of the fuel-efficient car. Today's vehicle engines are definitely more efficient than in the past; yet the relentless growth in number of cars and miles driven has cancelled out that gain. And the same logic holds across the board, from energy saving to pollution abatement and recycling; not to mention the fact that continuously staving off the destructive effects of growth in turn requires new growth. In fact, what really matters is the overall physical scale of the economy with respect to nature, not only the efficient allocation of resources. Herman Daly has offered a telling comparison:[12] even if the cargo on a boat is distributed efficiently, the boat will inevitably sink under too much weight – even though it may sink optimally! Efficiency without sufficiency is counterproductive; the latter must define the boundaries of the former.

However, the rambling development creed impedes any serious public debate on the moderation of growth. Under its shadow, any society which decides, at least in some areas, not to go beyond certain levels of commodity-intensity, technical performance, or speed, appears to be backward. As a result, the consideration of zero-options, that is, choosing not to do something which is technically possible, is treated as a taboo in the official discussion on global ecology, even to the point of exposing some agreements to ridicule. Take, for example, Agenda 21's (chapter 9) section on transport: although the 'population' of cars grows at the present rate four times faster than the population of humans, Agenda 21's authors were incapable of suggesting any strategies for avoiding and reducing traffic, or of course, any option for low-speed transport systems. There are many reasons for this failure, but on a deeper level, it shows that the development syndrome has dangerously narrowed the social imagination in the North as well as in the South. As the North continues to set its sight on an infinite economic future, and the South cannot free itself from its compulsive mimicry of the North, the capacity for self-mobilized and indigenous change has been undermined worldwide. Politics which choose intermediate levels of material demand remain outside the official consensus; the search for indigenous models of prosperity, which de-emphasize the drive for overdevelopment, has become an apostasy. Clearly, such a perspective would in the first place be at the expense of the wealthy, but without a politics of sufficiency there can be neither justice nor peace with nature.

The hegemony of globalism

'Sustainable development', though it can mean many things to many people, nevertheless contains a core message: keep the volume of human extraction/emission in balance with the regenerative capacities of nature. That sounds reasonable enough, but it conceals a conflict that has yet to win public attention, even though such fundamental issues as power, democracy and cultural autonomy are at stake. Sustainability, yes, but at what level? Where is the circle of use and regeneration to be closed? At the level of a village community, a country, or the entire planet? Until the 1980s, environmentalists were usually concerned with the local or the national space; ideas like 'eco-development' and 'self-reliance' had aimed to increase the economic and political independence of a place by reconnecting ecological resource flows.[13] But in subsequent years, they began to look at things from a much more elevated vantage point: they adopted the astronaut's view, taking in the entire globe at one glance. Today's ecology is in the business of saving nothing less than the planet. That suggestive globe, suspended in the dark universe, delicately furnished with clouds, oceans and continents, has become the object of science, planning and politics.

Modesty hardly seems to be the hallmark of such thinking. The 1989 special issue of the *Scientific American*, with the programmatic title 'Managing Planet Earth', sets the tone:

> It is as a global species that we are transforming the planet. It is only as a global species – pooling our knowledge, coordinating our actions and sharing what the planet has to offer – that we may have any prospect for managing the planet's transformation along the pathways of sustainable development. Self-conscious, intelligent management of the earth is one of the great challenges facing humanity as it approaches the 21st century.[14]

Perceiving the earth as an object of environmental management is, on the cognitive level, certainly an outcome of space travel, which has turned the planet into a visible object, a revolution in the history of human perception.[15] But there is a political, a scientific and a technological reason as well. Politically, it was only in the 1980s that acid rain, the ozone hole and the greenhouse effect drove home the message that industrial pollution affects the entire globe across all borders. The planet revealed itself as the ultimate dumping ground. Scientifically, ecological research, after having for years mainly focused on single and isolated ecosystems like deserts, marshes and rain forests, recently shifted its attention to the study of the biosphere, that envelope of air, vegetation, water and rocks which sustains life globally. Technologically, as often in the history of science, it was a new generation of instruments and equipment which created the possibility of collecting and processing data on a global scale. With satellites, sensors and computers, the technology available in the 1990s permits the biosphere to be surveyed and modelled. As these factors have emerged simultaneously, human arrogance has discovered the ultimate dominion: planet Earth.

Only a few years ago, invoking the wholeness of the globe meant something else. Environmentalists waved around the picture of the earth taken from outer space, in order to remind the public of the majestic finiteness of the earth and to spread the insight that there is in the end no escape from the consequences of human action. While they appealed to the reality of the planet, inviting people to embrace humility, a new tribe of global ecocrats is ready to act upon the newly-emerged reality of the planet, imagining that they can preside over the world. Research on the biosphere is rapidly becoming big science; spurred by a number of international programmes,[16] 'planetary sciences', including satellite observation, deep-sea expeditions, worldwide data processing, are being institutionalized in many countries.

With this trend, sustainability is increasingly conceived as a challenge for global management. The new experts set out to identify the balance between human extractions/emissions on the one side, and the regenerative capacities of nature on the other, on a planetary scale, mapping and monitoring, measuring and calculating resource flows and biogeochemical cycles around the globe. According to Agenda 21:

> This is essential, if a more accurate estimate is to be provided of the carrying capacity of the planet Earth and of its resilience under the many stresses placed upon it by human activities.[17]

It is the implicit agenda of this endeavour to be eventually able to moderate the planetary system, supervising species diversity, fishing grounds, felling rates, energy flows, and material cycles. It remains a matter of speculation which of these expectations will ever be realized, but there is no doubt that the linkage of space travel, sensor technology and computer simulation has vastly increased the power to monitor nature, to recognize human impact, and to make predictions. The management of resource budgets thus becomes a matter of world politics.

Satellite pictures scanning the globe's vegetative cover, computer graphs running interacting curves through time, threshold levels held up as worldwide norms are the language of global ecology. It constructs a reality that contains mountains of data, but no people. The data do not explain why Tuaregs are driven to exhaust their water-holes, or what makes Germans so obsessed with high speed on freeways; they do not point out who owns the timber shipped from the Amazon or which industry flourishes because of a polluted Mediterranean sea; and they are mute about the significance of forest trees for Indian tribals or what water means in an Arab country. In short, they provide a knowledge which is faceless and placeless; an abstraction that carries a considerable cost: it consigns the realities of culture, power and virtue to oblivion. It offers data, but no context; it shows diagrams, but no actors; it gives calculations, but no notions of morality; it seeks stability, but disregards beauty. Indeed, the global vantage point requires ironing out all the differences and disregarding all circumstances; rarely has the gulf between observers and the observed been greater than between satellite-based forestry and the *seringueiro* in the Brazilian jungle. It is inevitable that the claims of global management are in conflict with the aspirations for cultural rights, democracy and self-determination. Indeed, it is easy for an ecocracy which acts in the name of 'one earth' to become a threat to local communities and their life-styles. After all, has there ever, in the history of colonialism, been a more powerful motive for streamlining the world than the call to save the planet?

Yet the North faces a problem. For the bid for global management has been triggered by a new historical constellation. Ever since Columbus arrived in Santo Domingo the North has by and large remained unaffected by the tragic consequences which followed his expansion overseas; others had borne the burden of sickness, exploitation and ecological destruction. Now, this historical tide seems about to turn; for the first time the Northern countries themselves are exposed to the bitter results of Westernizing the world. Immigration, popuation pressure, tribalism with mega-arms, and above all, the environmental consequences of worldwide industrialization threaten to destabilize the Northern way of life. It is as if the cycle which had been opened by Columbus is about to be closed at the end of this century. As a result, the North devises ways and means for protection and risk management worldwide. The rational planning of the planet becomes a matter of Northern security.

The celebrated control of (Western) man over nature leaves much to be desired. Science and technology successfully transform nature on a vast scale, but so far, with unpleasant as well as unpredictable consequences. In fact only if these consequences were under control would it be possible to speak of having accomplished domination over nature. It is here that technocratic environmentalism comes in. Seen from this angle, the purpose of global environmental management is nothing less than control of a second order; a higher level of observation and intervention has to be installed, in order to control the consequences of the control over nature. Such a step becomes the more imperative as the drive towards turning the world into a closely interrelated and expanding economic society continues unabated. Given that the continuing force of the development syndrome is an impediment to restraining the dynamics of worldwide industrialization, the obvious task is to prepare for regulating the transformation of nature globally in an optimal fashion. It is in that light that the *Scientific American* can elevate the following questions to key-issues for future decision-making:

> Two central questions must be addressed: What kind of planet do we want? What kind of planet can we get? . . . How much species diversity should be maintained in the world? Should the size or the growth rate of the human population be curtailed . . . ? How much climate change is acceptable?[18]

If there are no limits to growth, there surely seem to be no limits to hubris.

Notes

1. See the entry for 'underdeveloped' in the *Oxford English Dictionary* (1989), vol. XVIII, p. 960. Extensive inquiries into the history of the development discourse can be found in Wolfgang Sachs (ed.) (1992) *The Development Dictionary: a guide to knowledge as power*, London, Zed Books.

2. Beijing Ministerial Declaration on Environment and Development, 19 June 1991.

3. For these reasons, I do not follow proposals to make a distinction between growth and development. It seems to me that 'development' cannot be purified of its historical context. For a distinction, see Herman E. Daly (1990) 'Toward Some Operational Principles of Sustainable Development', in *Ecological Economics*, Vol. 2, 1990, p. 1.

4. *World Development Report 1992* (1992), Oxford University Press (for the World Bank), New York, p. 34.

5. See for instance Salah El Serafy, 'The Environment as Capital', in R. Costanza (ed.) (1991) *Ecological Economics: the science and management of sustainability*, New York, Columbia University Press, pp. 168–75.

6. The title of a major document, published jointly by IUCN, UNEP, and WWF in Gland, Switzerland, in 1991.

7. This change has been observed for the domestic scene by Ulrich Beck (1987) *Risikogesellschaft*, Frankfurt: Suhrkamp.

8. Frederick Buttels et al. (1990) 'From Limits to Growth to Global Change: constraints and contradictions in the evolution of environmental science and ideology', in *Global Environmental Change*, Vol. 1, No. 1, December, pp. 57–66.

9. Karl Polanyi, in 'The Two Meanings of Economic', in his *The Livelihood of Man*, New York, Academic Press, 1977, has identified the optimization imperative as the core of modern economic thinking.

10. World Development Report 1992, op. cit., p. 114.

11. Robert Goodland et al., *Environmentally Sustainable Economic Development. Building on Brundtland*, The World Bank, Environment Working Paper No. 46, July 1991, p. 14.

12. Herman E. Daly, 'Elements of Environmental Macroeconomics', in R. Costanza (ed.), op. cit., p. 35.

13. For instance Ignacy Sachs (1980) *Stratégies de l'écodéveloppement*, Paris, Les Editions Ouvrières, 1980; or *What Now?* (1975), the report of the Dag Hammarskjöld Foundation.

14. William C. Clark, 'Managing Planet Earth', *Scientific American*, Vol. 261, September 1989, p. 47.

15. For an elaborate analysis of this aspect, see Wolfgang Sachs (1992) *Satellitenblick. Die Visualisierung der Erde im Zuge der Weltraumfahrt*, Berlin, Science Centre for Social Research.

16. For an overview see Thomas F. Malone (1986) 'Mission to Planet Earth: integrating studies of global change', in *Environment*, Vol. 28, No. 8, pp. 6–11, 39–41.

17. Chapter 35.1 in the section 'Science for Sustainable Development'.

18. Clark, op. cit., p. 48.

2.   Foxes in Charge of the Chickens

Nicholas Hildyard

The Earth Summit debacle

The United Nations Conference on Environment and Development, the self-styled Earth Summit, finished where it began. After ten days of press conferences, tree planting ceremonies and behind-the-scenes wheeling and dealing, the diplomats went home to their various other assignments and the politicians to their next round of international talks. Rio gave way to the Economic Summit at Munich and the more familiar territory of GATT, G-7 power politics and interest rates.

For the major players, the Earth Summit was a phenomenal success. The World Bank not only emerged with its development policies intact but with control of an expanded Global Environmental Facility (GEF), a prize that it had worked for two years to achieve. The US got the biodiversity convention it sought simply by not signing the convention on offer. The corporate sector, which throughout the UNCED process enjoyed special access to the Secretariat, also got what it wanted: the final documents not only treated TNCs with kid gloves but extolled them as key actors in the 'battle to save the planet'. Free-market environmentalism – the philosophy that TNCs brought to Rio through the Business Council on Sustainable Development – has become the order of the day, uniting Southern and Northern leaders alike. For many environmental groups, too, the Summit was a success: careers have been made, credibility achieved (some even having seats on government delegations) and their concerns are no longer marginalized. They are now recognized as major players themselves.

In brief, the Summit went according to plan. The net outcome was to minimize change to the status quo, an outcome that was inevitable from the outset of the UNCED process three years ago. Unwilling to question the desirability of economic growth, the market economy or the development process itself, UNCED never had a chance of addressing the real problems of 'environment and development'. Its Secretariat provided delegates with materials for a convention on biodiversity but not on free trade; on forests

but not on agribusiness; on climate but not on automobiles.[1] Agenda 21 –
the Summit's 'action plan' – featured clauses on 'enabling the poor to
achieve sustainable livelihoods' but none on enabling the rich to do so; a
section on women but none on men. By such deliberate evasion of the
central issues which economic expansion poses for human societies,
UNCED condemned itself to irrelevance even before the first preparatory
meeting got under way.

Conflicting interests, differing perceptions

In that respect, the best that can be said for the Earth Summit is that it made
visible the vested interests that stand in the way of the moral economies that
local people are seeking to re-establish in the face of day to day degradation
of their rivers, lakes, streams, fishing grounds, rangelands, forests and
fields. For those who rely on the commons, such degradation means a loss of
dignity and independence, security, livelihood and health. Defending the
commons is thus often a matter of life and death. By contrast, figures in
government, business and international organizations whose livelihoods do
not depend directly on what is around them tend to view environmental
degradation and the protests it provokes as threats to their political interest.
For them the environment is not what is around their homes but what is
around their economies. Northern leaders within UNCED, for example,
were preoccupied with how to keep a growing South from tapping resources
and filling up waste sinks which the North has grown accustomed to using,
while simultaneously maintaining the global capital flows which would help
the global economy expand. Southern leaders, responding to prodding from
Northern capital and hoping to benefit themselves as well, were equally
preoccupied with extending the boundaries of their economies by bringing
more land under the plough, logging more forests, diverting more water to
industry and so on.

Not surprisingly, the three groups approach environmental degradation
differently. For those who rely on the commons, the only response that
makes sense is to concentrate on what has proved to be effective in the past,
a response that entails maintaining or creating a space in which local
commons regimes can root themselves. Such a strategy entails pushing for
an erosion of the power of those who would undermine the commons, so
that capital flows around the globe can be reduced, local control increased,
consumption cut and markets limited. The demands of grassroots groups
are thus not for more 'management' – a buzzword at Rio – but for agrarian
reform, local control over local resources, the power to veto developments
and a decisive say in all matters that affect their livelihoods. For them, the
question is not *how* their environment should be managed – they have the

experience of the past as their guide – but *who* will manage their environment and in *whose* interest. They reject UNCED's rhetoric of a world where all humanity is united by a common interest in survival, and instead they ask, 'Whose common future is to be sustained through the conventions and deals cut at UNCED?' Their struggle is not to win greater power for the market or the state, but to reinstate the community as the ultimate source of authority – in effect, to reclaim the commons.

By contrast, the preferred response of world leaders and mainstream environmentalists is to seek further enclosure of the commons by the market and the state, in the hope that whatever troublesome environmental damage has been caused by previous enclosure can be remedied by more far-reaching enclosure in the future. This approach seeks to preserve economic expansion through a programme of global management of both the environment and people. It has never been attempted before on the scale proposed. Previous less ambitious attempts, moreover, have not only failed to arrest environmental degradation, they have exacerbated it. Nonetheless, it is this path which has been chosen by the Secretariat and virtually all delegations at UNCED, as well as by the major multilateral development agencies and many scientific and conservation organizations.

The threat of environmentalism

The issues under discussion at UNCED were not new: on the contrary, from the smokestacks of Victorian Britain to the logged-out moonscapes of modern-day British Columbia or Sarawak, environmental degradation has gone hand-in-hand with economic expansion, as commercial interests have sacrificed local livelihoods and environments in order to obtain raw materials, transform them into commodities, market them and dispose of the wastes. Nor has the destruction gone unchallenged. In the South, local cultures have fought successive attempts – first by colonial regimes and then by their 'own' post-independence governments, acting in consort with commercial interests and international development agencies – to transform their homelands and themselves into 'resources' for the global economy. Timber operations have been sabotaged, logging roads blockaded, dams delayed, commercial plantations uprooted, factories and installations burned, mines closed down and rallies held in a constant effort to keep outside forces at bay.

Likewise in the North, the history of protest against the ravages of industrialism is a long one, coalescing initially around the machine-breaking and public health movements of the 19th century and emerging latterly in the many and diverse groupings now challenging environmental pollution, declining food quality, countryside destruction, health hazards in the home and workplace, and the erosion of community life. As in the South, such movements have expressed their concerns using whatever channels are available to them – from civil disobedience to legal challenges, boycotts and alliances with like-minded groups. Toxic waste dumps have been picketed, sites for nuclear power plants occupied, polluting pipelines capped, companies boycotted, whaling ships buzzed, and media campaigns mounted in an attempt both to combat environmental degradation and to put the environment on the political agenda.

Where environmental destruction was limited to the local level – a clear-cut forest here, a leaking toxic waste dump there, a polluted river here, a salinized tract of land there – and where protest was restricted to isolated movements, the threat that they posed to established patterns of power could be contained with relative ease. Commercial and industrial interests were able to follow a strategy of simply denying the problem or of justifying the destruction in the name of 'the greater good' or the 'national interest'. Opposition could be met by force or played down as 'uninformed', 'reactionary', 'luddite' or subversive. The reaction of the Velsicol Corporation to the publication in the early 1960s of Rachel Carson's *Silent Spring*, the book which in many respects launched the 'green' movement in the North, is illustrative. In a five-page letter to Carson's publishers, Velsicol accused her of being in league with 'sinister influences, whose attacks on the chemical industry have a dual purpose: (1) to create the false impression that all business is grasping and immoral, and (2) to reduce the use of agricultural chemicals in this country and in the countries of western Europe so that our supply of food will be reduced to east-curtain parity.'[2]

Crude as such attacks are, they still persist. Recently, Bill Holmes, a former member of the California State Board of Forestry, told the 1991 Redwood Region Logging Conference:

In California we continue to plunge toward new ill-fated experiments in socialized timber management. The Hollywood crowd and other people in the US who hate America while worshipping Russia and its totalitarian system have jumped into bed with their environmental friends who welcomed them with open arms. They already had a great deal in common because, although not all left-wing radicals are environmentalists, certainly all environmentalists embrace some form of left-wing radical collectivism. As a result, the greatest threat to you, to me, to our communities, to our state and to our nation is no longer communism, it is not drugs, not AIDS, not crime, not poverty, not even liberal democrats, but radical environmentalism.[3]

Bill Holmes' vision of a communist conspiracy is clearly absurd, but he is right to be worried by the way in which alliances are being formed between formerly isolated, local or national citizens' groups, in order to resist the powerful interests that are threatening their commons. Indeed, it is arguably only as a result of such alliances that the previously marginalized discourse of environmentalism has been forced into the political mainstream, transforming ecological destruction from a 'side issue' that corporations and governments felt able to disregard, into lost markets and lost votes. If timber companies are now making noises about moving towards 'sustainable' logging practices, it is not because they have suddenly become aware of the damage they are causing to the environment (in many instances, they still deny the problem) but because timber boycotts and local protests have forced them to respond to growing public outrage over their activities. Likewise, if the landfilling of toxic wastes in the US is now being phased out, it is not because US companies themselves view landfill as an environmentally unacceptable means of waste disposal (US companies see no problems in landfilling their wastes in Britain or the Third World, for instance, where standards are lower) but rather because the spread of popular protest in the US had made it clear that 'not in my backyard' means 'not in anybody's backyard', leaving corporate executives with no option but to seek other waste disposal strategies. As Andrew Szasz notes:

> Community-based popular organization was the key factor. Indirectly, community protest pushed Washington to strengthen regulatory controls. Directly, local opposition . . . blocked the expansion of waste disposal and treatment capacity. . . . Popular pressure worked on two levels: in Washington, mainstream environmental groups and members of Congress facing constituency pressure recognized how salient and volatile the issue was and supported stronger regulations. At the same time, local opposition to new facilities interacted with these stronger regulations to drive up disposal costs, and thus to raise economic pressures for waste reduction.[4]

The threat of economic contraction

But the threat of environmentalism goes deeper than simply upsetting individual corporate apple carts. Tighter environmental standards – not to speak of environmental degradation itself – now threaten the *throughput* of resources in the global economy. As the Brundtland Commission, whose report *Our Common Future* initiated the UNCED process, puts it: 'We have in the past been concerned about the impacts of economic growth upon the environment. We are now forced to concern ourselves with the impacts of ecological stress . . . upon our economic prospects.'[5]

It is not clear whose 'economic prospects' Brundtland is referring to (at the local level, environmental degradation has been threatening local economic prospects for many decades): what is clear, however, is that environmental stress – and the pressure to ease it – is already denying *resources* to the global economy, whilst simultaneously depriving it of *sinks* into which the waste products of industrialism can readily (and cheaply) be disposed. As soils are eroded, so land is taken out of production; as the seas are overfished and rivers polluted, so fisheries crash; as forests are logged out or succumb to damage from air pollution, so timber supplies are threatened; and as the economic costs of mitigating damage rise, so capital is diverted away from productive growth. In the US alone, soil compaction – the direct result of modern mechanized agriculture – is estimated to have cost farmers some $3 billion in lost yields in 1980 alone. The damage already incurred through acid rain and pollution-related forest die-back in Europe and the US has been put at $30 billion, whilst the estimated cost of cleaning up the 2,000 worst polluting toxic waste dumps in the US has been put at $100 billion. No realistic figure can even be put on the social and economic disruption that will be incurred through global warming and ozone depletion. The likely loss of species alone makes the price tag incalculable.

Both Northern and Southern governments – voicing the concerns of industrial interests – argue that such costs could not be borne without sending the global economy into a tail-spin. For those whose livelihoods are being daily undermined by the growth economy, however, economic contraction is not the threat that the mainstream would have us believe: on the contrary, it brings the possibility of reclaiming the commons, of restoring what development has destroyed, and of living with dignity. As Gustavo Esteva, a social activist living in Mexico City, reports:

> With falling oil prices, mounting debts, and the conversion of Mexico into a free trade zone so that transnational capital can produce Volkswagen 'Beetles' in automated factories for export to Germany, the corruption of our politics and the degradation of Nature – always implicit in development – can finally be seen, touched and smelled by everyone. Now the poor of Mexico are responding by recreating their own moral economy. As Mexico's Rural Development Bank no longer has sufficient funds to force peasants to plant sorghum for animal feed, many have returned to the traditional intercropping of corn and beans, improving their diets, restoring some village solidarity and allowing available cash to reach further. In response to the decreasing purchasing power of the previously employed, thriving production co-operatives are springing up in the heart of Mexico City. Shops now exist in the slums that reconstruct electrical appliances; merchants prosper by imitating foreign trademarked goods and selling them as smuggled wares to tourists. Neighbourhoods have come back to life. Street stands and tiny

markets have returned to corners from where they had disappeared long ago. Complex forms of non-formal organization have developed, through which the barrio (village) residents create protective barriers between themselves and intruding development bureaucracies, police and other officials; fight eviction and the confiscation of their assets; settle their own disputes and maintain public order.[6]

But whereas economic contraction provides a space in which the commons can regain some of its authority, it poses a direct threat to those whose power rests on the ability to sustain productive growth. The prospect of such contraction becoming a *permanent* feature of the economy as a result of environmental degradation and environmental protest has thus caused alarm bells to ring in corporate headquarters and other centres of power. Indeed, in a leaked memorandum, the US Environmental Protection Agency has described America's 'environmental justice movement', best known for its work in opposing toxic waste dumps, as the greatest threat to political stablity since the anti-war movement of the 1960s.

Containing challenges

It is not the first time in history that movements for social change have threatened the power of established commercial and political élites. As in the past, the ability of those élites to survive with their power intact will ultimately depend on how far they are able to turn that challenge to their advantage. Now that it has become clear that environmentalism and environmental degradation can no longer be ignored, outright resistance to change is giving way to strategies for *managing* that change.

At one level, the emphasis has been on blocking those demands that cannot be contained without loss of power. Within UNCED, for example, elaborate manoeuvring enabled individual industries to head off measures that would impose too heavy a cost on their activities. Most notably, corporate interests effectively blocked discussion of the environmental impact of Transnational Corporations (TNCs): recommendations drawn up by the UN's own Centre for Transnational Corporations (UNCTC), which would have imposed tough global environmental standards on TNC activities, were shelved and instead a voluntary code of conduct, drawn up by the Business Council on Sustainable Development, a corporate lobbying group, was adopted as the Secretariat's input into UNCED's Agenda 21. The UNCTC's carefully crafted proposals were not even circulated to delegates. Meanwhile, a few months before the Rio Summit, the Centre itself was quietly closed down. Instead of being subject to a mandatory code of conduct, negotiated multilaterally, the TNCs emerged from UNCED without their role in causing environmental destruction even having been scrutinized in the official process, let alone curtailed.

On the contrary, governments, both North and South, have done everything in their power to protect the interests of their industrial and commercial lobbies. The US government's negotiating position, for example, has consistently reflected the close ties between the Bush administration and corporate interests: the guidelines issued to US delegates negotiating the Climate Convention faithfully reflected the position of the oil industry. Delegates were advised that it was

> not beneficial to discuss whether there is or is not warming, or how much or how little warming. In the eyes of the public, we will lose this debate. A better approach is to raise the many uncertainties that need to be understood on this issue.[7]

Instead, the negotiators were told to stress that 'the world community is making great strides towards understanding the science of global change, but many fundamental questions remain unanswered'; and that 'the economic impacts of potential global changes and possible responses are not well understood – more work is needed.'

A similar approach was adopted in the negotiations on biodiversity, the main priority of US negotiators being to block any measures that might harm the interests of biotechnology companies or undermine the patenting of 'intellectual property'. During the fourth Preparatory Meeting for UNCED, for example, the US delegation insisted that references in Agenda 21 to the hazards of biotechnology should be deleted, arguing that the risks have been exaggerated. In this, the position taken by the US delegation was identical to that of the Heritage Foundation, an influential US think-tank with close links to the US administration. The US also deleted major sections of the Agenda 21 text which would have imposed safeguards against 'the experimentation with unsafe fertility regulating drugs on women in developing countries'. A proposed ban on 'medical technologies in developing countries for purposes of experimentation in reproductive processes' was similarly deleted at the US' insistence.

Capturing the debate

Beyond such wrecking tactics, however, UNCED saw a conscious attempt by corporate and other mainstream interests to 'capture' the debate on environment and development and to frame it in terms that suit their purposes. Here a number of strategies came into play:

First, there was a concerted effort on the part of government and industry to distance themselves from the destructiveness of 'past' policies. Constant references within the official documents to 'recent' satellite data, 'new' studies, 'latest statistics' and the like conveyed the impression that ecological degradation was a *recent* phenomenon – and one, moreover, that had primarily come to light through the diligence and foresight of *government* scientists, *international* institutions and *industrial* planners, thereby protecting the credibility and authority of those who bear prime responsibility for the activities that have created the current ecological crisis. The past disappeared from view, discreetly curtained off from scrutiny. Instead, the public was asked to look towards the future and with it, a new age of environmental awareness in which industry – now aware of the environment – had put its house in order to the satisfaction of earthworm and corporate executive alike. Industry's record was thus wiped clean: the fox could now be put in charge of the chickens.

Second, there was an attempt to deny the many conflicts of interests underlying the crisis. Neither the institutional framework of global society nor the material interests and values it reflects received serious scrutiny. Instead, the ills under discussion were cast as having somehow 'happened' by themselves. No one would appear to have promoted the destruction, except by way of lack of knowledge, foresight or alternatives. No one was gaining power or profit from current policies; no one stood in the way of solutions. Instead, UNCED promoted a rosy-tinted view of a world where all humanity is united by a common interest in survival, and in which conflicts of class, race, culture and gender are characterized as of secondary importance to humanity's supposedly common goals. Constant references to 'humanity's common resources', for example, neatly obscured the fact that the vast majority of people have no access to those resources, which they neither own nor control, and which are selfishly exploited for the narrow ends of a few. (In Brazil, for example, multinational companies own more land than all the peasants put together. In Britain, just nine per cent of the population owns 84 per cent of the land.) Likewise, the flows of resources from humanity's supposedly 'common resource base' are grossly unequal. In the last 50 years, the US has single-handedly consumed more fossil fuels and minerals than the rest of humanity has consumed in all recorded history. The US beef industry alone consumes as much food as the populations of India and China combined, an orgy of consumption that is possible only by starving other people.

Third, by removing environmental problems from their local setting and accentuating the global nature of the environmental crisis, UNCED gave currency to the view that *all* humans share a common responsibility for environmental destruction, either because of the demands they are currently placing on the environment or because of the demands they are expected to exert in the future. Thus, instead of ozone depletion being blamed – as it should be – on local corporate interests (Dupont, for example) using their global reach to globalize sales of CFCs and other ozone-depleting chemicals regardless of the known environmental impact, responsibility for the ozone hole was pinned on the future demand for fridges in the Third World.

Fourth, by portraying environmental degradation as a global problem requiring global solutions, UNCED gave added impetus to those multinational interests who would extend their global reach. By definition, only international institutions and national governments were up to the task in hand.

Fifth, and closely allied to the above, there was an attempt to frame environmental problems in terms of 'solutions' which only the North (and its allies in the South) can provide. Underpinning Agenda 21, for example, is the view that environmental and social problems are primarily the result of *insufficient capital* (solution: increase Northern investment in the South); *outdated technology* (solution: open up the South to Northern technologies); a *lack of expertise* (solution: bring in Northern-educated managers and experts); and *faltering economic growth* (solution: push for an economic recovery in the North). The prior questions of whether money can solve the environmental crisis, of who benefits from capital and technology transfers, and of *whose* environment is to be managed and on *whose* behalf, were simply sidelined. The development process itself went unchallenged and instead the environmental crisis was reduced to chequebook diplomacy: a big enough cheque and the Earth would be 'saved', too small a cheque and humanity would disappear down the tube. All of which was music to the ears of politicians, corporate executives, bankers and business interests in both North and South.

And *sixth*, UNCED attempted to inspire environmentalist and industrialist alike with a 'crisis management mentality', in which the need for action was deemed more important than settling differences on what action should be taken, by whom, on whose say-so and with whose interests paramount. Few environmentalists would argue that environmental degradation has reached critical proportions – destroying local livelihoods, condemning species to extinction, blighting landscapes, and (if climatic disruption occurs on the scale predicted by some climatologists) possibly threatening the very future survival of humans and other mammals. But within UNCED the critical nature of such threats was used to justify giving those currently in power still more authority; to legitimize programmes which would remove control still further from local people; and to sanction more management, more top-down development, more policing and still greater control of people. With 'crisis management' has come 'war-room environmentalism'. The environmental crisis, it has been argued by some commentators, should be treated as if it were 'a military threat to national security' requiring 'fast-acting intervention instruments, such as an international environmental police force which should intervene whenever and wherever ecological threats are posed in or by a given country for the international community of nations.'

UNCED's prescriptions: further enclosure

That such thinking has gone unchallenged by mainstream environmental groups – indeed, in many instances, it is part of their rhetoric too – reflects the degree to which élites have been able to capture environmentalism and use it as a tool to increase their power. In that respect, now that UNCED is over, any hopes NGOs may have entertained about working on an equal footing with representatives of industrial interests have been delusions: they have constantly been outmanoeuvred. Worse still, the rhetoric they have embraced in the hope of nudging business and government in a more green direction is now being used to legitimize an agenda that, if unchallenged, threatens a new round of enclosure as devastating to the interests of ordinary people as anything that has gone before it. Consider the likely outcome of the new management regimes, capital flows and technology transfers that UNCED has set in motion.

Whilst local peoples have long managed their environments to sustain their livelihoods and cultures, the new environmental managers behind Agenda 21 have very different priorities. What is to be 'managed' are those aspects of the environment that have value to the global economy – from germplasm for biotechnology to pollution sinks and other commodities that can be traded. Increasingly, environmental managers assume the right to 'protect' the environment from demands that conflict with the 'needs' of commercial interests – a formula that labels local people, the main 'competitors' for 'resources', as the prime agents of environmental destruction. Once that premise is accepted, it is easy to demean the ways local people traditionally care for their environment. The way is thus opened for new institutions, administered for the needs of trade and commerce, to assume environmental management at all levels.

Within agriculture, for example, the policies promoted by the UN Food and Agriculture Organization at UNCED forsee the best land in Third World countries being zoned for cash crops. Only in those areas where 'natural resource limitations' or 'environmental or socioeconomic constraints' preclude intensification would farmers be allowed to grow their own food for their own use. Coupled to this zoning policy is the recommendation that governments should 'evaluate the carrying and population supporting capacity of major agricultural areas', and, where such areas are deemed to be 'overpopulated', take steps to change the 'man/land ratio' (their terminology) by 'facilitating the accommodation of migrating populations into better endowed areas'.[8] Transmigration programmes are explicitly recommended as a possible way forward.

Peasants who have been forced onto marginal lands as a result of 'high potential areas' being taken over for intensive export-oriented agriculture will thus be liable to resettlement at the whim of any government that deems them a threat to the environment. Since it is admitted that there are few 'better endowed areas' that can be opened for agriculture, the majority of the new transmigrants will have no option but to move to the slums of large cities or to clear land in forests. Many of the displaced are likely to wind up as labourers or 'tied producers' growing cash crops under contract to large corporations. Predictably, perhaps, the proponents of such 'sustainable agriculture' policies do not consider the possibility that ecological stress in marginal areas would be better relieved by reclaiming 'high potential areas' for peasant agriculture.

The global managers thus threaten to unleash a new wave of colonialism, in which the management of people – even whole societies – for the benefit of commercial interests is now justified in the name of environmental protection. Whereas in the past 'crown sovereignty' and 'poverty alleviation' were used to legitimize the appropriation of local resources and the dismantling of local institutions for the national good, under the new regime, integral local practices are to be broken down yet further in the service of systemic goals. This time these goals are not simply to provide raw materials, cheap labour, and markets to an international economic system, but also to supply environmental repair or caretaker services to mitigate the problems that system itself has created. Carbon-dioxide-absorbing tree farms will supplant peasants' fields and fallows, tropical forests will be taken away from their inhabitants to provide services to Northern industry, researchers and tourists, and population control efforts will be redoubled as a way of taking pressure off Northern-controlled resources.

The new and additional financial resources agreed at Rio are likely further to reinforce that management strategy. The loans agreed during the pilot phase of the Global Environment Facility (GEF), which aims to 'help' developing countries to 'contribute towards solving global environmental problems', give an indication of how green funds will be used to further élite interests. At the time, GEF's terms of reference restricted it to funding environmental projects which are of 'global' – rather than local – significance and which would therefore be 'of benefit to the world at large', its four priorities being the 'protection of biodiversity', the mitigation of global warming, the control of pollution in international waters, and the management of stratospheric ozone depletion. Few would deny that these are all areas of major concern: it is also incontestable that the chief perpetrators of the destruction in all four areas are Northern interests, acting in conjunction with southern élites. But GEF has not singled out these areas in order to take on the world's dominant élites: rather it is concerned with securing control of those aspects of the environment – the atmosphere, the seas and biodiversity – that are necessary to the continued throughput of resources in the global economy. Thus, by designating the atmosphere and biodiversity as 'global commons', the GEF was able to override the local claims of those who rely on local commons and effectively assert that everyone has a right of access to them, that local people have no more claim to them than a corporation based on the other side of the globe. Pressing problems with a direct impact on local peoples – desertification, toxic waste pollution, landlessness, pesticide pollution and the like, all of which could be judged as being of 'global concern' – are thus pushed to one side while the local environment is sized up for its potential benefit to the North and its allies in the South. It is surely no coincidence, for example, that 59 per cent of projects approved under the first tranche of the GEF should have been for 'biodiversity protection'. Nor is it surprising that the chair of the GEF, Mohamed El-Ashry, singled out areas which 'include important gene pools or encompass economically significant species' as the priority for funding. Biodiversity protection is thus translated into protecting biodiversity not for its own sake but for the global economy.

Likewise, the GEF uses the notion of 'internalizing' ecological costs as a formula not for preventing inherently destructive projects but for providing additional resources to them in the guise of green funding. Thus, El-Ashry told *World Bank News*: 'We now know that the environmental costs of building dams can be considerable. The belief in the past was that environmental considerations were additional costs that could be postponed until a country became fully developed. But we've learned that these costs should be considered investments. Postponing these investments can only result in higher costs later on.'[9] The message to dam builders was clear: not only does the GEF believe it possible to mitigate the damage done by dams, but it is willing to pay for such mitigatory measures. Such cynicism in the face of the overwhelming evidence of the destructiveness of large dams is unforgivable. For, in reality, no amount of animal rescue schemes, education programmes, biosphere reserves or direct monetary compensation can undo the ecological damage done by dams, or make good the psychological and social rape inflicted by such projects on local people. Internalizing these externalities by reducing them to figures on a balance sheet that can then be magicked away by setting them against supposed benefits may be politically expedient but it does not make the projects any more defensible morally, ecologically or socially. For what the GEF refers to as 'externalities' are flesh and blood: they are real people, real animals. They are not simply 'germplasm' or 'biodiversity'. They bleed when bulldozers crush them. They cry when they are uprooted from their homes. They are 'externalities' only in the sense that they are 'external' to the interests of those who determine the GEF's priorities. They are in the way.

Nothing could be more revealing of the agenda that UNCED set itself to promote.

Notes

1. W. Sachs (1992) 'Theatre on the Titanic', *Guardian*, 29 May.

2. F. Graham (1980) 'The Witch-hunt of Rachel Carson', *Ecologist*, Vol. 10, No. 3, March.

3. Quoted in *Earth Island Journal*, Summer 1991, p. 48.

4. A. Szasz (1991), 'In Praise of Policy Luddism: strategic lessons from the hazardous waste wars', *Capitalism, Nature, Socialism*, Vol. 2, No. 1, Issue 6, pp. 17–43.

5. World Commission on Environment and Development (1987) *Our Common Future*, Oxford University Press, Oxford, p. 5.

6. G. Esteva (1991) 'Development: the modernization of poverty', *Panoscope*, November, p. 28.

7. World Commission on Environment and Development, op. cit.

8. UN Food and Agriculture Organization (1991) *SARD Draft Proposals*, 's-Hertogenbosch, The Netherlands, April, pp. 12 and 16; and FAO (1991) *The Den Bosch Declaration and Agenda for Action on Sustainable Agriculture and Rural Development*, 's-Hertogenbosch, The Netherlands, April, p. 9.

9. Mohamed El-Ashry (1991) 'Sustainable Development Requires Environmental Protection', *World Bank News*, 22 August.

3.   Politics of the UNCED Process

Matthias Finger

The UNCED-process has made nation-states managers for global environmental problems, using the process to develop their skills. In the 1970s the nation-states were attacked for not paying enough attention to ecological degradation because they were so focused on development. In fact, they became identified as development agencies. Today, UNCED tries to give them future control over the global environment and rehabilitates them as legitimate actors to deal with the ecological crisis. They in turn will abdicate it to the transnational corporations (TNCs) as the real engines of industrial growth.

Quite logically, the UNCED process sought to divide, co-opt, and weaken the green movement, a process for which the movement itself has some responsibility. On the one hand UNCED brought every possible NGO into the system of lobbying governments, while on the other it quietly promoted business to take over the solutions. Non-governmental organizations (NGOs) are now trapped in a farce: they have lent support to governments in return for some small concessions on language and thus legitimized the process of increased industrial development. The impact of the lobbying was minimal, while that of the compromise will be vast, as NGOs have come to legitimize a process that is in essence contrary to what many of them have been fighting for years.

UNCED's failure

UNCED was organized as a two-year process of a Preparatory Committee (PrepCom), composed of delegates of all nation-states, and supported by an UNCED secretariat. The process was to produce the outcomes indicated below. Exactly 20 years earlier a similar conference – the Stockholm Conference on the Human Environment – had taken place. It had been organized along the same lines and was headed by the same secretary-general: the Canadian 'businessman and leading environmentalist' Maurice

Strong. Let me briefly present and discuss here the main political outcomes of the UNCED-process, and in particular how these outcomes compare to the ones of the Stockholm Conference 20 years ago.

(1) UNCED was to produce an Earth Charter, that is, a 'series of principles to govern the relationship of people and nations with each other and with the Earth'. This Earth Charter was to be the equivalent of the 'Stockholm Declaration'. However, a consensus on such an Earth Charter appeared to be impossible in Rio. As a result, the negotiating countries finally settled for a very much watered down 'Rio-Declaration'. Its basic message is to 'better take care of mother Earth in the future'.

(2) UNCED was to produce an Agenda 21, that is, 'a programme of action for the implementation of the principles enunciated in the Earth Charter'. Agenda 21 was to be the equivalent of the 'Stockholm Principles of Action'. As a result of the UNCED-process, Agenda 21 is a 800-page document categorized into natural resources and environmental risks management, whose translation into action remains to be seen.

(3) UNCED was also to produce an agreement on financial resources, that is, 'measures for financing the actions provided for in Agenda 21', in particular for financing environmental management, capacity-building and technology transfer. Both financial and technological transfers seemed to have lower priority at Stockholm. The UNCED secretariat had calculated that roughly US$70 billion, on top of the US$55 billion currently given by the North for development projects, will be required to implement Agenda 21. At UNCED, the negotiating parties managed to secure US$2 billion towards this goal. This money will be contributed to specific development projects via the newly created Global Environmental Facility (GEF).

(4) UNCED was to produce institutional outcomes, that is, 'measures for strengthening existing institutions, notably the United Nations Environment Programme (UNEP)'. To recall, UNEP is already the institutional outcome of the Stockholm Conference. For this and many other reasons, UNCED did not produce any new institutional outcome, neither did it lead to strengthening UNEP. And until the decision of the UN General Assembly in September 1992 the institutional follow-up of the UNCED-process will remain unclear. In any case, it will be minimal.

(5) In addition and in parallel to the UNCED-process, two separate negotiations were under way: the Intergovernmental Negotiating Committee's negotiations on climate change and on biodiversity. A convention on forests, in discussion in the beginning of the UNCED

process, had been abandoned quickly. The climate convention contains neither timetable nor specific targets, and is therefore of limited value. The biodiversity convention, on the other hand, is certainly the most substantive outcome of the UNCED-process. But it is also of limited value, as the United States and India have refused to sign it.

In short, the outcomes of the two-year UNCED-process can hardly be called a success. Rather, one could say that, considering these outcomes, UNCED was an outright failure. This failure can be explained largely by the fact that UNCED was an almost perfect remake of the UN Conference on the Human Environment 20 years earlier: an identical preparatory process taking place 20 years later, on similar dates, often in the same places, and sometimes with the very same persons as 20 years before. And this applied even to the UNCED agenda: under a very similar influence of Northern conservationist NGOs (especially IUCN, WWF, and influential US conservationist NGOs), UNCED, like the Stockholm Conference, worked on the basis of a natural resource conservation and environmental protection agenda, and promptly ended up with the same North vs South, or environment vs development cleavage. Again, this cleavage could be overcome only by the North pledging additional development aid to the South.

The very fact that UNCED was basically a repetition of the 20 years earlier Stockholm Conference merely illustrates to what extent nation-states continue to consider themselves to be the most pertinent actors when it comes to dealing with the challenges of global ecology. The facilitating process can be traced back to UNEP's ten year review conference in 1982. At that moment, and considering in particular the severe critiques addressed to UNEP by some governments of the North, in particular the United States, the idea of an independent World Commission on Environment and Development (WCED) surfaced. This Commission should be analogous in nature to the Brandt Commission on the North–South relations and the Palme Commission on the nuclear predicament. After a lot of politicking and US pressures, the WCED was created in autumn 1983 (UN General Assembly resolution 38/16) as an independent Commission reporting directly to the UN General Assembly. Gro Harlem Brundtland, then parliamentary leader of the Norwegian labour party, was appointed chair of the Commission by the UN Secretary-General. Maurice Strong, along with 22 others, also (re)appeared as a member of the Commission. After a three-year process and 14 public hearings around the globe, the Commission published in 1987 the so-called Brundtland report, officially entitled *Our Common Future* (WCED, 1987). The report is essentially a document that defines the main global environmental problems; indicating how one must look at them, and outlining some very general recommendations of how to deal with them.

It remains still relatively obscure what actually happened in the UN-system between autumn 1987 – the adoption of the Brundtland report – and December 1989 when the same General Assembly decided to convene a UN Conference on Environment and Development (UNCED) for June 1992. This was to be a process independent from the already existing UN Environment Programme, in charge of examining, among other things, 'the state of the environment and the changes that have occurred since the UN Conference on the Human Environment' (UN General Assembly Resolution 44/228, p. 5). In the meantime, Brundtland had established, with private funds, a promotional institution called the Center for Our Common Future, employing many of the former staff of the WCED, and located at the same place as the former WCED (Geneva). The Center's 'sole agenda (was) to further the messages contained in the (Brundtland) report and broaden the understanding, debate, dialogue, and analysis around the concept of sustainable development. The Center would move that debate into as many sectors of society and as many countries as possible', says Warren Lindner, the Director of the Center, and former administrator and secretary of the WCED (in Lerner, 1991:241). In fact, and as I will show later, the Center's main role was the promotion of a new way to think politics in the age of global ecology.

Yet, UNCED, though being an institutional repeat of the Stockholm process seeking to perpetuate nation-states as pertinent and legitimate actors, however took place, 20 years later, in a very different context than that which prevailed at Stockholm in the late 1960s and early 1970s. This was the context of the new global ecology and the emergence of a corresponding new global environmental awareness. Much more than the global ecological crisis, it is this new context which comes, via the awareness of citizens, as a new major threat to nation-states and their governments. I can refer here to the existing legitimation crisis and erosion of traditional politics, a process which has been further accelerated by trends towards globalization, especially by global ecology.

It is therefore not astonishing that nation-states seek to reaffirm their legitimation, by responding to, and to a certain extent even by incorporating, some of the new aspects global ecology has given rise to. Above all, the UNCED-process must be seen as an attempt by nation-states and their governments to rehabilitate themselves as pertinent and legitimate actors in the eyes of their citizens. Before showing how they went about doing this through UNCED, let me briefly outline how the new global ecology has actually challenged nation-states and their governments.

Global ecology – a threat to nation-states and their governments

One central feature of modernization and industrial development is without doubt the fact that both have been accompanied by parallel processes of globalization, for example: the case of growing transnational economic activity, development of the media worldwide, increasing information flow, homogenization of culture, and many others. Since the 1980s, the environment must be added as a new dimension to this globalization trend. Overall, these dimensions pose threats to nation-states and their governments, but for reasons that lie beyond the scope of this chapter, the globalization of environmental issues might prove to be the most difficult dimension that nation-states will have to deal with.

Indeed, since the beginning of the 1980s – in particular since the emergence of the theory of the nuclear winter in 1982 and the end of the Cold War in the mid-1980s – environmental issues increasingly come to be seen as global, therefore considerably accelerating the trend towards globalization. A new type of scientists, in particular atmospheric chemists, geologists, oceanographers, and climatologists, are about to define a new type of ecology, which I would like to call 'global ecology'. In fact and for the first time, the world looks at planet Earth so-to-say from a satellite perspective, a perspective with cultural implications that are still difficult to assess. More specifically, global ecology leads to conceiving planet Earth as a single, complex, more or less self-regulating system of bio-geo-chemical cycles. Global ecologists moreover demonstrate how these cycles are increasingly disturbed by so-called 'anthropogenic effects', that is, effects of industrial development upon the biosphere as a single system. This new global ecological look suddenly makes us aware that environmental problems are not only much more global than we previously thought, but also much more serious and much more urgent. Moreover, they are now all seen as being highly interlinked, possibly having synergistic effects.

Global ecology therefore, at least to a certain extent, short-circuits the more traditional views on environmental problems as promoted by conservationist ecology as well as by political ecology. Indeed, in 1972 at the time of the Stockholm Conference it was still possible to frame environmental problems in traditional political terms. And political systems, by definition limited to national boundaries, were still perfectly able to handle most of these problems. A proof is the fact that even the anti-nuclear and the green movements of that time addressed their demands before all to their respective national governments, which partly responded by a series of national environmental policies and regulations. These generally took the form of measures to better manage environmental resources, as well as of policies to better control specific pollutants.

Nation-state politics, at that time, was considered to be a substantial means for solving environmental problems.

This, however, radically changes in the age of global ecology: traditional nation-state politics increasingly comes to be seen as part of the problem, rather than part of the solution. But global ecology, the view of planet Earth as one single system, inevitably calls for some sort of global 'political' action yet to be defined. This global action, however, is certainly not identical to the sum of or to the compromises of national political actions. But how to move on from specific national environmental policies to global political action remains unclear. Clearly, therefore, nation-states face considerable difficulties in effectively responding to the challenges of global ecology. I would argue that global ecology is, indeed, a threat to nation-states. As a result, there is today a discrepancy between the new awareness among citizens resulting from global ecology on the one hand and the traditional means of political action (nation-state politics) on the other. In short, global ecology has created a 'political' vacuum, which waits to be filled by a new form of 'global politics' yet to emerge.

When thinking about this vacuum, it is essential to take note of the rapid growth of a new global environmental awareness. Indeed, new increasingly global environmental values and attitudes have now become so widespread, that in almost all industrialized countries global environmental degradation is recognized as the No. 1 problem. Furthermore, public opinion research shows that citizens with high global environmental awareness are increasingly sceptical of their governments' willingness and capability to deal with the global ecological crisis.

The UNCED process took place in the midst of this transformation towards global ecology and, as such, it sought to respond to the new challenges it posed. Rather than addressing the global ecological crisis in its own right, however, the UNCED process basically addressed the threats global ecology posed, via the citizens' increasing global environmental awareness, to the nation-states and their governments.

In order to show how the UNCED process dealt with these threats, I will separate the Brundtland Commission's preparatory process from the UNCED process in the strict sense. The first process, I argue, tells concerned citizens of the world how the new global environmental problems must be looked at, whereas the second process puts this worldview into practice.

The Brundtland process

The Brundtland Commission's main function, its subsequent report, and after 1988, its institutionalization in the Center for Our Common Future was to define how global environmental problems were to be interpreted –

in, of course, the perspective of how they were to be dealt with in the future, that is in the UNCED process. The fact that Maurice Strong, member of the Brundtland Commission, became Secretary-General of UNCED was just one illustration that the approach developed by the Brundtland Commission would be applied throughout the UNCED process.

In order to understand this approach, it should be remembered that the Brundtland Commission was created in the midst of the new Cold War, at the beginning of the 1980s. There are good reasons to believe that, at the time, the environmental problems *per se* did not attract world leaders' attention. Rather, the environment seemed to be a vehicle for fostering co-operation among nation-states in general and between the East and the West in particular. As Brundtland explained in the preface of her report: 'After a decade and a half of standstill or even deterioration in global cooperation, I believe the time has come for higher expectations, for common goals pursued together, for an increased political will to address our common future' (Brundtland in WCED, 1987:x). Was the environment, at that time, simply a means to promote international co-operation, as well as to rehabilitate governments' status and credibility? Indeed, governments, especially in Western Europe, looked particularly powerless, caught as they were in the Cold War dynamic.

By locating the Brundtland Commission within the context of the new Cold War we can better understand the main features of its way of looking at environmental problems. More specifically, this worldview can be broken down into the three elements briefly presented below: what I will call the 'same boat' ideology, the slogan of 'sustainable development'; and the idea of 'global environmental management'.

(1) The 'same boat' ideology says that environmental degradation – like nuclear weapons before – is a threat to all inhabitants of planet Earth alike. We are, therefore, all in the same boat, with no choice but to dialogue and co-operate: we will either win or lose together.

(2) The slogan of 'sustainable development' implies that there is no contradiction between ecological sustainability and economic development. Traumatized as they were by a potential nuclear conflict, the members of the World Commission on Environment and Development anticipated a potential new conflict arising from increasingly global environmental degradation: the South–North conflict. In the light of the 'same boat' ideology they therefore tried to pre-empt this potential conflict by promoting a corresponding 'argument'. As a result, the sustainable development slogan has come to mean that ecological sustainability is good for economic development, and economic development is good for ecological sustainability. Instead of promoting

co-operation, however, the slogan of sustainable development promotes, above all, fuzzy thinking.

(3) Combining both previous elements, the Brundtland Commission concluded that 'global environmental management' would be the answer to the challenges of global ecology. Global environmental management basically means that self-appointed global environmental managers will promote sustainable development with the approval and support of the world's citizens (cf. same boat ideology). Again, we detect the reference to the nuclear weapons' crisis of the early 1980s; as the nuclear arms race had become a threat to human survival, it must be managed on the highest possible level, preferably through a summit dialogue among heads of states. As in the case of disarmament talks, dialogue on 'management' has become a goal in itself.

Analysts of the Brundtland report have generally limited their critiques to the slogan of 'sustainable development', highlighting in particular the effects of the report on ecology, namely reducing it to a 'higher form of efficiency' (Sachs, 1988:33). However, sustainable development is only one of three elements of the Brundtland Commission's approach to dealing with global environmental problems; and, I would argue, maybe not even the most important one. Indeed, the Brundtland Commission's implicit conception of 'global politics' might be at least as important an outcome. Combining the three above elements, it can be concluded that the main characteristics of successful global politics are personal charisma, leadership skills, and political will; 'political will' meaning the world citizens' unconditional support for their global environmental managers. Note also that global managers are considered most efficient when they happen already to be in key positions, such as heads of state and industrial bosses. Environmental management solutions, in turn, are considered most efficient if they are a-cultural, a-political, and do not imply socio-economic structural changes. There is, therefore, above all, good reason to suspect that the new global politics envisioned by the Brundtland Commission will mean 'business as usual'.

When analysing the Brundtland report, one can identify three distinct elements of such a-political global 'politics': (1) the dialogue among enlightened individuals; (2) global environmental awareness-raising and corresponding ethics; and (3) planetary stewardship, a typical New Age expression (Brundtland, in Starke, 1990:65). All three elements are a direct outcome of the Brundtland report's failure to identify the real causes of today's global ecological crisis, and can be related to the preoccupation with Cold War problems. As a result, one is left with the impression that the only reason why sustainable development has not yet occurred is due to a lack of dialogue between citizens and leaders, between leaders themselves, between representatives of ecology and economy, and so on. And dialogue, it must be recalled, is never considered a matter of structure or power relations, but rather a matter of goodwill. No wonder that the Brundtland Commission came to very optimistic conclusions: 'We have the power to reconcile human affairs with natural laws. And to thrive in the process. In this, our cultural and spiritual heritages can reinforce our economic interests and survival imperatives' (WCED, 1987:1).

In short, the Brundtland Commission promotes 'dialogue' as the miracle solution to the global ecological crisis. But if dialogue was, perhaps, an efficient means to end the Cold War, it has become, within the UNCED process, an efficient means to persuade civil society to support their political leaders' transformation into global managers. Therefore, far from solving the global ecological crisis, global politics as promoted by the Brundtland Commission has primarily helped nation-states and their governments reduce the threats posed to them by global ecology and the global ecology movement.

The UNCED process

Non-governmental organizations (NGOs) – also called 'independent sectors' – have been attributed by the Brundtland Commission and the UNCED process the key role in this new global politics. They are now seen as collaborators with governments, 'providing the services that governments are unable to' (Starke, 1990:65). Moreover, along with industry and science, they are said to be partners in the dialogue, as well as multiplicands of environmental awareness, carriers of planetary responsibility, and signs of hope (Starke, 1990). Warren Lindner, director of the Center for Our Common Future, calls them '1000 points of light'. Therefore, considering their crucial intermediary role between the concerned and aware citizens on the one hand and the global managers on the other, some NGOs have been, quite logically, promoted to the role of key actors in the new global politics.

In this respect, the two-year long UNCED preparatory process was essentially designed to achieve two things: (1) to build a so-called UNCED-constituency by getting NGOs, and even more so NGO-coalitions, to publicly support UNCED; and (2) to identify some NGO or independent sectors' leaders to become associates in global management. For these two purposes the UNCED secretariat created a special NGO-liaison office, whereas in June 1990, the Center for Our Common Future created an International Facilitating Committee (IFC). Both, plus the accreditation procedure that easily enabled all interested NGOs to become part of the UNCED process, was to help build a strong UNCED constituency and select the potential working partners in global management. Of course this was not easy because the NGOs did not readily relinquish all their sovereignty. But in the belief that they were winning ground inch by inch, they failed to notice that they were becoming part of the system. In fact not all NGOs are equal but in making them work together it became possible to influence them altogether and let them play into the hands of Northern domination and industrial development.

Building a strong UNCED constituency

In order to achieve this first objective, Public or Global Forums, where 'governments hear the voices of the people' (*Brundtland Bulletin*, Oct. 1990:9) have been set up. Fourteen of these Forums were held during the elaboration of the Brundtland report. But probably the most illustrative one took place in October 1990 when some 1,000 people gathered in Moscow at the Global Forum on Environment and Development for Human Survival 'to hear almost every leading environmentalist, "green" politician, and religious authority in the world' (Starke, 1990:158).

The IFC, since its creation in June 1990, has held 12 Public Forums where citizens and NGO representatives can 'dialogue' with world leaders, and express their anxieties, fears and concerns. Leaders are supposed to listen to these citizens, take up their concerns, and feed them into the negotiating process. But this remains often an illusion because world leaders do not actually conduct the negotiations. At best, they are able to repeat these citizens' concerns in their own speeches or publications, as did the Brundtland report. At last in Rio it became clear that the Global Forums and other NGO-mobilizing events have hardly anything to do with negotiations: the citizens' summit – significantly called Global Forum – was parallel to and entirely separate from the Earth Summit. In this respect, the build-up of an UNCED constituency – which ideally should have comprised all citizens of the planet – was essentially a public relations exercise, mainly designed to legitimize the global managers in the role of real actors in the UNCED process.

One of the most important tools to build this UNCED constituency and certainly a unique phenomenon in UNCED, was the build-up of NGO coalitions. These organizations do not really promote a particular political project, except in so far as generally referring to the Brundtland report's view of sustainable development and global politics. As such, they sought other NGO organizations to adopt these views and to become involved in the UNCED process. Examples for this are numerous: on the international level is the IFC, but to a certain extent even ELCI (Environmental Liaison Center International) whose major event was the Paris NGO meeting in December 1991. And on a national level, for example, the Brazilian NGO Forum, the US Citizens' network, the Canadian NGO Coalition for

UNCED, the US Global Tomorrow Coalition, the Norwegian Campaign for Environment and Development, and many others.

Whether they promoted the Brundtland report's view and sought to mobilize citizens and/or NGOs into UNCED, or whether they tried to do exactly the opposite, all NGOs involved in and around UNCED became caught in what I call the 'UNCED visibility trap': no matter whether they promoted or protested against the idea of sustainable development, whether they sought to feed into Rio or organize alternative meetings, they all did what Maurice Strong and before him Gro Harlem Brundtland wanted, namely, increase the visibility and ultimately the legitimation of the UNCED process and participating nation-states. Moreover, many NGOs now themselves have a stake in this, as their own visibility has become dependent on UNCED.

Selecting working partners in global management

In this new view of global politics promoted by the Brundtland Commission and later implemented by and via the UNCED process, it is said that global environmental problems will ultimately be solved, once the world's governments establish a dialogue among themselves as well as with the main non-governmental actors. It was therefore essential that the right, that is the most influential, dialogue-partners were associated with the UNCED process. In general, it is these who can speak on behalf of a powerful constituency. In this regard, the concept of 'independent sector' as essentially used by the Center for Our Common Future is typical: the concept carries a technocratic bias, as it makes the assumption that the world leaders (the heads of governments) express the public interest, while the independent sectors aggregate private interests. Implicit in the use of this term is that all interests are by definition private, and therefore they all have an equal right to be heard by the world leaders, provided of course they represent a powerful constituency and have the means to make themselves heard. Consequently, the various independent sectors, such as women, indigenous people, youth, environmental NGOs, students, trade unions, business and industry, among others were asked to organize themselves into specific UNCED constituencies.

Inevitably, some partners in dialogue are more privileged than others to become associates in global management. The IFC and the UNCED secretariat promoted some independent sectors' organizations as privileged working partners of the UNCED process, whereas others, less organized and/or less powerful, were screened out. Yet, it is the business sector that has actually most profited from this new global politics. Business and industry successfully prepared themselves from 1984, the year of the First World Industry Conference on Environmental Management, to organize for UNCED; and in 1990 a Business Council for Sustainable Development was created. Quite logically, Maurice Strong appointed its chair, the Swiss millionaire Stephan Schmidheiny, as his personal adviser. It is no surprise that the new global politics stressing interpersonal dialogue and minimizing the role of changes in socio-economic structures, actually led to promoting the best organized and financially most potent independent sectors as UNCED's privileged working partners. This applied not only to business and industry, but also to some Northern, establishment-oriented environmental NGOs, in particular IUCN (World Conservation Union), WWF (WorldWide Fund for Nature), and WRI (World Resources Institute).

NGO coalition builders such as IFC, Environment Liaison Center International (ELCI), the European Environmental Bureau (EEB), the Brazilian NGO-Forum, the US Citizens' network, and others, also played into the hands of the UNCED secretariat by helping to co-opt parts of the movement, alienate others and destroy the remainder, while promoting themselves. These NGO bureaucrats are now, after Rio, a legacy for the movement to deal with. NGO demands have, moreover, been used effectively to serve the purposes of governments. For example, calls for equitable distribution of profits by Third World Network and other environment and development NGOs were used in UNCED by nation-states and TNCs as the key leverage to justify further industrial growth. If the North–South gridlock has been portrayed as the ultimate global crisis, this was only in order to allow further industrial development to miraculously emerge as the only solution to it.

Conclusion: towards a new 'green' order

UNCED has served to accelerate the process towards global management, in which the environmental crisis is used as a pretext to further hasten the build-up of a world technocracy managing resources and so-called 'environmental' risks, stemming generally from industrial development. In this view, global environmental problems such as resources depletion and pollution are seen as being caused by micro-actors, generally individuals in the South, but which, nevertheless, need to be managed globally. This will take the form of so-called global crisis management: environmental threats, along with individual fears and anxieties, will be used in order to legitimize a militaristic and technocratic approach, curing symptoms rather than causes and assembling power in the process. What remains is a profound absence of vision and leadership. No project is in sight to get us out of the crisis. It will need some time and catastrophes to get beyond UNCED. Further ecological degradations will be proof enough that UNCED has failed to deal with the crisis . . . but people, then, will only be more atomized, feel more insecure, and probably ready to accept more planetary technocracy.

References

Dawkins, K. (1991) 'Sharing Rights and Responsibilities for the Environment: assessing potential roles for non-governmental organizations in international decision-making', unpublished Master's thesis, MIT, Cambridge, MA.

Lerner, S. (ed.) (1991) *Earth Summit: conversations with architects of an ecologically sustainable future*, Bolinas, CA, Common Knowledge Press.

Lovelock, J. (1988) *The Ages of Gaia: a biography of our living Earth*, Oxford, Oxford University Press.

Sachs, W. (1988) *The Gospel of Global Efficiency*, IFDA Dossier, No. 68, pp. 33–9.

Starke, L. (1990) *Signs of Hope: working towards our common future*, Oxford, Oxford University Press.

UNCED Secretariat (1991) *In Our Hands*, Geneva, Earth Summit '92.

WCED (1987) *Our Common Future*, Oxford, Oxford University Press.

4. The Landscape of Diplomatic Conflicts

Tariq Banuri

When Chou En Lai was asked what he thought the effect of the French revolution had been on world history, he replied, 'It is too early to tell'. UNCED may not be in the same class as the French revolution (although many hoped that it would be a major turning point in our history) but even in its case three months are hardly sufficient to assess its impact. Nevertheless, now that it has come and gone we can at least begin to unravel its strands without fear of prejudicing the most immediate outcome.

UNCED can be approached from two different though interrelated directions: from the contrasting *perspectives* or the various *processes* in which participants and perspectives encountered each other.

Conflicting perspectives

UNCED is a tale of two cities. The North and the South, both government functionaries and NGO activists, entered the event with widely divergent perspectives, not only because of conflicts over economic or political interests, important as they are, but more importantly due to conflicts over meanings (on the larger issue of conflict over meanings, see Banuri 1990a, 1990b). The same event appears different from the two perspectives – as though people sitting in the same theatre were to be seeing two different plays.

Whereas more Northerners see UNCED as a welcome unfolding of collective action to save humanity, many Southerners, government functionaries as well as non-governmental organization (NGO) activists, albeit for different reasons, fear in it the emergence of a new imperialism, of new conditionalities, and of new obstacles to the alleviation of poverty and oppression. Northerners have lined up to take part in a drama of Noah building an ark to defend us against the deluge. But the South does not seem to belong in this story; it is in a theatre on the other side of the railroad tracks, where Jesus is being crucified to save humanity, where the poor have to suffer in their poverty so that the rich can enjoy their life-style. As a result, the meaning and significance of every building-block of UNCED – a political statement, a working paper or an inter-governmental treaty – can be apprehended only within its particular context. Let us not forget that the symbolism of a log of wood, too, depends not only on its shape and material but also on the story in which it figures, on whether in the end it will bear the weight of Jesus or Noah.

But UNCED is a tale of two cities in more ways than one. What for government officials was yet another process of inter-governmental negotiation, was for NGOs an occasion for networking and lobbying, for journalists a good story, for academics a paradoxical combination of folly and wisdom, for political leaders and celebrities a photo-opportunity, for environment ministries a chance to establish themselves at home as serious players, for foreign ministries another threat from ubiquitous global conspiracies against the national interest, for environmentalists hope and for developmentalists danger. Lastly, direct participants and distant observers seem to have experienced the event differently; and those who would hasten to conclude that the former's account must be more accurate should keep in mind the old Russian saying 'He lies like an eye witness'.

Juan Martinez-Alier prefaces his book, *Ecological Economics* with a quote from Gunnar Myrdal from a conference in 1968: 'I have no doubt that within the next five or ten years we are going to have a popular movement within the rich countries which is going to press Congress and the Administration to do many things for solving environmental problems. But the same will not be true in most, if not all, underdeveloped countries' (Martinez-Alier 1987: p. x). Martinez-Alier goes on to make two very important points. First, that although it would appear that Myrdal was right, this is not because ecology is a stronger force in the North than in the South, but because the latter is at a disadvantage in defining the international agenda. Second, the ability of the North to define the international agenda involves, *inter alia* an attempt to move the agenda away from the issue that the German geographer, Friedrich Ratzel (b. 1867), called *Raubwirtschaft*, namely the fact that environmental damage is caused primarily by the rich and not the poor. As Ratzel puts it, 'it seems particularly strange that characteristic devastation with all its grave consequences should especially accompany civilisation, while primitive folk know only milder forms of it' (quoted, Martinez-Alier 1987: xvii). The UNCED process reflects both issues raised by Martinez-Alier.

Paradoxically, the North is viewed as more conscious and respectful of environmental limits than is the South, when all available evidence shows that the environmental crisis has been precipitated almost exclusively by the North's wasteful and excessive consumption. Indeed, roughly 80% of the planet's resources, as well as its sinks, are being utilized by the 20% of the population living in Europe, North America, Oceania, and Japan (see Parikh et al., 1991). If the South disappeared tomorrow, the environmental crisis would be still with us, but not if the North disappeared.

Nevertheless, the perception of the North as more environmentally conscious is important. It has helped engender the belief that the North alone is capable of building Noah's ark to save us from the environmental crisis. As mentioned, Martinez-Alier has argued that this is a mistaken perception, that there are ecological roots and ecological contents in social movements by poor populations, in history as well as at present, and finally that ecology is potentially a stronger force in the South than in the North. He calls Southern egalitarian ecology 'ecological narodnism' or, following Ram Guha (1988) 'ecological socialism'. There is also an extensive literature documenting the environmental content of traditional systems of knowledge and their superiority in this respect over the modern system of knowledge (Banuri and Apffel Marglin 1993). The tendency to disregard or undervalue environmental movements in the South is best illustrated by the *Chipko* movement in India. As is now well known, *Chipko* began with the protest of a few village women against the felling of trees in their area. In the event, the publicity received by the action helped galvanize the movement and transform it into a national effort for environmental conservation, indeed, for a redefinition of the very notion of development.

Conversely, looking only at the number of movements explicitly committed to an environmental agenda in the North tends to overstate their influence and spread. These groups have been unable to enter the mainstream of political action, and their ability to influence the mainstream political agenda remains limited and derived from sensational events. For example, in Sweden, one of the most environmentally sensitive countries, the Green Party entered parliament in elections held in the aftermath of Chernobyl, but was ousted in the subsequent polls. Furthermore, no political party anywhere in the North seems willing to risk its electoral future by advocating policies that would help restrain consumption or reduce the growth rate. In other words, the supposedly higher environmental concern in Northern countries merits a closer look, and may prove to be based only on rhetoric.

This argument received inadvertent support from an opinion poll of attitudes towards the environment and economic growth, conducted by the Gallup Institute in June 1992 to coincide with UNCED (Dunlap, Gallup and Gallup 1992). It found no significant differences between North and South on the level of environmental concern. It also discovered that, except in Korea, a far larger proportion of people see the North rather than the South to be 'solely responsible' for global environmental problems (although 13 out of 22 countries held both North and South 'equally responsible'); and most interestingly, people from the South were just as likely to claim being active in the environmental movement or to have voted or worked for a candidate because of his/her position on environmental issues. In fact, the two countries where the highest proportion of the sample claimed to be active in the environmental movement were the Philippines (42%) and India (18%).

The misperception of North/South levels of concern is important. Because: (1) it explains the common view that the environment is a Northern issue, imposed on a reluctant South against its will; and (2) it has led to a view that the UNCED process was 'owned' by the North, a Northern initiative, driven and dominated by Northern concerns, and that its success was the North's responsibility. Even Southern governments and NGOs seemed to believe this and to act as if they were but guests at the event. As a result, their strategy became almost entirely reactive in character.

Raubwirtschaft, or who owns UNCED?

A more concrete result is that the UNCED agenda was responsive primarily to Northern concerns and views. Indeed, Martinez-Alier's cliam that the wealthy seek to move the agenda away from the issue of *Raubwirtschaft* is vindicated by the omission from the discussions of consumption and life-styles, debt and trade, or the nature of governance, and the obsession with population growth as the key to environmental degradation.

It is probably not subject to controversy that the environmental crisis represents an intolerable level of pressure, caused by unsustainable levels of human consumption, on a finite natural resource base; and therefore that environmental sustainability necessitates a change in behaviour patterns, in particular a reduction in overall consumption of energy, minerals and biomass. Controversies and differences arise in the elaboration. Reduction in consumption can be brought about either through changing the resource intensive life-style of richer countries, or through reductions in the consumption and/or the population of poor countries. While, obviously, both sides wish to avoid adjustments difficult for their people, the success of the North lies in its ability to set the agenda in a manner that would rule out the unacceptable option altogether.

A major factor in this success is the bracketing together of global and local resources. Here, the former term includes the atmosphere (and the oceans), which have been degraded through overuse because no one was responsible for them; and the latter covers say, forests or minerals, where degradation occurred in large part because those who had been responsible historically were dispossessed through processes of colonialism, development and nation-building. In the one case, the need is to establish a system of global governance in order to restrain those who overused the commons; while in the other case, the need is the opposite – to establish local governance and strengthen historic users in order that they may re-assume responsibility for their local environment. The confusion of local and global resources obscures the fact, argued elegantly by Lipietz (1992), that UNCED is after all an 'enclosures movement' to allocate rights to the global commons.

The North seems to be saying that global commons must be allocated on the basis of historic use, and local commons on the basis of ability to manage 'rationally'. Not surprisingly, both formulations favour the North. Southern interest, however, would have been served better if discussions of global commons employed the principles of justice and equity in the allocation of rights, historically as well as contemporarily. But it is not really a question of partisan interests. Justice and equity are necessary conditions for the inculcation of the value of restraint, and without restraint the environmental crisis will not be averted. Likewise, the allocation of rights to local resources on the basis of historical experience and responsibility not only favours the South generally, but also local over national interests within the South; more importantly, by allowing the emergence of an empathetic as opposed to an instrumental view of nature, it can allow a conservationist ethic to take root (Banuri and Apffel Marglin 1993).

Underlying the conflict over interests is also a conflict over language. The interests of the rich are served by the language of inertia: of national interest; foreign aid; financial transfers and business as usual; while the poor will benefit from the language of transformations and turning points: property rights; global commons; conditionalities (on the North); global inter-dependence; and global governance. UNCED discussions, from the outset, were dominated by the former language. Alternative languages crept into both UNCED and domestic political agendas in the South only incidentally and indirectly because of the actions of a few NGOs. For example, on global warming UNCED spent all its time debating whether industrialized countries, particularly the US, would agree to reduce greenhouse emissions to the 1990 level by the year 2000. The implicit assumption, that the 1990 level is somehow 'normal', is scarcely a ground for hope. A more appropriate approach for the South, as articulated in the critique of Agarwal and Narain (1991) would have been to ask for an equitable division of a tolerable level of emissions of greenhouse gases by the world population.

Similarly, in the language of inertia, issues become abstract and disembedded from their contexts. Population growth and poverty became the primary causes of environmental degradation, allowing decision-makers to drift into the complacent view that the solutions to the problems are known, needing only more money and more technical assistance. The point is not that these are not problems, nor that they are unconnected to the environment, but that attempts to address them without looking at the larger problems of inequity, injustice, and illegality, or without trying to understand the causes of the failure of earlier innumerable solutions are at best quixotic and at worst injurious.

All this is not, however, to assert that Southern governments were passive in the discussions. Far from it; they were united in accusing the North of precipitating the environmental crisis. But they used the confrontation not to bring about a change in underlying structural conditions, but to place moral pressure on the North to induce it to increase the level of financial transfers, provide technical and other assistance to facilitate the shift to sustainability even in local contexts, and forswear any moves towards the imposition of fresh conditionalities. The result is that what began as a dialogue quickly degenerated into unconnected monologues, one side intent upon saving the planet for everyone, and the other equally determined not to be sacrificed in the process of collective salvation.

Development without frontiers?
The positions taken by the South's governments in UNCED discussions cannot be understood without reference to the vision of an unending and expanding frontier that underlies their development policies (Banuri and Holmberg 1992). Resource constraints have almost never been important in this vision. The belief was that these constraints could always be overcome by better technology and organization – for example, by replacing green revolution technology with biotechnology. The need for restraining consumption in the North or in the élite sections of the South has nowhere been taken seriously.

The Malaysian example is instructive in this regard. In recent planning documents, the explicit objective of economic strategy is stated to be that when (not if) natural resources run out, the country should have a sufficient industrial and technological base to maintain its high living standard (Hurst 1990). This reflects an unconscious reliance on the model of growth and development provided by European countries, where for every unit of biomass produced locally a multiple is imported from other, mainly Southern, countries. The environmental crisis has been engendered precisely by the replication of this model around the globe.

In other words, the prevailing vision of development is based on the ability to access biomass either through political means or through better management and technology. Earlier, the political means went by the name of colonialism; today, they are subsumed under the widely accepted superiority of national over local interests. However, whether the means are political or economic, the assumption is that there exists a biomass-rich 'hinterland' that could be tapped to finance the development of the growing sector of the economy. Where such a hinterland does not exist, as in desert regions (for example, Central Africa) or in densely populated countries (such as Bangladesh) one senses a certain despair about developmental prospects.

The ubiquitous and hegemonic nature of this vision makes it clear why cynics in the South are entirely justified in their suspicion that concern for the environment is a ruse through which the North aims to halt the South's economic development. The North wants the South not to base its development on the replacement of indigenous with imported biomass. But this needs an altogether different model of development, and one that the North still appears to be unwilling to introduce in its own midst.

An associated factor here is the debt of history. In many places, the residual influence of colonial history includes the replication of colonial relationships in post-colonial societies, thus supporting Ashis Nandy's (1982) contention that the colonized seeks inevitably to become like the colonizer. Post-colonial governments and élites invariably saw economically backward and/or biologically rich regions and their inhabitants – aboriginal tribes, rural populations, or culturally non-cosmopolitan segments of societies – as colonies to be exploited for the 'national' benefit. There are striking similarities in the attitude of the Malaysian élites towards North Borneo, of the pre-1971 Pakistani élite towards East Pakistan (now Bangladesh), of the Indonesians towards East Timor, and of the Thai state, initially, towards its own rural citizens and rural areas, and increasingly towards neighbouring 'hinterland' regions (Banuri 1992). The export of colonial relations to a hinterland is particularly significant; as Thai citizens protest against unwise development projects, the Thai state finds it less costly (politically or economically) to, instead, persuade neighbouring states to undertake them and to treat *their* citizens in a manner that Thailand can longer treat its own.

Among other consequences, this vision of development produced a supporting system of centralized political rule in socialist as well as 'developing' societies, the interrelated myths of the nation-state and the national interest, and the degradation and outright hostility to local institutions, especially participatory ones. Another result is the low pricing of natural resources, especially of common resources such as forests; this again was the most extreme in the former Soviet Union, where natural resources were supposed to have a zero price (over and above the labour costs of exploitation), but others were not far behind (see Kollontai 1992). Lastly, and of most relevance to this discussion, it led the South's governments to acquiesce in the agenda framed by the North, being the only way in which the continuation of the development project could be justified.

As Goodland et al. (1991) have argued, the prevailing growth model in the twentieth century has been based on the assumption of an 'empty world': one where natural capital and human-made capital are substitutes, and where the natural resource frontier is expanding. In this model it makes sense to run down your natural capital in order to build up your human-made capital, thus shifting from a biomass-based economy to an industrial–technological economy. However, we are increasingly finding ourselves in a 'full world': where natural capital and human-made capital are complements, and where the natural resource frontier is shrinking. Here, running down natural capital is counter-productive because human-made capital would run out of natural resources to process. Thus, for example, in the initial stages it may make economic sense to sell your trees to set up sawmills, but when you start to run out of trees, your sawmills would have nothing to work with.

In fact, the environmental message is that at the global level we have already entered a full world, that is, one with a shrinking frontier. Therefore, we must start to live within our means. But this would be possible only if every country is willing to do so, in other words if every country were willing to accept the fact that its frontiers are shrinking. Thus, it makes sense to tell Malaysia and Indonesia that they cannot further deplete their forests; they must behave as if they have already run out of forests to deplete. Malaysia is, however, correct to assert that such restraint should begin in the North, which has been living beyond its means for over two centuries.

Moreover, and this is the implicit message of most Southern countries, if they are no longer allowed to deplete their natural capital to finance development, they can finance it only if they have access to other types of resources, namely: financial transfers and technical assistance from the North.

Concern and defiance

We should not, however, give the impression that every Southern government went to UNCED with the same concerns and hopes. Belief in the vision of development was itself conditioned by geography, resource endowment, and the nature of the political system. In particular, decision-makers are affected by whether they live in a world with an *expanding frontier* or a *shrinking frontier*. An expanding frontier will tend to reduce the willingness to compromise other objectives in the interest of environmental health, while a shrinking frontier is likely to make a country more open to a conservationist message.

In the former world are countries such as Indonesia, Japan, Korea, Malaysia, Singapore or Thailand, where the perception is of expanding possibilities for the growth of income and wealth. In Indonesia and Malaysia, it is because idle natural resources are believed to be available and exploitable for financing growth. Singapore and Korea, like industrialized countries (Japan for example), feel that they can access natural resources from other countries through trade, that is, through economic means. In Thailand, this confidence derives increasingly not from the country's own resource endowment but from that of neighbouring countries (Myanmar, Kampuchea, Laos). As long as Thailand can assert the superiority of a 'regional interest' over local interests, it can control natural resources in its hinterland directly.

Other countries (for example, Pakistan, India, Bangladesh) are less fortunate: they are beginning to see a *shrinking frontier*, that is, a growing set of limitations on growth because of resource constraints. In Pakistan four decades of development were made possible by dramatic increases in water and land. Now, however, there is no further water and no further land, and further growth will have to be based upon a static resource base. Neither have these countries reached the point where they could access natural resources through trade alone.

A second set of reasons that influenced countries' attitudes towards UNCED discussions is their relationship to the emerging global environmental crisis. Some countries are *concerned* (Bangladesh, Maldives) because they are clearly affected by global degradation. Others are *defiant* because they have been singled out as major contributors to global degradation (China, India, Japan, Malaysia). Most countries, however, began the day as *indifferent* to UNCED, partly because they were neither accused of contributing significantly nor felt exclusively threatened by the global environmental crisis.

The countries which responded most energetically to UNCED discussions, were those that saw themselves as unfairly targeted in the North's analyses and declarations on one or more UNCED issues. Malaysia took on the forestry issue because it had been identified as the most significant destroyer of tropical forests; China and India began to co-operate because the North identified them (mainly because of their size) as major polluters, even though on a per capita basis they were much less responsible than even middle-income countries. On the other side, industrialized countries, aware of accusations that their excessive consumption was responsible for the environmental crisis, repeatedly asserted the environmentally benign impact of their own consumption and industry, assertions that were often challenged by their own NGOs, unlike Southern NGOs, which support their governments on the issue of unfair accusation even when they oppose them on virtually everything else.

A third set of factors that influences attitudes along the axis of concern and defiance is the bargaining power of a country in the community of nations. Bargaining power is the opposite of conditionality; a country has bargaining power if the community of nations cannot impose conditionalities on it. In general, bargaining power depends on size, potential for pollution, expected growth, geopolitical situation and financial independence.

China and India are large countries and cannot be ignored or even brow-beaten publicly; both are major emitters of greenhouse gases (because

of their size and coal-based economies); and are relatively independent
financially. Both, therefore, have greater independence than, say, Pakistan
with its large debt burden, but since Chinese growth prospects are better, it
is in a far stronger geopolitical situation than India. Similarly, East Asian
countries have a high degree of bargaining power because of their virtual
economic independence.

NGOs and the democratic space

Another factor that has strongly influenced governments' perception of
environment and development, and through it their approach to UNCED
discussions, is the role of NGOs. The key determinant of the existence,
strength, and orientation of NGOs is what Korten (1990) has called the
'democratic space' in a country.

Both Northern and Southern NGOs made their presence felt, indirectly
(by pressuring their governments), and directly (by participating in
discussions). The effectiveness of a particular NGO depends on its
organizational strength, financial solvency and analytical capacity, as well
as the democratic space in its own country or in the global forum. The
UNCED Secretariat made considerable efforts to create such a space at the
global level, and this in turn opened up the space in individual countries.
NGOs are important partly because they can say things a government
cannot, partly because of their access to information at the micro level
(often not available to governments or international agencies), and perhaps
most importantly because they have begun to articulate a genuinely
alternative vision of development, one compatible with the new constraints
(see Agarwal and Narain 1989, Husain 1990, Guha 1993, PER 1991). As a
result, it is possible for them to speak with a greater degree of self-confidence
to the North's governments and NGOs than do the South's governments.

In those countries of the South where NGO activity is minimal (for
example, China, Korea, Singapore), governments have often tended to be
defensive and secretive about environmental problems, and therefore
reluctant to promote awareness of environmental issues. In many countries
(India for example) environmental problems were brought to light by active
and vigorous NGOs. This led to a more vigorous stand on global
environmental issues.

Similarly, government's openness to advice from and dialogue with
NGOs and other institutions of the civil society depends also on the strength
and ability of research institutions outside the government. In China and
Singapore, for example, where research and analysis are almost entirely
controlled or dominated by the state NGOs are at a disadvantage in the
dialogue. Where, as in India, the government's ability to analyse has
weakened over time, and civic groups have become increasingly organized,
a certain degree of equality is introduced into the picture. Lastly, where the

services of non-governmental research institutions are available to NGOs as well as to other private groups, they are able to base their arguments on analyses of a high quality. This depends partly on the efficiency of the government departments entrusted with the responsibility, and partly on the existence of effective independent research institutions.

While Southern NGOs, such as the Centre for Science and Environment, India, or the World Rainforest Movement, Malaysia, have supported the demand for additional financial transfers (and even provided concrete suggestions on how this could be done), their attention concentrates on how the resources would be allocated internally. Thus, they demand a transformation of domestic governance into a decentralized and participatory one. They also seek to establish the basis of global governance on a new set of parameters, including a dramatic transformation in the nature of the aid relationship. Needless to say, these views are hardly welcomed in the North.

NGOs have also been less concerned than have their governments about conditionality, largely because they see the basis of existing conditionalities to be the ineffectiveness of centralized governmental action. In other words, they see most conditionalities emerging on the one hand because of governments' corruption, inefficiency and incompetence, and on the other hand because of their illegitimate and non-representative nature. Governments therefore need to be coaxed into performing socially desirable tasks. An alternative, decentralized, vision of society, one based on the centrality of the civil society rather than the state, would avoid this problem. In this alternative vision, desirable social goals would be decided not by expatriate consultants but by society itself through decentralized and participatory collective institutions.

Nevertheless, while NGOs were (at UNCED) generally more responsible and more committed to the resolution of problems, their perception of global problems was also (naturally) influenced by their national or regional contexts. This does not mean simplistically that NGOs were partisans of their national interests – which they often were – but that they viewed their own experiences as definitive, not only for themselves but also for others from very different backgrounds. Given the self-righteousness of NGO activists, this often made a cross-country dialogue between NGOs more difficult than that between governments or between NGOs and governments. It is perhaps in recognition of this point that Gustavo Esteva, a well-known social activist from Mexico, called NGOs the last frontier of arrogance.

Sites of encounter at UNCED

In the first section we looked at the various perspectives that UNCED participants brought to bear upon the process. But just as UNCED does not represent a single vision of environment or development, neither does it represent a single, monolithic process. Indeed, UNCED can be viewed as a collection of sites where people with different perspectives and different agendas encountered each other. Four sites are particularly salient, the mass media site, or the most expensive adult education exercise in history, which brought together NGOs, activists, writers, academics, and journalists from various countries; a site for inter-governmental diplomatic negotiations aimed at identifying and protecting national interests in the face of imminent changes; and a site for the articulation and evolution of leadership or vision required for global cooperation to combat the environmental crisis.

In Rio, these sites were also physically distinct. The adult education exercise was conducted out of press briefing rooms, the offices and facilities of local and international news media, and through the newspapers and TV screens around the globe. The negotiations were carried out in the assembly halls and smaller meeting halls of Riocentro, the *mela* (Urdu – roughly meaning festival) took place in the Global Forum. The leadership exercise was confined to the last two days of the conference.

Many people have commented on the anti-climactic nature of the UNCED summit. Although a number of protagonists have tried to put on a brave face, it is widely conceded that UNCED was a failure in terms of the high expectations it had aroused. Yet, it could be said that this failure was not monolithic either, since some processes succeeded in meeting or even exceeding whatever expectations could reasonably have been attached to them. The adult education programme was successful beyond expectations, and the negotiations process as well as the *mela* achieved exactly what they had set out to achieve. However, and this is the main reason for the disappointment and disillusion, the leadership exercise was a total failure. The massive disappointment accompanying the last days of the Rio conference was nothing but the recognition that the so-called global movement lacked both the vision and the leadership needed to face the future.

Negotiations and conventions
The main plank in UNCED was seen to be the bureaucratic one, namely the actual process of negotiation between government representatives that led to the elaborate conventions and agreements signed at the Summit. The purpose of the diplomatic negotiations can be seen as protection of the national interest of each country from the impact of imminent changes, both because of the environmental crisis, and from steps that the global community will take as a defence against it. In other words, these negotiations can help mark out the limited area of co-operation that would

be available even if no country was willing to yield anything. It can be said that this process was fairly successful. The prolonged negotiations helped outline the very limited area of global co-operation still possible in an uncooperative environment. While this does not get us very far, even outlining the area of agreement is useful. The limited nature of the agreements are a testament not to the failure of the bureaucratic process, but to the absence of trust between various countries, particularly those of the North and the South. The former believed that the South was out to undermine their way of life, partly by asking for compensation for past and present threats posed by Northern actions to the global environment, partly by insisting upon changes in the North's consumption and life-styles, and partly by refusing to protect the biological diversity that is necessary to sustain the North's high consumption. Southern countries seemed to believe that the North wished to hoodwink them by attempting to take over control of their natural resources, diverting resources away from poverty eradication and income expansion, and using every means possible to maintain the existing disparity in consumption levels. In this environment, both groups of countries were unwilling to agree on anything that posed the slightest threat, real or perceived, to their national interest, narrowly defined.

The South's initial position in the UNCED process was indifferent and fragmented. Most countries did not see the issues as very relevant to their concerns. Environment was (and to a certain extent still is) seen by many governments as antithetical to development. Although several civic groups and NGOs articulated alternative views, they were generally treated rather cavalierly by governments and powerful élites. Interest was also limited by the scarcity of concrete knowledge about the possible impact of global changes on local living conditions and development prospects. More importantly there was and continues to be an enduring pessimism about the potential of a North–South dialogue on issues of global import. As a result, most of the South's governments entered into the discussions to pursue narrowly parochial agendas – the most obvious being to seek financial gains for themselves, rather than trying to influence the structural features of the situation.

By the third PrepCom, however, a number of regional discussions and agreements (for example, the ESCAP Ministerial Declaration, the Beijing Declaration, the Commonwealth Declaration) had helped bring these countries together, with the result that common themes began to emerge relatively forcefully. One reason for the emerging North–South divide is that the process of convergence of positions took place in forums whose composition did not cut across the North–South divide (or, even where it did, the representatives of the other group were not very vocal or effective, for example, Japan at the ESCAP meetings). Be that as it may, the positions of the Group of 77 (G77) countries and China were virtually identical by the time the prepartion of National Reports for UNCED began in earnest in early 1991. Note that China is not a member of G77.

Yet, a number of issues have not been taken up forcefully by the South. First, the need to link the discussions in UNCED, UNCTAD and GATT: the South has more or less accepted the fact that these discussions take place in different forums, even though it hurts countries with limited financial, analytical and professional resources. Next, the ability to set the agenda has nowhere been visible; there has been no attempt to seek a binding convention on poverty, or on the global distribution of consumption, on debt, or on sharing the benefits of technology. Biodiversity is another issue on which the South's positions have not emerged sufficiently clearly. After raising the issues of biotechnology and the rights of local farmers in the gene pool, neither the South's positions nor internal Southern discussions have progressed very far. (In contrast for example, discussions within Southern countries over the climate change issue are far more detailed and sophisticated.) Lastly, there does not appear to be a clear recognition that UNCED was essentially a discussion of global property rights. Neither National Reports (with the exception of Pakistan's) nor the Beijing Declaration adequately recognized this point.

The Beijing Declaration focuses almost exclusively on the issue of North–South conflict of interest. It lays the blame for the global environmental crisis on the North, identifies poverty and basic needs as the fundamental issues facing the South, and emphasizes the importance of 'new and additional resource flows' and 'transfer of technology on concessional terms' to promote sustainable development in the South. With the exception of Japan and Singapore, the position of virtually all Asian countries at UNCED was informed by the Beijing Declaration.

It is in large part because of the positions taken at the Beijing conference, and the strong advocacy and support of Southern NGOs that UNCED ended up with conventions and agreements that clearly lay the blame for the environmental despoliation on the North. This kind of an agreement was inconceivable two years ago.

The adult education exercise

In Isaac Bashevis Singer's story, 'Sabbath in Gehenna', the condemned of the earth talk among other things about starting a magazine, because 'When you sign a petition the angels throw it away. . . . But a magazine they would read. The righteous in paradise expire from boredom.' Southern governments did not really undersand the power of the media in UNCED, they kept presenting petitions, which the angels kept throwing away; but they never thought of starting a magazine.

However, the fact that the magazine was there affected outcomes far more than all the king's horses and all the king's men could have done. This very important role of the mass media needs to be highlighted in its own right. As Gro Harlem Brundtland has put it, 'The media is the mechanism'. This was abundantly clear in the UNCED process, where the ability of the media to create a sense of a moral community was very important.

UNCED represented a transformation in thinking along a number of dimensions: on 'development' which is gradually being transformed into 'sustainable development'; on the concept of the global commons, which has become more concrete; on the nature of the global order, and on relationships between sovereign states; on the appropriate role of the UN and other international agencies; on trade and development; on governance and domestic issues of political economy; on the relationship between the state and civil society, and specifically between government departments and NGOs; and on the appropriate balance between decentralized and centralized decision making.

Through the mass media, UNCED was able to focus attention on the emerging environmental and developmental problems in a manner that was inconceivable even a few years ago. Part of the reason for this was the UNCED Secretariat's decision to involve NGOs in discussions. NGOs helped create a 'civil society' at the discussions, they managed to keep a check on diplomats from their own and even other countries. They were often better informed and more articulate than government representatives, and better at obtaining and disseminating information than were the journalists themselves. They also engaged themselves in writing and speaking openly and forcefully on the issues involved, and lastly they were also more capable of creating the drama which makes good copy. For all these reasons, the eyes of the world became focused on the event, and therefore on the ideas behind the event.

The media's effectiveness may also have helped Southern delegations disproportionately. These delegations were often not in a position to access and digest the vast amount of material emerging from the conference and were clearly assisted in the process by the media's analytical capacity. At Rio itself, the UNCED media brigade was generally favourably inclined towards environmentalist positions, and particularly towards the South's positions. This was clearly not the case as far as the media in the countries themselves were concerned; for example, while the special UNCED newspapers were unanimously critical of George Bush's speech at the Rio summit, the US newspapers gave it a more favourable coverage.

The NGO *mela*
An element in the discussions was the expanding role of NGOs, both in challenging their own governments in domestic forums, and in presenting alternative perspectives and solutions in global discussions.

Besides acting as grist for the journalists' mill, the NGO *mela* had other important functions. It enabled people from different countries and different organizations to meet each other, to exchange notes, to learn about other activities in their field, to argue, to buy and sell goods, artifacts, books, papers, exchange ideas, and to acquire the confidence to deal with their governments at home. At Rio itself, the process was somewhat diluted by the fact that the main NGO event, the Global Forum, was located 40 kilometres away from Riocentro, the site of the governmental conference. Thus, journalists or observers were forced to choose between the two events, to the detriment of the quality of both.

Nevertheless, the greater involvement of NGOs in the negotiations process had some very positive results. For one, as a leading activist put it, 'Pity the leader who tells a lie', because their NGOs would be present to catch them at it. Second, it strengthened and gave teeth to the extremely visible and effective role played by the mass media. NGOs often provided the knowledge and information that gave journalists the right leads. Third, it strengthened governmental ability and effectiveness, because government delegations began to call on their NGOs for assistance and support. This applied especially to Southern countries, where government officials do not normally have adequate backup to ensure that they keep abreast of the issues. In short, NGO involvement may have tilted the balance ever so slightly towards the normally weak Southern delegations.

The NGO Forum, an initiative to draft alternative treaties on the various issues before UNCED seemed too strongly dominated by Northern NGOs; therefore, a few NGOs and individuals (mainly from Asian countries) tried to co-operate to introduce the South's perspectives and concerns into the debate. Specific issues addressed were those of poverty and environment, the role of consumption, and the issue of local rights, especially in forests.

Leadership: a failure of vision

A major conclusion that emerges from this process of observation is that the so-called growing concern over global problems is mere rhetoric. The primary objective of government representatives seemed not to be the resolution of global problems but the protection of their countries from the costs of global environmental degradation as well as global clean-up. This is probably the key reason why the region of agreement in UNCED was so limited in scope and consequence.

The real failure of the conference was in the area of leadership. The environmental crisis needs a co-operative response, and co-operation becomes possible only when participants agree to constraints on their behaviour, in other words if they are willing to sacrifice something in the short run. If everyone responds positively, such sacrifices are beneficial to all, and are therefore not costly in the long run. But for this to happen, effective leadership is essential. For a number of historical reasons, it was expected that the US would provide such leadership by accepting restraints upon itself, and inviting others to respond positively. In the event, the US was the most laggard in responding. Europe was too concerned about its own internal unity to provide leadership. Nordic countries took a moral stance, but given that they, too, refused to do anything more than they were already doing, they were unable to assume a leading role. Japan seemed unwilling to take up the position so recently vacated by the US. And finally, Southern countries decided to take a reactive rather than a proactive position. The result was that the Summit (though not the conference) became something of a farce.

Hegemony in the Gramscian sense includes both the ability to bring people within a group together on one platform, and also to be able to forge alliances with other groups. Hegemony is partly a question of self-confidence. The governmental élites of only a few Southern countries believe that they have the right to define moral and political questions in the international arena; others take the moral perspective of the industrialized world as the definitive framework for discussing global issues, and thus focus only on technical or financial concerns.

The greatest obstacle to the establishment of hegemony, in the above sense, is an absence of trust between the North and the South. The global concerns that led to UNCED demanded global co-operation and global institutions. But properly functioning and legitimate global institutions require the existence of a global *political* community – namely a community in which individuals recognize their interdependence. It is fair to say that such a sense of community is absent even within many Southern countries, let alone between Southern and Northern countries. More importantly, trust requires the existence of a global *moral* community – namely a sense of shared values of equity and justice across the globe. This, too, is absent at the global level, and even in most national states. This lack of trust between the North and the South militates against the possibility of arriving at agreements that call for co-operation, mutual sacrifice and inter-temporal as well as inter-regional redistribution.

This absence of trust is most evident whenever the issue of global consumption patterns is raised. The fact that there is a strong resistance against serious consideration of this issue in industrialized countries, including Japan and Singapore, and that there is no significant social movement to reduce the North's consumption levels suggests that such reduction, in order to maintain global sustainability, is not on the cards. Respectable initiatives in Japan (such as the Global Economic Forum 1991) do not advocate a decline in consumption levels, but rely on moral suasion to bring about necessary changes. This must mean that people in the North expect the South to provide the bulk of the adjustment to the crisis. As the

Beijing Declaration pointed out, however, the UNCED agreement could only be based on the principle that basic survival needs have priority; in other words that the needs of the poor should take precedence over the non-essential needs of the rich. Indeed, even within a Southern country, the rich would probably be reluctant to dispense with their own consumption patterns in favour of their own poor. The rich fail to see the political importance of providing for the basic consumption needs of the poor, mainly because they do not perceive an interdependence between their own interests and those of the poor.

The absence of trust can lead in two different directions: 1) it can be used to argue for decentralized decision-making, and for the gradual construction of global institutions; 2) alternatively, poor countries could renounce any interest in issues of global governance. The existing discussions have taken the second route.

This explains why the South in general, and Asian countries in particular, have not taken advantage of the opportunity provided by UNCED's discussions to confront the need for global governance. On the contrary, their main effort has been to use the occasion to ensure guaranteed financial transfers from the North, and to assert the importance of maintaining their developmental momentum. These notions have entered the discussion as common themes put forward by G77 and in other assemblies of Southern nations.

References

Books and articles

Agarwal, Anil and Sunita Narain (1989) *Towards Green Villages: a strategy for environmentally sound and participatory rural development*, Delhi, Centre for Science and Environment (CSE).

Agarwal, Anil and Sunita Narain (1991) *Global Warming in an Unequal World: a case study of environmental colonialism*, Delhi, CSE.

Apffel Marglin, Frédérique and Stephen A. Marglin (eds) (1990) *Dominating Knowledge*, Oxford, Clarendon Press.

Banuri, Tariq (1990a) 'Development and the Politics of Knowledge', in Apffel Marglin and Marglin (1990).

Banuri, Tariq (1990b) 'Modernization and its Discontents', in Apffel Marglin and Marglin (1990).

—— (1992) 'Decision Making on Sustainable Development in Asia', Paris, UNESCO (mimeograph).

Banuri, Tariq and Frédérique Apffel Marglin (eds) (1993) *Who Will Save the Forests?*, London, Zed Books.

Banuri, Tariq and Johan Holmberg (1992) *Governance for Sustainable Development*, London, International Institute for Environment and Development (IIED).

Dunlap, Riley, E., George H. Gallup, Jr., and Alec M. Gallup (1992) *The Health of the Planet*, Princeton, NJ, Gallup International Institute (mimeograph).

Global Environmental Forum (1991) *Towards the Creation of an Environment-friendly Culture*, Tokyo, Global Environmental Forum.

Goodland, Robert, Herman Daly, Salah El Sarafy, and Bernd von Droste (1991) *Environmentally Sustainable Development: building on Brundtland*, Paris, UNESCO.

Guha, Ramachandara (1988) 'Ideological Trends in Indian Environmentalism', *Economic and Political Weekly*, XXIII (49).

——— (1993) 'The Malign Encounter: the Chipko Movement and competing visions of nature', in Banuri and Apffel Marglin (1993).

Hardin, Garrett (1968) 'The Tragedy of the Commons', *Science*, 162 (13 December), pp. 12, 438.

Hurst, Philip (1990) *Rainforest Politics*, London, Zed Books.

Husain, Tariq (1990) *Managing the Environment: social organization, the informal sector and participatory approaches*, Islamabad, National Conservation Strategy (NCS).

Khor Kok Peng (Martin Khor) (1991) various articles in *Resurgence*, No. 14/15 (October–November).

Kollontai, Vladimir (1992) 'Environment and Development Problems in the USSR', Paris, UNESCO (mimeograph).

Korten, David (1990) *Getting to the 21st Century: voluntary action and the global agenda*, West Hartford, CT., Kumarian Press.

Lipietz, Alain (1992) 'La préparation de la CNUED comme processus de négociation: rapport à l'UNESCO', Paris, CEPREMAP (mimeograph).

Martinez-Alier, Juan (1987) *Ecological Economics*, Oxford, Basil Blackwell.

Nandy, Ashis (1982) *The Intimate Enemy*, Delhi, Oxford University Press.

Parikh, Jyoti, Kirit Parikh, Subir Gokarn, J. P. Painuly, Binhas Saha, and Vibhooti Shukla (1991) *Consumption Patterns: the driving force of environmental stress*, Bombay, IGIDR.

PER (Project for Ecological Recovery) (1991) *People and the Future of Thailand's Forests*, Bangkok, PER.

WRI (World Resources Institute) (1991) *A Guide to Global Environment*, New York, Oxford University Press.

Government documents

China, *National Report to UNCED*.

Japan (1991) 'Japan's Contributions to the Solution of Environmental Problems', Tokyo, Ministry of Foreign Affairs (mimeograph).

Japan (n.d.) *How Japan is Dealing With Global Environmental Issues*, Tokyo, Ministry of Foreign Affairs.

Pakistan, *National Report to UNCED*.

Singapore, *National Report to UNCED*.

Thailand, *National Report to UNCED*.

International declarations

Beijing Ministerial Declaration, Beijing, 17 June 1991.

ESCAP Ministerial Declaration, Bangkok, 16 October 1990.

5. Winners and Losers in Climate Change

Klaus M. Meyer-Abich

So far the efforts to describe oncoming climate changes have been mainly directed towards climatology. However, even if we had a complete description of climatic developments in climatological terms (temperature, pressure, and humidity), this would still not allow a judgment with respect to the impacts of such changes and even less to their desirability or non-desirability. Therefore, political implications must be based on further reasoning. Particularly, if some climate change has been described in the language of climatology, this description must be translated into terms of:

- ecology, i.e., into changes in the habitat of different species, or ecosystems;
- economy, i.e., into advantages or disadvantages and their implications for particular sectors like construction, tourism, and agriculture;
- political science, i.e., into advantages or disadvantages and their implications for particular groups, or interests, and countries.

Descriptions of climate change in these terms have come to be called impact studies. This wording is somewhat unfortunate because in an anthropogenically-caused climate change, the impact is not directed from non-human natural developments to humankind but the other way around; thus humankind is making an impact on itself by means of the rest of the world. Compared to climatological studies, impact studies (in the general sense) have been enormously neglected so far. To put it in terms of research funds: while expenses for climate modelling have reached the billion dollar level, those for impact studies have been left almost two orders of magnitude behind. Even with limited funds, however, considerable progress has been made by the United Nations Environment Programme (UNEP) IIASA study (Parry et al. 1988) and the report of the Intergovernmental Panel on Climate Change (IPCC), set up in 1989 jointly by the UNEP and the World Meteorological Organization (WMO) (Tegart et al. 1990). The following description of the implications of climate change for humanity draws mainly on the IPCC report, particularly on the impact assessment.

The following considerations refer to a climate change scenario in which an effective doubling of CO_2 in the atmosphere between now and 2025 to 2050 implies:

- an equilibrian increase of global mean temperature in the range of 1.5°C to 4.5°C and a 1°C increase over current temperatures by the year 2030;
- an unequal global distribution of this increase with the tropical regions warming by about half, and the polar regions by about twice the global average;
- a global mean sea-level rise of 0.3 to 0.5 m by 2050 and about 1 m by 2100.

These changes go together with a shifting of climate zones to the poles and to higher elevations, with modifications in ocean circulation (and, therefore, in carbon dioxide [CO_2] absorption), and with changes in the variability of climate (frequency and intensity of exceptional weather). Further details are given in modelling simulations.

The following analysis refers to a number of individual predictions given in the IPCC impact assessment. Considering the state of the art in regional forecasting, it is fairly improbable that these predictions bear much certainty individually. The overall picture, however, may be taken as a good indication of how the world may be affected by climate change. While this paper is not concerned with changes in individual countries but with aggregate impacts on different parts of the world, references to individual countries may still serve: (1) as illustrations for concreteness: (2) as an indication of risks; and (3) as a reminder that in any case global developments will ultimately spell down to individual situations and interests.

Changes in ecology

The next step in making an evaluative judgment of the implications of climate change is to describe the presumed change in terms of ecology. The poleward shifting of climate zones now means that the boundaries of vegetation zones (e.g., boreal tundra, temperate forests, grasslands, etc.) may be expected to shift correspondingly several hundreds of kilometres over the next 50 years. For instance, in the northern parts of Asiatic Russia, the vegetation zone may move 500–600 km to the north. Permafrost degradation may allow the growth of deeper rooted, broadleaved species and the establishment of denser forests of coniferous species. Again, in European Russia the forest–steppe sub-zone might change while in southern portions of western Siberia the forest–steppe boundary may move up to 200 km. More to the south, in the arid zones of the Mediterranean, climate change may result in desertification of the North African and near Eastern steppes.

Considering agriculture, its climatic limits in some parts of the world are estimated to shift poleward by 200–300 km per degree of warming. Upward shifts in the mountains could be in the order of 150–200 metres. Of course, the given soils as well as the terrain may not allow any advantage to be taken from this change. Also, the climatic conditions, both at high-latitude and low-latitude boundaries of temperate and northern forests, may shift hundreds of kilometres poleward, but the forests may not be able to follow their climate because the change will occur too quickly. After all, temperatures are expected to rise between 15 and 40 times faster than in past glacial–interglacial transitions.

Generally speaking, different climate regimes may be more or less hospitable for terrestrial ecosystems so that they will bring advantages to some and disadvantages to others. To what extent plants will be able to migrate with the climate again depends on its rate of change. The rates of the movement of species are in the range of only 10–100 m/yr, depending on specific abilities to disperse and on the existence of geographical barriers. The rates of projected climate changes are likely to be faster than the ability of many species to respond. Of course, corresponding to the degree of warming, the changes in vegetation zone are projected to be greatest in polar deserts, tundras, and boreal forests.

The expected changes in climate are so large and fast that a severe disruption of ecosystems must be expected in any case, even if some species might spread. Global biological diversity is, therefore, expected to decrease as a result of climate change. Also, ecosystems will not move as units but change their structure when species distributions and abundances are altered. These changes could be aggravated by increased pest outbreaks and fire.

Most sensitive to climate change are: (1) species at the edge of (or beyond) their optimal range; (2) geographically localized species (e.g., on islands, mountains, or in parks and reserves); (3) genetically impoverished species; (4) specialized organisms with specific niches; (5) poor dispersers; (6) very slowly reproducing species; and (7) localized populations of annual species. Particularly at risk are, therefore, montane and alpine, polar, island, and coastal communities as well as heritage sites and reserves.

Considering the oceans, the sea ice, for instance, is an essential element of the habitats of many marine mammals (e.g., seals, polar bears, penguins) and birds, and its reduction will also deprive land animals of migratory and hunting routes. In general, global warming will change the thermal budget of the world's oceans and shift the global ocean circulation, also affecting its capacity as a sink of atmospheric heat and CO_2.

Where land and water meet, a too rapid sea-level rise could reduce or eliminate many coastal ecosystems, drown coral reefs, reduce biological diversity, and disrupt the life cycles of many economically and culturally important species. Wetlands, like salt, brackish and fresh marshes as well as mangrove and other swamps, are vital to the ecology and economy of coastal areas. Coral atolls, too, are important ecological habitats with high biodiversity. If the rate of sea-level rise exceeds the maximum rate of vertical coral growth (8 mm/yr), inundation and erosive processes may begin to dominate.

Changes for humanity

Implications of climate change for humankind concern different countries, men and women, the rich and poor, different professional groups, owners and tenants, different communities, and do not affect all of them equally. On the contrary, even the smallest changes generally go together with advantages for some and disadvantages for others. The most basic experience in politics is that no action is equally in everybody's interest or disinterest, so that some will be in favour while others are against it. Considering this elementary fact of life, nobody should expect that a far-reaching process like climate change will have equal implications for everybody all over the world. It must be assumed, therefore, that there will be advantages for some and disadvantages for others, or advantages as well as disadvantages for everybody but not to the same extent. Even if, as frequently believed, in the long run the disadvantages will outweigh the absolute advantages for everyone, it must be expected that some will have lesser disadvantages than others, and that these will still be *relative* advantages. *Absolutely or relatively, there will be winners and losers.*

With respect to climate change, it is often emphasized that we are all in the same boat, but this is exactly what one must expect to hear from those who are looking forward to being the winners. The one-boat metaphor, even if well-meant, should not, therefore, be accepted without reservations. On the other hand, confidence in regional estimates of critical climatic factors is low so that, for instance, precipitation and soil moisture cannot yet be reliably predicted, and data on the regional effects of climate change on crop yields, livestock productivity and production costs or other economic parameters cannot be given so far. To indicate such data would be the simplest way of assessing winners and losers. But this is not the only way. Instead, *risks* can be assessed; even if the economic data were available, *vulnerabilities* need also to be taken into account.

Most vulnerable to climate change are those countries which:

- depend heavily on agriculture since this is obviously the economic sector most dependent on climate;
- cannot help themselves easily when agricultural production is detrimentally affected;
- already suffer from droughts or otherwise depend on climate variability;
- will suffer from flooding when the sea level rises.

Some or all of these conditions apply to the Third World. By contrast, some industrialized countries depend on climate to some extent but can in any case help themselves. Expected flooding may even prove to be an incentive for some economic sectors. Already from this general analysis it is easily seen that the Third World must once more be expected to be on the loser's side in oncoming climate change, while the industrialized countries again tend to be the winners, at least relatively.

This is shown to be even more so when the general patterns of anthropogenic climate change are taken into account. Again, I refer mainly to the impact part of the IPCC report. While individual forecasts in the IPCC analysis generally do not bear any certainty, the analysis may to some extent still be taken as an assessment of risks (probable losses) rather than a forecast of what will definitely happen. One is doing harm to others, however, not only by inflicting a definite (deterministic) loss upon them, but by exposing them to a (probabilistic) risk as well. Risks are facts, particular kinds of entities existing in the world. For instance, when I am at risk of losing my life in a specific situation, I am better off as soon as the risk is over. Also the value of an economic good is reduced when a risk is burdened upon it. As soon as low-lying countries such as the Maldives, Tuvalu, and Kiribati are exposed to the risk of disappearance as sea levels rise, this risk in itself is harmful for them because property is depreciated and they will have different conditions for long-term credits. Thus apart from deterministic damages, *risks are a second category of doing harm to others.* In the following analysis I deal with both categories together, because distinctions between damages expected with certainty or with significant probability are not sufficiently warranted by current knowledge.

The IPCC impact report leaves no doubt that the implications of climate change will be regionally different and is surprisingly explicit with respect to impacts on specific regions. Distributional inequalities depend on the following factors:

(1) Throughout the world 'the most vulnerable populations are in developing countries, in the lower income groups, residents of coastal lowlands and islands, populations in semi-arid grasslands, and the urban

poor in squatter settlements, slums and shanty towns, especially in megacities.'

(2) 'Change in drought risk represents potentially the most serious impact of climate change on agriculture at both regional and global level.' With respect to the socio-economic implications in agriculture and forestry, 'it is concluded that climate change could more likely exacerbate most current and near-term issues and tensions rather than relieve them.'

(3) Generally there is no doubt that changes will differ among countries and that some countries are better able than others to cope with the impacts. Particularly, the capacity of developing nations to adapt to likely climate changes and to minimize their own contributions to it through greenhouse-gas emissions is constrained by their limited resources, by their debt problems, and by their difficulties in developing their economies on a sustainable and equitable basis.' This implies a special responsibility of the industrialized countries even apart from the question of who is causing climate change. The high vulnerability of the Third World with respect to climate fluctuations has already been shown in several cases by the IIASA–UNEP study (Parry et al. 1988).

(4) 'The impacts of climate change on human settlement and related socio-economic activity, including the energy, transport and industry sectors, will differ regionally, depending on regional distribution of changes in temperature, precipitation, soil moisture, patterns of severe storm, and other possible manifestations of climate change.' Particularly, global warming can be expected to affect the availability of water resources and biomass, both major sources of energy in many developing countries. 'These effects are likely to differ between and within regions with some areas losing and others gaining water and biomass.' Climate change will also affect the regional distribution of other renewable energy resources such as wind and solar power.

(5) Further distributional effects will be that:
- an increase in average temperature and any change in the distribution of seasonal wetlands will alter the temporal and spatial distribution of diseases such as malaria, filariasis, and schistosomiasis since wetlands (particularly seasonal wetlands in warmer regions) provide habitat for the breeding and growth of vectors of these diseases;
- the predicted change of the patterns of cloud cover, stability in the lower atmosphere, circulation, and precipitation could concentrate or dilute pollutants and change their distribution patterns and transformation rates in regional or local sectors;

- changes in coastlines will mean that some people get beach-front property while others lose it.

  These are just a few examples to which many others could be added by further studies on the relevance of climate for human habitats.

(6) The effects of changes in ocean circulation, upwelling zones, etc. will vary geographically with changes in habitats, a decrease in biological diversity, and shifts in marine organisms. As a result of these changes, a redistribution of productive zones must be expected. Regional shifts in fisheries will have major socio-economic impacts.

Beyond these general statements, the IPCC report indicates specific changes in different regions of the world. These are not generally detrimental, or even catastrophic.

Implications for industrialized countries

Evidently the poleward shift of climatic zones may bring a warmer climate and, therefore, advantages to human living conditions in the higher latitudes. The course of history has been such that the industrialized countries have developed in these latitudes. They may, therefore, become beneficiaries of climate change to some extent. This has been generally confirmed by some of the IIASA–UNEP case studies (Parry et al. 1988) and is again pointed out in the IPCC analysis. Generally speaking, towards the northern edge of current core agricultural and forestry regions, warming may enhance the productive potential in climatic terms. Northern Europe and the higher latitudes of North America as well as of Russia and Japan could considerably benefit from these increases, even if they are limited by soils and terrain.

Apart from agriculture and forestry, which are only of minor importance for the economic welfare of industrialized societies, considerable benefits may emerge through more favourable living conditions, such as more sunshine and warmer winters. Together with the cultural environment, these general factors of human habitat (including recreation possibilities) are becoming more and more important for business decisions (where to settle or where to expand). Just as, for instance, a century ago the industrial economy developed where resources like coal and iron were mined, the economic shift from material and energy centredness to communication and information technologies is accompanied by an economic trend to siting in clean and culturally, as well as climatically, attractive regions. At present, in central and northern Europe for instance, these comparative advantages for the south have led to migration from the other parts. Climate change seems to imply that the privileged regions will be extended further to the north.

A surprising result of the IIASA–UNEP study (Parry et al. 1988) indicated that not only could less damage be expected for the industrial economies than for the Third World but that even advantages could come about with climate change. For instance, it is expected that:

- Crop yields estimated for doubled atmospheric CO_2 concentrations will be above the present-day average, a result that can be attributed to large predicted increases in precipitation, offsetting the increased water demand from crop transpiration caused by markedly higher temperatures. Parry et al. (1988) suggest that there may not be a sufficient capacity to collect and store the greater output;
- The relative profitability of different crops will change, and thus the optimum patterns according to which they are grown in different regions. With CO_2 doubling, some crops can be expected to do better than others. For instance, in the Moscow region of Russia, crops with greater thermal requirements (such as maize) may show a greater increase in yield than cold-region crops (such as potatoes and oats);
- The enhanced growth rates of boreal (northern) forests, in the long run, may lead to increased supply of forest products on the world market.

Correspondingly, a similar study of the US Environmental Protection Agency (EPA 1988) refers to economic modelling results, showing that the production capacity of US agriculture appears to be adequate to meet domestic needs, even under the more extreme climate change scenarios. 'Only small to moderate economic losses are estimated when climate change scenarios are modelled without the beneficial effects of carbon dioxide on crop yields.' Of course, agricultural production will have to shift northward, for instance to Minnesota, Wisconsin, and northern Michigan. The farmers in Appalachia, the south-east and the northern Great Plains in the US will not be happy about this. However, as long as the discriminated south is part of the same country that benefits from gains in the north, this is a national problem which does not ask for too much solidarity compared to the current status of political ethics.

A clear-cut advantage is predicted by the IIASA–UNEP study for Iceland. The model calculation for a doubled CO_2 concentration in the atmosphere predicts that the mean annual temperature and precipitation will be 4°C and 15% above the 1951–80 baseline; the onset of the growing season is brought forward by 48 days; hay yields increase by 66% and pasture yields by 49 to 52%; the sheep-carrying capacity of improved grassland increases by 253% and of range lands by 64 to 66%; lamb carcass weight increases by 12% and sheep-feeding requirements decrease by 53%. Fairly pleasant expectations, if one accepts these preliminary calculations, can also be held for Finland and Japan. In both of these countries, again, the north appears to be comparatively better off than the south. For instance, in northern Japan the rice-growing area could be doubled.

With respect to the ex-USSR, the study also suggests fairly favourable developments with climate change. For instance, in the central region, winter-wheat yields are expected to increase by 30% while barley yields decrease 4%. Estimates also suggest a substantial (17%) increase in spring-wheat yields for the northern part of the country. I would not be surprised, therefore, if the fairly positive assessment of the oncoming climate change, which the well-known Russian climatologist, M. I. Budyko, gave at the Hamburg Congress on Climate and Development in November 1988, had some political relevance in his country (Budyko and Sedunov 1988).

A more favourable human habitat cannot be denied as a general long-term perspective, but as soon as one looks at the changes which must be expected in the near future the probable advantages are balanced by numerous disadvantages:

- Current stands in boreal forests will mature and decline during a climate to which they are increasingly poorly adapted. Owing to physical stress, mortality will increase, as will the susceptibility to insects, diseases, and fires.
- In the northern mid-latitude regions, where summer drying may reduce productive potential (e.g., in the south and central US and in southern Europe), yield potential in agriculture is estimated to fall by 10–30% under a doubled CO_2 climate by the middle of the next century.
- In western Europe, southern US, and western Australia, surplus production of cereals could be reduced so that exports are at risk.
- Horticultural production in mid-latitude regions may be reduced owing to insufficient accumulated winter chilling.
- Temperature increases may extend the geographic range of some insect pests, diseases, and weeds, allowing their expansion to new regions as they warm and become suitable habitats.
- Vector-borne and viral diseases such as malaria, schistosomiasis, and dengue can be expected to shift to higher latitudes under warmer climatic conditions.
- General circulation model simulations for Europe show that precipitation and run-off may increase in the North (possibly causing flooding problems) while the Mediterranean countries of Europe may experience a decline in run-off, thereby increasing the already serious and frequent water supply shortages there. Agriculture will probably suffer the most adverse effects.
- Flooding problems could arise in many northern rivers of the ex-USSR. Increased run-off would notably improve the water quality of the Caspian Sea but not suffice to save the Aral Sea.

- In the US the arid and semi-arid regions, like similar areas in the world, may be most severely affected by global warming. A special study has shown that the Delaware River's run-off would decline by 9–25%, causing problems for the water supply of Philadelphia and New York.
- Further water circulation effects are expected to be prolonged periods of droughts and shorter periods of intense precipitation in Japan, an expansion of the summer-dominant rainfall area of Australia and considerably more rain in Great Britain.
- Of course, the area of snow cover (seasonally 62% of the Eurasian continent and all of North America 35°N) is expected to decrease with global warming. Reductions in both the temporal and spatial seasonal snow cover will again inadvertently affect the availability of water. Particularly sensitive may be areas such as the Alps and Carpathians, the Altai mountains of Central Asia, the Syr Dar'ya and Amu Dar'ya region of the ex-USSR, the Rocky Mountains, and the North American Great Plains, all of which are dependent on snowmelt for the majority of their spring and summer water resources. Changes in snow cover will also affect tourism and recreation-based industries and societies.
- At present, about 20–25% of the land surface of the Earth contains permafrost. Although in the permafrost region, global warming may result in expansion of human settlement poleward, thawing of the permafrost may also disrupt infrastructure and transport and adversely affect the stability of existing buildings, as well as the conditions for future construction. The socio-economic consequences of these changes should not be underestimated. It is expected that a 2°C global warming would shift the southern boundary of the climatic zone currently associated with permafrost over most of Siberia north and north-east, by at least 500–700km. However, the southern extent of permafrost will lag behind this, moving only 25–50 km in the next 40–50 years. During this period the depth of the active layer is expected to increase by about one metre.
- Last but not least, as the sea level rises, much of the infrastructure in low-lying urban areas may be affected, requiring major engineering design adjustments and investments. In particular, storm water drainage and sewage systems of many cities will be affected. Coastal protection structures, highways, power plants, and bridges may require redesign and reinforcement to withstand increased flooding, erosion, storm surges, wave attack, and seawater intrusion.

All of these changes are undesirable; many of them would inflict high costs on the countries concerned. As long as the West Antarctic ice sheet does not collapse, however, none of them seems to pose a catastrophic threat. In fact, all of these problems have, in principle, been successfully handled in the past, though not as quickly as countries should respond to climate change. In some cases, losses may already have been balanced by gains elsewhere, during this transition period to the future climate, e.g., agricultural losses in the southern US may have been balanced by gains in the northern states. In other cases, infrastructures in need of renewal or modernization, with respect to climate change, can be adapted slowly over decades. In any case, the actual costs will represent only a fraction of what has been spent for military armament. Therefore, if some of the industrialized countries decided that their poleward expansion was an economic incentive for approaching new frontiers by means of climate change, they would be able to pursue this goal actively since the economic resources would be available.

Climate policies of the industrialized countries then will have to balance uncertain but possible long-term advantages against fairly certain short-term disadvantages. To prevent climate change, therefore, implied short-term disadvantages outweigh the risk of losing long-term advantages. If governments decided (as they usually do in environmental matters) to prefer short-term gains to reasonable long-range considerations, this kind of rationale might lead to the prevention of climate change. This is by no means a clear case, however, since a lot of money would have to be spent to prevent further climate change. By contrast, the countries of the Third World are in a completely different position.

Implications for the Third World

Even a scrupulous evaluation of the IPCC impact report produces no hint that the situation of the Third World could be generally improved by climate change in some respects. The same is true for the earlier report by Parry et al. (1988). Of course, comparative advantages of some Third World countries with respect to others may come up, e.g., in fisheries due to changes in oceanic upwelling. However, these generally do not seem to help the poor relative to the rich. There are, however, general aggravations the other way around. The Third World is not only more vulnerable than the industrialized countries, it will be hit harder.

• Climatically induced changes in natural terrestrial ecosystems will have far-reaching socio-economic implications, especially in those regions of the globe where societies and their economies directly depend on the integrity of those systems for their welfare. Changes in the availability of food, fuel, medicine, construction materials, fibre products, recreational attractiveness, and general income must be expected when those ecosystems no longer provide what they used to do.

- 'One can reliably predict that certain developing countries will be extremely vulnerable to climate changes because they are already at the limits of their capacity to cope with climatic events' (IPCC 1990). These include populations in low-lying coastal regions and islands, subsistence farmers, populations in semi-arid grasslands, and the urban poor. Their vulnerability to the adverse implications of climate change is high because of limited access to the necessary information, infrastructure, human expertise, and financial resources. According to IPCC, the adaptive capacity of 'developing' economies is generally very low (not only in agriculture), and there is some evidence to suggest that their industries may also be particularly vulnerable to climatic change.
- In agriculture, according to the IPCC impacts report, two broad sets of regions appear to be most vulnerable to climate change: (1) some semi-arid, tropical and subtropical regions (such as western Arabia, the Maghreb, western West Africa, Horn of Africa and southern Africa, eastern Brazil); and (2) some humid tropical and equatorial regions (such as South-East Asia and Central America). Also, the productive capacity of South America and other net exporters of cereals could decline.
- Increase in drought risk is probably the most serious impact of climate change on agriculture. Those countries suffering from drought already will suffer even more in the future. These are mainly countries of the Third World. Increased drought frequency also implies forest degradation and more fire risk.
- A regional case is that in the semi-arid, arid, and hyper-arid ecoclimatic zones of the Mediterranean, greenhouse-gas-induced climate change 'will reduce plant productivity and result in desertification of the North African and Near Eastern steppes owing to increased evapotranspiration. The upper limit of the deserts would migrate under the influence of climate change and most likely extend into the area that currently corresponds to the lower limits of the Semi-Arid Zone (i.e., foothills of the High, Mid and Tell Atlas and Tunisian Dorsal in Northern Africa, and of the main mountain ranges of the Near-Middle East: Taurus, Lebanon, Alaoui, Kurdistan, Zagros and Alborz)' (IPCC 1990).
- With respect to water resources, the regions that appear to be at greatest risk, by climate change, in terms of serious threats to sustaining the population, are:

  (1) Africa: Maghreb, Sahel, the north of Africa, southern Africa;
  (2) Asia: western Arabia, South-East Asia, the Indian subcontinent;
  (3) America: Mexico, Central America, south-west US, part of eastern Brazil;
  (4) Europe: the Mediterranean zone.

In many instances, it can be expected that changes in hydrologic extremes in response to global warming will be more significant than changes in hydrologic mean conditions. 'Water shortages caused by irregular rainfall may especially affect developing countries, as seen in the case of the Zambezi river basin' (IPCC 1990) Biomass (fuel, wood) provides more than 90% of the energy in most of the countries of sub-Saharan Africa. Changed moisture conditions in some areas, reducing this biomass, could pose grave problems for domestic energy needs as well as for the construction of shelter. Increased scarcity of water will also have health impacts, especially in large urban areas.

- Climate change may make some present hydroelectric power facilities obsolete. Changes in cloud cover, precipitation and wind intensity will also affect the availability of other forms of renewable energy.

- In the short term, fisheries could benefit when marshes flood, die, and decompose; however, 'in the longer term, by 2050, the overall impact on fisheries and wildlife is likely to be negative.' Regional shifts will also have major socio-economic impacts.

- Climate change imperils the existence of entire countries (such as the Maldives, Tuvalu, and Kiribati) by a rise of only a few metres in sea levels. Populous river delta and coastal areas of such countries as Egypt, Bangladesh, India, China, and Indonesia are threatened by inundation from even a moderate global sea-level rise. For instance, if it rose one metre, 12–15% of Egypt's arable land and 14% of Bangladesh's net cropped areas would be below sea-level, and tens of millions of inhabitants could be displaced by inundation. Also, low-lying urban infrastructure would be destroyed, freshwater supplies contaminated, and coastlines altered. Again, like in the industrialized countries but in a very different economic situation, coastal protection structures, highways, power plants, and bridges may require redesign and reinforcement to withstand increased flooding, erosion, storm surges, wave attack, and seawater intrusion.

Taking these implications together suggests that greenhouse-gas-induced climate change will severely aggravate the general situation of the Third World. Even if some countries may expect relative advantages with respect to others, which could be defined by further regionalizing climate modelling simulations, on the whole there is little to be seen that is positive for the Third World in these projections.

Considering the quality of regional climate projections at present, I expect that further studies will modify, as well as make more specific, the changes in individual countries mentioned in the above assessment. However, there is no reason to believe that the general result will be changed if some names and data were exchanged for others. With respect to equities and inequities then, we have to face the fact that the Third World is the prospective loser. Could this picture be changed by an adequate political response? And may such a response be expected?

Climate politics and the new inequality

To consider political responses to inequities induced by climate change, the basic observation is that not only are the implications of such change unevenly distributed internationally, but also its causes. Countries, however, are not affected according to their share of responsibility for the climate change. Taking CO_2 as the predominant greenhouse gas, the average per capita consumption in 1985 in the industrialized countries was almost ten times as high as in the Third World, namely 3.12 and 0.36 t carbon/person. This imbalance is demonstrated in Table 5.1.

The foregoing analysis shows that those who cause about three-quarters of the climate change will be least affected by the implications or will even have absolute advantages. Those who will suffer from it most, share the responsibility only to the extent of about one-quarter. This picture remains about the same when the other greenhouse gases are also taken into account. Of course, with respect to the future, the projections are that the share of Third World countries in causing climate change would rise with economic welfare (according to IPCC 1990a, to 44% of 12 billion tons in 2025), but this depends on the degree of welfare to be expected.

Table 5.1
The emissions of carbon by sectors of the world community due to the combustion of fossil fuels (after PCC 1990)

	Gt/yr	% of Total Global
Industrialized Countries	3.83	74
Western Europe	0.85	16
North America	1.34	26
OECD Pacific	0.31	6
Centrally planned Europe	1.33	26
Third World Countries	1.33	26
Africa	0.17	3
Latin America	0.22	4
South and East Asia	0.27	5
Centrally planned Asia	0.54	10
Middle East	0.13	3

If an international sovereign could apply the 'polluter pays principle', generally so well accepted within industrial market economies, the political response clearly would be:

(1) that the industrialized countries, through preventive technologies as soon as possible, must reduce greenhouse-gas emissions to a level so that they would no longer live at the expense of the welfare of others and of future generations;

(2) that the industrialized countries should be made liable for the harm they are doing to Third World countries as far as this has already happened or can no longer be prevented. With respect to future emissions, worldwide per capita allowances could be made tradable.

When will the 'developing' countries bring this argument to bear in debt negotiations? While the 'polluter pays principle' is sometimes difficult to apply because those who are liable cannot be identified, this is not the case with respect to climate change, since the CO_2 emissions of different countries are known more or less.

As in national environmental liability issues, those who might be held responsible may argue that, scientifically, some questions remain open. This is what some national governments have been doing from conference to conference, particularly the government of the US. However, even if this argument is accepted, climate change should still be prevented for reasons similar to 'Pascal's bet'. His argument was as follows:

(1) If God exists and I believe in him, it's all right.

(2) If God does not exist and I do not believe in him, it's equally all right.

(3) If God does not exist and I believe in him, I will refrain from certain actions but this will not hurt me too much.

(4) If God exists and I do not believe in him, I will be damned, subject to an eternal catastrophe. Since no action is worth eternal damnation, it's prudent to believe in God.

Transferring Pascal's bet to the climate discussion, the issue is to believe or not to believe in the existence or non-existence of the threat that climate will change due to greenhouse-gas emissions, as has been described in the preceding section. The four cases to be compared are:

(1) Greenhouse-gas-induced climate change exists and everything is done to prevent globally harmful developments in the future. This is the ideal case, generally well above the actual performance of even the best political systems.

(2) Greenhouse-gas-induced climate change does not exist and nothing is done to prevent globally harmful development in the future. This is the ideal case for the political propensity to do nothing except symbolic politics.

(3) Greenhouse-gas-induced climate change does not exist and everything is done to prevent globally harmful developments in the future. This means that, for instance,

- burning fossil fuels will be considerably reduced so that valuable resources are saved for more sophisticated uses in the future;
- energy conservation will be enforced, which seems to be generally beneficial for technological modernization of the economy. As far as this means to increase energy prices, it should be kept in mind that empirically, economic performance is fairly well correlated with energy prices (both decreasing from Japan to Europe to the US to the ex-USSR);
- 'development' policies will be cancelled and economic policies fitted into a new economic world order instead;
- emissions of chlorofluorocarbons banned so that the ozone hole gets a chance to fill up within the next century;
- tropical forests will be saved to some extent through the help of the industrialized countries, which have already cut their trees in the past and now legitimately compensate others for not proceeding in like manner.

It may be difficult to imagine any reasonable action in favour of preventing climate change which is not at the same time beneficial for others. Perhaps it has not happened so far because global interests are not easily observed by the many national and international authorities taking care of world issues. This case then deserves to be positively denoted like the former two. Also, in politics it is fairly common for a decision to be right but not necessarily implemented for the right reasons.

(4) Greenhouse-gas-induced climate change exists and nothing is done to prevent globally harmful developments in the future. This means that the loser will be the Third World. Famines of a hitherto unknown dimension may take place and tens of millions of people may be displaced from their countries. When this happens it will be too late to do anything, except on the charity level. Most of those who are responsible for the catastrophe will no longer be alive.

The result of evaluating the 'climate bet' seems to be even more conclusive than that of Pascal's original bet. The argument shows that if there were an international sovereign, its duty would be to prevent greenhouse-gas-induced climate change because, if it happens, present inequities would be irresponsibly increased. If this authority also considered the heritage of future generations, the argument would be enforced because, with still rising inequities, more and more human beings would be born into a world with decreasing chances of equity. Ethically, this is a clear case because the basic rule: *neminem laede*, do no harm to others, is violated by inflicting climate change risk or definite climate change or both (described in terms of human habitat) upon others. In this sense, no further philosophical discussion is required. The problem, however, is that there is no international authority to protect the disadvantaged from the advantaged in the context of anthropogenic climate change.

Is there any chance that political perception of the consequences of climate change will lead to a response which prevents the inequity increases at least to some extent? From past experience this may not be expected. The Third World is already suffering and it is expected that it will suffer even more with climate change. There are famines as well as millions of environmental refugees crossing national borders already, and nothing appears likely to change the situation. To the contrary, wealth is transferred from the poor to the rich as World Bank data show. Conceiving climate change in political terms which are considered realistic at present, therefore, the situation can be likened to that of someone who has to cross a river which is 1,000 m wide but is strong enough to swim no more than 100 m and now additionally finds out that the river is not 1,000 m but 2,000 m wide. In present politics, the climate issue is reasonably perceived as (white) 'chalk on the white wall' (Meyer-Abich 1980).

Governments, so far, have not been particularly sensitive to environmental protection so that their political reasoning must be expected to correspond to the institutional framework, i.e., simply to their national interests. These are:

(1) Not to compensate other countries for the losses one's national activities have inflicted upon them as long as such compensation can be avoided without losing one's own reputation.

(2) To be aware of national advantages, be they absolute or relative, which might be brought about by climate change.

To defend national interest, following point (1), we should expect a government to respond to the climate issue as late as possible and then to insist on scientific uncertainties so that much more research would have to be done before any decisions could be made. To soothe public worries one should emphasize that in any case we are all in one boat, so that everybody must be equally interested to prevent or mitigate climate change. The one-boat argument also helps to conceal national interest (2) with the implication to suppress arguments on winners and losers as long as possible.[1] All of this could happen. Considering political perception, it is also easily seen that expectations (absolute or relative) of advantages through climate change can become political facts in themselves, be they scientifically justified or not.

Within current political rationality, it is reasonable to shift any response to oncoming climate changes as far as possible into the future because:

- it is anyway the propensity of governments to shift costs so that others (in this case, future generations) will have to pay;
- the responsibility, or liability, issue will look different in the future, when the debts from the past become larger than those politically in charge can be expected to cover. This is a way of 'socializing losses' globally as well as intergenerationally.

Both strategies, therefore, as a rule will be favoured by current political institutions. The implication for international as well as intergenerational equity is that *everything will be done to do nothing at present*. Inequities will increase the more current political institutions succeed in doing nothing. Traditional political rationality has become unreasonable at the present stage of global interrelations.

We are not, however, left completely without hope that a response to climate change might reduce the inequities which seem inevitable so far. One reason is an increasing awareness that as an output of industrial economy wealth is more and more balanced by newly emerging risks. Climate change is certainly one of them, and the growing uneasiness regarding accepting new burdens of risk may help to support policies of preventing climate change, even devoid of international considerations.

Second, a lack of political rationality that usually leads to a preference for short-term goals may become helpful in climate politics. For instance, even if the possible long-term advantages of climate change for the industrialized countries would by far exceed the short-term disadvantages of the migration of some part of the population from one to another part of the country, these disruptions could be decisive for the fate of particular governments. Shortsightedness in this case, therefore, could be advantageous for the prevention of climate change. Usually in environmental policies, long-term losses are accepted for short-term gains. In the case of climate, the same bias – paradoxically enough – could help to prevent changes at the expense of the Third World.

Finally, our political institutions were developed well before the industrial revolution took place and cannot be adequate at the present stage of global interrelations. While in the 19th century social inequity was mitigated at the expense of disruption of the environment, climate inequities are brought about by disruption of the environment. This may imply a chance that the social and environmental issues are no longer considered separately. The task then is to conceive a political philosophy of humankind in the community of nature beyond that of the 17th and 18th century, which considers peace within the nations but not peace between them and peace with nature. Such a philosophy could support the emerging forms of international solidarity when nations fall back to where, basically, they still are.

Notes

1. The first international conference on the winner's and loser's issue took place in 1990. The report is written in a fairly restrained language which may reflect administrative expectations (Glantz et al. 1990).

References

Budyko, M. I. and Y. S. Sedunov (1988) 'Anthropogenic Climate Changes', prepared for the World Congress on Climate and Development, Hamburg, 7–10 November 1988 (manuscript).

Deutscher Bundestag (1990a) *Zweiter Bericht der Enquete-Kommission 'Vorsorge zum Schutz der Erdatmosphäre' zum Thema Schutz der tropischen Wälder, Protecting the Tropical Forests: a high-priority international task* (Second Report of the Enquete-Commission 'Preventive Measures to Protect the Earth's Atmosphere' of the Eleventh German Bundestag (Bundestagsdrucksache 11/7220, Bonn, 24 May 1990), Bonn, Bonner Universitäts-Buchdruckerei.

Deutscher Bundestag (1990b) *Dritter Bericht der Enquete-Kommission 'Vorsorge zum Schutz der Erdatmosphäre' zum Thema Schutz der Erde, Protecting the Earth: a status report with recommendations for a new energy policy* (Third Report of the Enquete-Commission of the Eleventh German Bundestag 'Preventive Measures to Protect the Earth's Atmosphere'), two vols. (Bundestagsdrucksache 11/8030, Bonn, 2 October 1990), Bonn, Bonner Universitäts-Buchdruckerei.

EPA (United States Environmental Protection Agency) (1988) 'The Potential Effects of Global Climate Change on the United States: executive summary', edited by Joel B. Smith and Dennis A. Tirpak, Draft, October.

Flohn, H. (1990) 'Treibhauseffekt der Atmosphäre: neue Fakten und Perspektiven', *Rheinisch-Westfälische Akademie der Wissenschaften Vorträge*, No. 379, Opladen, Westdeutscher Verlag, pp. 11–14.

Glantz, M. H., M. F. Price and M. E. Krenz (eds.) (1990) *Report of the Workshop 'On Assessing Winners and Losers in the Context of Global Warming', St Julians, Malta, 18–21 June 1990*, Boulder, Environmental and Societal Impacts Group, National Center for Atmospheric Research.

Houghton, J. T., G. J. Jenkins and J. J. Ephraums (eds.) (1990) *Climate Change: the IPCC scientific assessment*, prepared for the Intergovernmental Panel on

Climate Change by Working Group I, WMO/UNEP, Cambridge, Cambridge University Press.

Intergovernmental Panel on Climate Change (IPCC) (1990a) *Potential Impacts of Climate Change*, report from Working Group II to IPCC. Chairmen Yu. A. Izrael, M. Hashimoto, W.I. McG. Tegart. See Tegart et al. 1990.

Intergovernmental Panel on Climate Change (IPCC) (1990b) *Policymaker's Summary of the Formulation of Response Strategies*, report prepared for IPCC by Working Group III.

Meyer-Abich, K. M. (1980) 'Chalk on the White Wall? On the Transformation of Climatological Facts into Political Facts', in J. Ausubel and A. K. Biswas (eds.) *Climatic Constraints and Human Activities*, International Institute for Applied System Analysis (IIASA) Proceedings Series Vol. 10, pp. 61–73. Oxford, Pergamon.

Meyer-Abich, K. M. (1984) *Wege zum Frieden mit der Natur – Praktische Naturphilosophie für die Umweltpolitik*, München, Hanser.

Parry, M. L., T. R. Carter and N. T. Konjin (1988) *The Impact of Climatic Variations on Agriculture*, Vol. 1: *Assessment in Cool, Temperate and Cold Regions*. Vol. 2: *Assessments in Semi-Arid Regions*, Dordrecht, Kluwer Academic Publishers.

Sachs, W. (1990) 'The Archaeology of the Development Idea, six essays', *Interculture*, No. 109, XXIII. 4, pp. 2–37.

Tegart, W. J., G. W. Sheldon and D. C. Griffiths (eds.) (1990) *Climate Change: the IPCC impacts assessment (Working Group II)*, WMO/UNEP, Canberra, Australian Government Publications Service.

World Development Report (1988) *Opportunities and Risks in Managing the World Economy: Public Finance in Development, World Development Indicators*, New York, Oxford University Press.

World Meteorological Organization (WMO) (1989) *Conference Proceedings. The Changing Atmosphere: Implications for Global Security*, Toronto, Canada, 27–30 June 1988 (WMO/OMM – No. 710), Geneva, WMO.

Part II
Confusion Over Sustainability

6.   Making Development Sustainable

Paul Ekins

Defining sustainable development

The extent to which talk of resolving the environmental crisis is now couched in terms of 'sustainable development' makes it absolutely imperative that this term is clearly defined in a way that commands widespread agreement. Unfortunately this is very far from being the case.

'Sustainable development' as a concept was popularized by the Brundtland Report[1] as that which 'meets the needs of the present without compromising the ability of future generations to meet their own needs' (p. 43), an imprecise formulation which makes no distinction between the vastly different 'needs' in the First and Third Worlds nor between human needs and the consumer wants towards the satisfaction of which most First World consumption, at least, is directed. There have been many subsequent attempts to define 'sustainable development' more precisely; indeed, the Pearce Report[2] gives a 'gallery' of such definitions, but the term remains subject to many different assumptions and conclusions. An area of considerable continuing uncertainty is the relationship of 'sustainable development' to economic growth (interpreted for the moment as growth in GNP, but see below).

It was Mrs Brundtland herself who had linked these two concepts, when, in her introduction to the Brundtland Report, she called for 'a new era of economic growth – growth that is forceful and at the same time socially and environmentally sustainable' (p. xii).

The Report later seeks to clarify the link:

> The concept of sustainable development does imply limits – not absolute limits but limitations imposed by the present state of technology and social organisations on environmental resources and by the ability of the biosphere to absorb the effects of human activities. But technology and social organisation can be both managed and improved to make way for a new era of economic growth. (p. 8)

This final sentence is in fact little more than an article of faith, but its sentiment is now widely interpreted, especially by the business community, to mean that sustainable development and GNP growth are not in conflict. Thus the International Chamber of Commerce (ICC)'s 'Business Charter for Sustainable Development'[3] proclaims: 'Economic growth provides the conditions in which protection of the environment can best be achieved, and environmental protection, in balance with other human goals, is necessary to achieve growth that is sustainable.' A similar sentiment was expressed by Stephan Schmidheiny, Chairman of the Business Council for Sustainable Development (BCSD), formed to give advice from a business perspective to the 1992 UN Conference on Environment and Development, at the BCSD's launch: 'Sustainable development combines two key objectives, environmental protection and growth.'[4] In an earlier interview with the newspaper *Neue Zurcher Zeitung* (8/9 December 1990), however, Schmidheiny himself had admitted the very shaky basis on which this proposition was founded when, in response to the question, 'Isn't this combination (of growth and environmental protection) just a dream, because it means bringing together things that don't match?', he replied, 'For the time being that's true.'

An equation introduced by Paul and Anne Ehrlich[5] indicates the scale of the technological challenge if both sustainability and GNP growth are to be achieved. They relate environmental impact (I) to the product of three variables: population (P), consumption per capita (C), and the environmental intensity of consumption (T). This last variable captures all the changes in technology, factor inputs and the composition of GNP. Thus: $I = PCT$.

The contemporary concern with sustainable development indicates that current levels of I are unsustainable. With regard to energy consumption and climate change, the Intergovernmental Panel on Climate Change (IPCC)[6] calculates that carbon dioxide emissions will quickly have to fall by a minimum of 60% to halt global warming. Three other greenhouse gases – N_2O, CFC-11, CFC-12 – also need cuts of more than 70%. With regard to other environmental problems, the Dutch National Environmental Policy Plan[7] argues for cuts in emissions of 80–90% for SO_2, NO_x, NH_3 and waste-dumping, 80% for hydrocarbons and 100% for CFCs. Thus with regard to I overall, it seems conservative to suggest that sustainability demands that it should fall by at least 50%. With regard to population, the UN's latest projections indicate a global figure of 10 billion by about 2050[8] about twice today's level. With regard to consumption, what is considered a moderate economic growth rate of 2–3% results in a quadrupling of output over 50 years. Thus, where subscript $_1$ indicates the quantity now and subscript $_2$ indicates the quantity in 50 years' time, we have:

$I_2 = 1/2 \times I_1$ (for sustainability)

$\left. \begin{array}{l} P_2 = 2P_1 \\ C_2 = 4C_1 \end{array} \right\}$ (by assumption)

For the Ehrlich equation to hold, this means that $T_2 = 1/16\ T_1$. In other words the environmental impact of each unit of consumption would need to fall by 93% over the next 50 years to meet the rather conservative definition of sustainability that has been adopted. This is a very tall order indeed, and one does not have to be a technological pessimist to entertain serious doubts as to its feasibility.

The facile linking of sustainable development with GNP growth not only tends to obscure the scale of the technological challenge that is actually involved in rendering these two concepts compatible. It also fails to address the all-too evident past contradictions between GNP growth and a wider concept of development; and it tends to gloss over those areas where GNP growth and environmental quality are at present in irreconcilable conflict (e.g. transport) with the danger that, in these areas, minimum levels of environmental quality will be continually eroded; and, as with the early Brundtland definition of sustainable development (SD), it makes no distinction between the development needs of North and South.

The resolution of these problems can be achieved only by a far more focused attention on the two components of SD: *Sustainability* and *Development*.

Sustainability

In order for economic activity, or a human way of life, to be environmentally sustainable, certain conditions need to be rigorously adhered to, concerning the use of renewable and non-renewable resources, the emission of wastes and associated environmental impacts. These conditions can be enumerated as follows:

(1) Destabilization of global environmental features such as climate patterns or the ozone layer must be prevented;

(2) Important ecosystems and ecological features must be absolutely protected to maintain biological diversity;

(3) Renewable resources must be renewed through the maintenance of soil fertility, hydrobiological cycles and necessary vegetative cover. Sustainable harvesting must be rigorously enforced;

(4) Non-renewable resources must be used as intensively as possible by designing for durability and the maximum feasible practice of repair, reconditioning, re-use, and recycling (the 'four Rs');

(5) Depletion of non-renewable resources should proceed on the basis of maintaining a minimum life-expectancy of the resource, at which level consumption would have to be matched by new discoveries of the resources. Furthermore, all depletion of these resources should involve the

contribution to a capital fund to help finance research for alternatives and the eventual transition to renewable substitutes. The size of the capital fund can be calculated from a formula given by El Serafy,[9] which splits the receipts from a non-renewable resource into two streams, a capital and an income stream, the relative size of which depend on the life expectancy of the resource and the discount rate applied. Ekins[10] has worked out the sums involved for the depletion of the UK's North Sea oil, whereby the UK government should, by 1990, have had a fund of £25 or £43 billion (at 10% or 5% discount rates respectively) to invest in the production of a substitute for the depleted oil. No such fund exists, of course. In this, and in other cases, the oil and other non-renewable resources have simply been unsustainably consumed.

(6) Emissions into air, soil and water must not exceed the capability of the earth to absorb, neutralize and recycle them, or lead to life-damaging concentrations of toxins.

(7) Risks of life-damaging events from human activity must be kept at very low levels. Technologies, such as nuclear power, which threaten long-lasting ecosystem damage at whatever level of risk, should be forgone.

On the basis of these sustainability conditions, sustainability standards need to be set for all environmental functions, combining the best scientific knowledge and the precautionary principle, which stresses prudence in the face of uncertainty and potentially large costs or damaging irreversibilities. These standards, formulated in terms of maximum sustainable yield, emission, concentration, use or carrying capacity, can then be converted into policy targets. Examples of such targets are the reductions in the emissions of greenhouse gases recommended by the Intergovernmental Panel on Climatic Change (IPCC) or the proposed cuts in emissions in the Dutch National Environmental Policy Plan, which were quoted earlier. The implications of such targets for different industrial sectors need to be evaluated and strategies for achieving them devised, including both time-scales and budgets. To be credible, rhetorical commitments to sustainability or sustainable development should always be accompanied by commitments to targets, time-scales and budgets. The first principle of SD is that achieving these targets and time-scales must have absolute priority over GNP growth, where these objectives conflict.

Development
The relationship between growth and development is no less complex than that between growth and sustainability. At its simplest level, as Daly has argued, 'growth is quantitative increase in physical scale while development is qualitative improvement or unfolding of potentialities.'[11]

This useful distinction is, however, blurred by two considerations. Firstly, it may be that 'qualitative improvement or unfolding of potentialities' depends in some circumstances on a quantitative increase of something. That is, development may depend on growth. This is almost certainly the case in situations characterized by acute material deprivation. It is not so obviously the case in affluent societies. Secondly, it may not be so simple to distinguish quantitative and qualitative change when it involves such aspects of life as utility or welfare, or the environment.

Thus it seems necessary first of all to differentiate between different kinds of growth:

Production growth: this is normally indicated by an increase in the GDP or GNP figures, but non-monetary production should also be included if an economy's total output is under consideration. GDP or GNP growth is often termed 'economic growth' but this is not strictly correct as it wrongly identifies the essential subject matter of economics as concerned with production rather than scarcity (Hueting 1992 has made a clear exposition of this point).[12]

Environmental growth: this can lead to an increase in environmental resources for consumption (e.g. fuelwood) or for environmental services (e.g. forests for climatic control). The generation of biomass involved leads to the concept of a Gross Nature Product. This is not a mere subset of GDP for two reasons: 1) a considerable portion of the Nature Product may not enter into money transactions; and 2) it generates utility for people (through the environmental services yielded) independently of its consumption.

Growth of utility or **welfare**: this is the kind of growth which Hueting[13] defines categorically as economic growth, with welfare's contributory factors including at least production, employment, environment, working conditions, leisure, income distribution, health and safety of the future. Production is assumed to contribute to welfare in and of itself, but it is quite possible for it also to cause negative feedbacks into other factors (e.g. polluting wastes, environmental destruction, erosion of community) which outweigh its positive contribution. Thus, production growth can be associated with a decrease in welfare.

Distinguishing between these different kinds of growth clarifies the relationship between growth and development. Development, as a qualitative improvement, is closely associated with an increase in welfare. From the discussion above, therefore, development may or may not occur with GDP growth; and GDP may or may not increase with development. It is still very much an open question as to how much production growth, if any, is possible without engendering utlity-cancelling negative feedbacks. This is especially true in high-consumption, high-polluting industrial countries, where negative environmental feedbacks are already significant, and extra income, because of its diminishing marginal utility, does not yield as much extra welfare as in poorer countries.

Development as achievement of potential largely depends on access to resources – ecological, organizational, human and manufactured (I have elsewhere given an exposition of a four-capital model of wealth-creation).[14] They need to satisfy their felt needs. Except perhaps in emergencies, the most important component of development is not income, but access to the various forms of capital, and opportunity to participate in the economy, so that people can generate their own incomes.

Achieving sustainable development

The brief discussion above leads to three clear new directions for economic policy if sustainable development is to be achieved. They will be taken in turn under the following headings:

(1) Differentiation between North and South
(2) Justice in the global economy, and participatory development.

Differentiating between North and South

The differences between North and South in terms of economic structure, levels of affluence and contribution to global environmental degradation make it imperative that they adopt different pathways to sustainable development. In the North the emphasis must be on setting ambitious targets, time-scales and budgets to achieve the sustainability conditions described earlier. Achieving these conditions will be a tough process lasting several decades and entailing lifestyle changes as well as enormous technological innovation. The implications of such a strategy for GNP growth are unclear, but clarifying and coping with them are probably the most important tasks of macro-economic management in the transition to sustainability. Sustainability will not be achieved unless these conditions are given priority over GNP growth.

For the South there must, in the short- and medium-term at least, be an emphasis on balanced, sustainable growth through a twin focus on environmental regeneration and careful industrialization using the most environmentally advanced technologies. The environmental regeneration must be such as to lead to an increase in biomass that will both foster environmental stability and contribute to the sustainable livelihood security of the rural poor. Careful industrialization, implying considerable technology transfer from North to South, must be undertaken in full recognition of the difficulties of such transfer between different cultural milieux, and with appropriate modifications to the technologies, and design of the transfer programmes, to take account of this. This is not at all the same process as that recommended by the Report of the South Commission (South Commission 1990), the principal emphasis of which is the need for rapid economic growth and rapid industrialization.[15]

Development, moreover, is still broadly equated with modernization, which is in turn conceived as a process to be imposed on people (although requiring their 'participation') rather than one to be generated by them in the course of their seeking to improve their lives on the basis of their own knowledge and resources. Furthermore, the 'growth' in question is still conceived as GNP growth, with no mention at all of the environmental growth and associated growth in non-monetary production that will be necessary if the rural poor are to secure their livelihoods.

There are few, even among environmentalists, who dispute the need for GNP growth and industrial development in the South, but unless both these processes are based on environmental regeneration rather than continued environmental degradation, then they will be neither sustainable nor sustained and will undermine the South's populations' conditions even of survival. No one knows how fast GNP or industrial growth based on environmental regeneration can proceed, but it is certain that it will be achieved only if the emphasis is put on regeneration, rather than growth *per se*, with local people being both responsible for and the principal beneficiaries of the regeneration.

Justice in the global economy and participatory development
I have elsewhere argued[16] that the three principal institutions of global economic interdependence – trade, aid and debt – have worked and are working systematically to the benefit of the North at the expense of the South. These arguments cannot be rehearsed here, but, in response to the fact that these institutions are now proving deeply inimical to the interests of the poor, there has been an eruption of popular organization to promote a different sort of 'development'. Bertrand Schneider's analysis identifies three principal tasks for this 'barefoot revolution' aimed at improving the quality of life of the rural poor, whom he calls 'the real challenge of the development process':[17]

(1) The removal of the 'factors of impoverishment afflicting rural populations'. Such factors essentially comprise misguided policies, corruption or outright repression by their own governments, or destructive 'development aid' by others.

(2) The definition by villagers of their basic needs and how they can best be met.

(3) The development by villagers, with appropriate external assistance, of the necessary factors of production to meet these needs in the desired fashion (p. 223).

Schneider considers that the new popular movements and non-governmental organizations are the only possible executors of such a development strategy. He calculates that these organizations currently benefit some 100 million people out of the two billion rural poor with whom he is principally concerned, and have brought them great benefits at a cost of only some $6.50 per head per year (p. 213). He then calls for an annual investment of $13 billion per year to reach the other 1.9 billion people in his target group (p. 236). Schneider does not say whether he considers this should be 'new money' or resources transferred from existing allocations. He does make clear, however, that it should be an investment in rural areas in small-scale activities in which the beneficiaries 'retain the initiative, choice and responsibility for development decisions which are aimed at answering their real needs'. Such large-scale projects as may still be necessary will then proceed from a quite different motivational, practical and political basis, in which 'the starting point of development efforts is the village or community' (p. 226).

A group of South Asian scholars has studied in detail the various processes and conditions by which the development envisaged by Schneider under (3) above can be achieved:

A social transformation of enormous magnitude has to be envisaged. In Third World countries the critical structural changes relate to a shift of decision-making power towards the poor by initiating a 'bottom-up' process, the village becoming the focal point of development, and a change in the education system redirecting it towards raising mass consciousness and remoulding élites. There is in the light of this no easy way to bring about the structural changes required, which themselves have to be supported by an integrated process of total mobilisation, involving raising people's consciousness and the inculcation of democratic values, the transformation of labour-power into the means of production, the fullest utilisation of local natural resources and the systematic development of appropriate technology.[18]

Furthermore, as one of the scholars quoted above has noted elsewhere:

A truly participatory development process cannot be always generated spontaneously, given the existing power relations at all levels, apathy, and the deep-rooted dependency relationship between rich and poor, common in most countries of the South. It often requires a catalyst or initiator who can break this vicious circle, a new type of activist who will work with the poor, who identifies with the interests of the poor and who has faith in the people.[19]

Many Southern countries exhibit the same division internally between small rich élites and poor marginalized masses as the global economy displays internationally between countries. The maintenance of such divisions is incompatible with the participatory development of the majority of those countries' people, and therefore with sustainable development. More equitable and democratic social systems in the South, with the state acting as the enabling servant of people and their organizations, rather than their overbearing master, are essential for sustainable development to be achieved.

Conclusion

The foregoing arguments can be drawn together into the following principles:

(1) The Northern establishment must recognize its countries' primary responsibility for the present environmental crisis and determine to take radical action to address it.

(2) The North must further recognize that current structures of interdependence, of trade, aid and debt, make Southern sustainable development impossible. They must, therefore, embark on wholesale reform of such institutions as GATT, the World Bank and IMF.

(3) Southern élites must recognize that the principal concern of sustainable development is with the poorest people in their countries and determine to let these people lead their development process by giving them equitable access to resources and support for their grassroots movements.

From these three principles a strategy for sustainability begins to emerge. In accepting its essential responsibility for the environmental crisis, the North should undertake a root and branch, sector by sector analysis of the environmental impacts of its economies, in terms of resources (renewable and exhaustible) used, wastes emitted and biosystems affected. It should then take the necessary steps to bring these impacts within defined sustainability criteria through a massive programme of conservation, resource-efficiency and pollution control in its own countries. This would certainly involve major lifestyle changes, such as curbing the use of the private motor-car.

Such a programme would be unlikely to lead to aggregate GNP growth. It would certainly bring about a radical restructuring of production and consumption in which polluting or depleting activities were either made more efficient or curtailed, while activities without such environmental impacts enjoyed a relative price advantage. Organic agriculture would benefit over the intensive chemical variety. Cyclists and those using public transport would gain over private motorists. Investment in energy conservation and efficiency would yield a greater return relative to energy use. This could not be a Pareto process, for some people would inevitably be worse off. Some prices would rise and some activities diminish. This would reduce production growth and there is no guarantee that substituting activities or technologies would fully compensate for this.

This can be illustrated by returning to the $I = PCT$ equation, again assuming that environmental impacts must be halved over 50 years, that population will double and that Third World consumption per head must quadruple. This time, however, let a further assumption be that rich countries experience no growth in consumption. Using figures from the World Bank,[20] and with all future population growth in the Third World, average per capita consumption there will still be less than one-fifth of per capita consumption in rich countries. I have calculated that, to attain sustainability, *technology must then decrease the environmental impacts of each unit of consumption by 78%.*[21] This is still an ambitious target. It may just be achievable and certainly represents the greatest technological challenge in human history, in meeting which technologists will need all the support of green consumerism, environmental taxes and regulation that Northern societies are able to muster. It is simply unrealistic for Northern societies to expect GNP growth as well. They should instead concentrate on navigating the difficult transition to, in Daly's terminology, a steady-state economy.[22]

In also recognizing the constraints on sustainable development in the South caused by the world economic system, the North should undertake its systematic reform, involving debt cancellation, fairer trading relationships (involving issues such as commodity prices, protectionism against Southern manufactures, corporate codes of conduct, exploitation of the global commons) and far greater Southern influence in global economic institutions. The North should also agree to the concessional transfer of clean, efficient technologies for appropriate Southern industrialization, and of resources for Southern environmental regeneration. It is inconceivable that governments of populations, a large proportion of which are living in absolute poverty, are going to be able successfully to demand sacrifices from both their poor and middle classes for a sustainability the benefits of which may not be apparent for two or three decades, unless they are perceived to be receiving real backing for the future from the rich world, while it simultaneously puts its own house in order.

However, this programme of Northern reform must have fundamental conditions for Southern élites, expressed by the words justice, democracy and sustainability. Justice demands the return of illegal flight capital from Northern banks to its countries of origin to fulfil the development tasks for which it was intended. It also demands a recognition of peasant and indigenous land rights through comprehensive and effective programmes of land reform. Democracy demands that people become the controllers of their development rather than its passive instruments or, worse, its victims. This involves the option of rejecting certain development patterns as well as full participation in those chosen. Sustainability involves absolute respect for and conservation of critical global resources such as rainforests, as well as rigorously sustainable use of all renewable resources and strict adherence to internationally agreed emission quotas.

Developing countries should continue to strive for greater production and productivity, but only on the basis of the increased sustainable production of biomass from a regenerated environmental base. As Robert Chambers has observed,[23] many degraded Third World environments can become sustainably productive again, but only with appropriate investment, and above all, the full participation and in the control of the intended beneficiaries of the increased production. This would have the further beneficial effect of stemming the flow of the people from the countryside to the towns and so contributing to the solution of another major social development problem. It is evident that the sort of development strategy which concentrates almost exclusively on the participatory rural regeneration of ecosystems to yield sustainable livelihoods, is about as different a strategy from the current priorities of most developing country governments and multilateral institutions, like the World Bank, as it is possible to imagine.

Such a programme would cost the North large sums of money which could probably be found only by plundering arms budgets. It certainly implies curtailment of the international arms trade. It would also include lifestyle shifts and a likely drop in Northern incomes. It would cost the Southern élites their autocratic power and many of their Northern lifestyle trappings. It would give new life and hope to the rural poor worldwide. It would also give the human race a secure future.

At present it is an unfortunate fact that, with regard to the three principles discussed above: differentiated and unequivocal strategies for sustainability in North and South; reform of international economic institutions in favour of the South; and a commitment to participatory development – not one is close to being given practical effect. Northern countries continue to put GNP growth as an objective well ahead of sustainability; they continue also to condone, and profit from, the global economy's injustices; and there is no evidence of willingness to transfer conserving technologies or investment to the South on the necessary scale. Southern countries continue to degrade rather than regenerate their fragile environments. Nor are many of their governments much concerned with diminishing internal equalities or with empowering their marginalized citizens. If these are the real issues at the heart of sustainable development, then the agenda has hardly been set, much less systematically addressed.

For Southern countries that wished to address such an agenda in the absence of general Northern co-operation, a priority, and probably a prerequisite, is very close co-operation with others in the South. Actions that would be likely to be necessary include: determined mobilization of their own people and technological capability to provide where possible for their own needs, with special reference to food security; participatory environmental investment in rural areas, based on small-scale landholdings with secure tenure; trade for mutual self-reliance with sympathetic partners in the South or North; the introduction of resource-saving technologies into industrial production wherever financial resources and indigenous capability permitted; and the formation of multi-state areas of economic co-operation to get the benefits of economies of scale in large internal markets.

It is a formidable programme for both North and South. But it is hard to see how sustainable development can be achieved with less.

Notes

1. WCED (World Commission on Environment and Development) (1987) *Our Common Future* (The Brundtland Report), Oxford, Oxford University Press.
2. D. Pearce, A. Markandya and E. Barbier (1989) *Blueprint for a Green Economy*, London, Earthscan, pp. 173—85.
3. ICC (International Chamber of Commerce) (1990) *The Business Charter for Sustainable Development: principles for environmental management*, Paris, ICC.
4. BCSD (Business Council for Sustainable Development) (1991) 'Top World Business Leaders Support Major New Initiatives on Environment and Development', Geneva, BCSD, press release 19 February.
5. P. and A. Ehrlich (1990) *The Population Explosion*, London, Hutchinson, p. 58.
6. J. Houghton, G. Jenkins and J. Ephraums, J. (eds.) (1990) *Climate Change: the IPCC scientific assessment*, Cambridge, Cambridge University Press (for the IPCC – Intergovernmental Panel on Climate Change), p. xviii.
7. MOHPPE (Ministry of Housing, Physical Planning and Environment) (1988) *To Choose or to Lose: national environmental policy plan*, The Hague, MOHPPE.
8. N. Sadik (1991) *The State of the World Population 1991*, New York, UNFPA (UN Fund for Population Activities), p. 3.
9. S. El Serafy (1989) 'The Proper Calculation of Income from Depletable Natural Resources', in Y. Ahmad, S. El Serafy, and E. Lutz (eds.) *Environmental Accounting for Sustainable Development*, Washington DC, World Bank.

10. P. Ekins (1992) 'Sustainability First', in P. Ekins and M. Max-Neef (eds.), *Real-Life Economics: understanding wealth creation*, London, Routledge.

11. H. E. Daly (1990) 'Toward Some Operational Principles of Sustainable Development', *Ecological Economics* 2: 1–6, p. 1.

12. R. Hueting (1992) 'Growth, Environment and National Income: theoretical problems and a practical solution', in P. Ekins and M. Max-Neef (eds.), *Real-life Economics: understanding wealth creation*, London, Routledge.

13. Ibid.

14. P. Ekins (1992) 'A Four-capital Model of Wealth-creation', in P. Ekins and M. Max-Neef (eds.) *Real-life Economics: understanding wealth creation*, London, Routledge.

15. South Commission (1990) *The Challenge to the South*, New York, Oxford University Press, pp. 80, 91–2, 272.

16. P. Ekins (1991) 'A Strategy for Global Environmental Development', *Development* 1991:2, Rome, Society for International Development.

17. B. Schneider (1988) *The Barefoot Revolution: a report to the Club of Rome*, London, Intermediate Technology Publications, p. 229.

18. G. De Silva, W. Haque, N. Mehta, A. Rahman and P. Wignaraja (1988) *Towards a Theory of Rural Development*, Lahore, Progressive Publishers, p. 22.

19. P. Wignaraja (1988) 'Participatory People-centred Development', Geneva, mimeo for the South Commission, October.

20. World Bank (1990) *World Development Report 1990*, New York, Oxford University Press.

21. P. Ekins (1991) 'The Sustainable Consumer Society: a contradiction in terms?', *International Environmental Affairs*, Vol. 3, No. 4.

22. H. E. Daly (1977) *Steady State Economics*, San Francisco, W. H. Freeman.

23. R. Chambers (1988) *Sustainable Livelihoods, Environment and Development: putting poor rural people first*. Discussion Paper 240, Brighton, Institute of Development Studies, University of Sussex, January, pp. 17ff.

7.   Scarcity and Sustainability

Hans Achterhuis

> We sailed from Peru (where we had been staying for the span of one
> year) across the Pacific Ocean towards China and Japan and took
> victuals for twelve months with us. During more than five months we
> had light and gentle winds. Then however the wind rose.

This is how Francis Bacon starts his description of the voyage of the
discovery of the New Atlantis.[1] Bacon designed his technological utopia, the
New Atlantis, at the beginning of the 17th century. In his imagination Bacon
anticipated the kind of society the West has been building over the last few
centuries; commentators generally agree that Western civilization has taken
the course that Bacon's utopia foreshadowed.

From this point of view two aspects of New Atlantis are significant.
Firstly, the New Atlantean culture, especially its science and technology,
acknowledged no limits. In New Atlantis there is a kind of scientific
academy, Solomon's House, whose purpose is 'the enlarging of the bounds
of human empire, to the effecting of all things possible'. The so-called
technological imperative, that what is possible should be realized, shining
through this purpose, leads to the second important aspect of the culture of
New Atlantis: nature has been eliminated and largely subjugated. The New
Atlanteans have literally created 'a second nature', that improves upon the
original and makes it superfluous. For example, people are obtaining new
food from matter 'not in use', they regulate the climate with their 'Chambers
of Health', and are even 'making new species'.

Finally, Bacon summarizes the new discoveries and inventions in which
the transgression of all limits combined with mastery over nature become
evident. At the beginning we find: 'the prolongation of life, the restitution of
youth in some degree, the retardation of age and the curing of diseases
counted incurable'.[2] Here the dreams of modern Western mankind are
clearly spelled out. And, as in Bacon's utopia the project of modern Western
culture and technology was, from the outset, directed toward the
transgression of every cultural and natural limit. As a reality in its own right

nature has disappeared, culture is regarded as some kind of device to enable humankind to live as long and as fully as possible. In all the earlier utopias, from Plato to Thomas More, the ideal society was always described within certain cultural limits and in relation to nature's reality. But in the New Atlantis nature is totally subjected to the power of mankind, or more precisely, of the technocrats of Solomon's House, and limits exist only in order to be transgressed.

What underlies this societal urge that characterizes modernity? Why have modern societies, for several centuries already, moved inexorably in this direction? And why does the non-Western world increasingly seek to follow this march of Western mankind? The answer lies quite simply in the notion of progress. Modern society simply wants a better and longer life. This sounds attractive and Bacon seemingly provided a perfect expression of the positive aspects of the idea of progress. But with the help of two other philosophers I propose to show that, from the beginning, the idea of progress was contaminated by negative aspects – aspects that, long hidden, are now emerging to threaten the future of our world. These negative aspects might also be the cause of our present incapacity to accept limits and to find another way of dealing with nature. This complex of feelings and social structures behind the idea of progress I have described as 'the reign of scarcity'[2]. A short inquiry into this reign may shed new light on Bacon's famous voyage of discovery and on our modern plight.

Hobbes: power as a comparative phenomenon

For me the philosophical articulation of the reality of scarcity, a phenomenon largely unknown before modernity, starts in the 17th century with the thought of Thomas Hobbes, a former secretary of Bacon, who in some respects can be considered his disciple. The best approach to the subject can be found in Hobbes' theory of power developed in *Leviathan*.[3] According to Hobbes, power manifests itself in all kinds of social institutions and structures. Already, like Michel Foucault in the 20th century, he states that every social phenomenon is based on power relations between individuals and groups.

For Hobbes power is a comparative phenomenon; it originates from a comparison between different people. The goods, the objects one seeks to obtain, are pursued not for their own sake, but because someone else also tries to get them. For example, when Hobbes writes of 'covetousness', the 'desire of riches', he remarks that this 'name is always used in signification of blame', 'because men contending for (riches), are displeased with another attaining them'. It is clear that people desire riches not because they want them directly for themselves; they are important only in comparison with what others have. The possibility of being content with the riches one possesses seems to be excluded, otherwise it is difficult to understand why the fact that others are rich also should be a source of displeasure.

Starting from this triangular comparative principle, society for Hobbes becomes a vast arena of conflicts. 'Competition of riches, honour, command or other power enclineth to contention, enmity and war: because the way of one competitor to the attaining of his desire is to kill, subdue, supplant, or repell the other.'[4] That, for Hobbes, society is a zero-sum game is evident. Everything one attains is realized at someone else's cost. The power that people desire is always power over others, power at the expense of others. Or in short, because of the comparative relations between people, everything in the universe of Hobbes potentially becomes a scarce good; his definition of power makes it impossible that there will ever be enough of it. Scarcity, the relation between limited means and unlimited ends is, according to Hobbes, caused by the continuous comparisons and strife between individuals and groups. The ends are unlimited because one must always surpass the ends of others.

As a philosopher Hobbes reflected on a new kind of social relations that he saw emerging in his time. Most modern scholars agree that in Hobbes' writings there is apparent a radical rupture with his philosophical predecessors. He turns the world of Plato, Aristotle and the medieval thinkers upside-down. In my opinion, this radical rupture is best expressed by the emergence of the theme of scarcity. Before the rise of modern economic society no one suggested that unlimited desire was a natural quality of man. Scarcity arising out of this limitless, triangular desire is, in this general sense, an invention of modernity. This is not to deny that the European Middle Ages, in common with non-Western cultures, experienced many periods of shortage and insufficiency. But up until the 19th century, even in Western Europe, the noun 'scarcity' mostly expressed an episode of shortage, a period of insufficiency. Only at the end of the 19th century did the concept of scarcity begin to signify a general condition of humankind. This modern usage of the term was foreshadowed by Hobbes.

Society for Hobbes became a lifeboat in which all the passengers fought each other. Survival, not the good, the right life, became the ultimate value. Out of the fear of scarcity it is necessary to be the first to strike at or throw out the other. The relations between individuals and groups that Hobbes describes as war and that I conceptualize as scarcity, are characterized by fear, competition and envy. Fear, especially, is predominant for Hobbes. Fear largely regulates human behaviour. In order to escape fear, men create by covenant 'the great Leviathan', a semi-absolute state, that keeps its subjects in awe and that prevents the permanent scarcity from developing into outright war.

Locke: growth and expansion

The other philosopher concerned with scarcity, John Locke, at the end of the 17th century, gave us the modern images of nature and the idea of unlimited progress and growth mentioned above.[5] Locke, as well as Hobbes, was aware of the threat of scarcity and he also described it as a state of war. But rather than identifying its origins in human social relations, his view of scarcity – which became the accepted view of modernity – was that of an economic, a quasi-natural fact, a perpetual relation between people and nature. For him scarcity simply spelled out the fact that earth and nature fail to provide enough for all. Therefore, we have only to produce more to alleviate or even to end scarcity. Economic growth and expansion are the answers to the threat of scarcity. With Locke, humanity, at least Western humanity, starts a rush forward in order to escape scarcity.

In this rush forward, nature, that Hobbes, however mechanical a philosopher he was, still saw as our 'common mother', became the primary enemy. Nature does not give enough and humanity has to struggle and labour with it, to subdue the earth, in order to produce more and more. In many of Locke's comparisons in his 'Second Treatise', nature loses its traditional connotations, it is devalued against the cost of labour. He asks, for instance, what is the difference between an acre of land planted with tobacco or sugar and the same acre of land held in common and unhusbanded? This comparison will reveal 'that of all the things useful to the life of man, when he divides what in them is purely owing to nature and what to labour, he shall find that in most of them ninety-nine hundredth were wholly to be put on the account of labour'.

In Locke's philosophy the themes of progress and of the devaluation of nature are closely linked with the fear of scarcity. The European Enlightenment and the myth of progress can thus be partly interpreted as a flight from scarcity.

The same can be said of European expansion. For Locke, America was an empty continent that could help alleviate the effects of scarcity in Europe. Colonialism and expansion find their legitimation in scarcity. Cecil Rhodes, the greatest imperialist of the 19th century, openly stated that imperialism was necessary in order to avoid a class war in England. And he already dreamt about the necessity of an ongoing expansion into the universe: 'I would annex the planets if I could', he wrote.[6] To give one more example, former President Reagan, in his speech at the launching of *Discoverer*, after the failure of the *Challenger*, told the American people that it was essential to conquer space in order to overcome 'war, scarcity and misery on earth'. The same argument as Locke's in the 17th century.

Unlike Locke, Hobbes never saw the flight forward into 'empty' space as a possible way to escape scarcity. In chapter 24 of *Leviathan* he wrote extensively about plantations or colonies, but nowhere suggested that the perpetual war among men could be solved by expansion. He knew that scarcity originated in human relations and that people trying to escape it will inadvertently spread and propagate it to the ends of the earth – and even beyond.

The original myth of modern economy

Locke makes many comparisons between the Europeans who have subdued nature by way of rational labour and, for instance, the American Indians 'who are rich in land, but poor in all the comforts of life', because they don't work. They have the same fertile land, 'yet, for want of improving it by labour, have not one hundredth part of the conveniences we enjoy, and a king of a large and fruitful territory there feeds, lodges and is clad worse than a day labourer in England.'[7]

In this kind of comparison we can already discover the original myth of the modern economy. According to this myth, that will be fully worked out by Adam Smith in the 18th century, scarcity is the original condition of all humankind. Because of nature's scarcity, humanity must wrestle with it, first in order to survive and later to live fully. This myth projects the typical modern relation to a scarce and hostile nature back to the whole history of humanity. Nature becomes the scapegoat of modernity, nature's scarcity becomes the source of violence. Hobbes' competitive desires do not create scarcity, the guilt lies with nature. When nature can be subdued and conquered by labour, then peace and abundance will be the future lot of humankind.

This last idea is forcefully expressed by maybe the greatest economist of the 20th century. In 1930 John Maynard Keynes prophesied that within two generations industrial societies might finally realize what, according to him, had always been the purpose of humankind: an end to the problem of scarcity. Keynes saw contemporary society still struggling in the dark tunnel of scarcity, but the future would bring the light in the form of the satisfaction of all their basic needs. At that time a change in moral codes would also be possible.

> We shall be able to rid ourselves of many of the pseudo-moral principles which have hag-ridden us for two hundred years, by which we have exalted some of the most distasteful of human qualities into the position of the highest virtues . . . The love of money as a possession . . . will be recognised for what it is, a somewhat disgusting morbidity, one of these semi-criminal, semi-pathological propensities which one hands over with a shudder to the specialists in mental disease.

When scarcity is overcome we shall be able 'to return' to the traditional virtues of mankind. 'We shall honour those who can teach us how to pluck the hour and the day virtuously and well'.[8]

These well-known phrases of Keynes have important implications not foreseen by their author. Firstly, Keynes suggests that the tunnel of scarcity has a beginning. Before that beginning, somewhere in the past, virtuous living was apparently possible. With the coming of modern economy, however, it seems that the world was turned upside-down. The promise of modern economy is that in future it will again be possible to live humanely and virtuously. But Keynes warns his contemporaries that before that time comes, they should continue to live in their upside-down world of scarcity. For maybe 100 years we must tell ourselves and each other that honesty is mean and meanness is honest. Meanness is useful and necessary, and honesty is not. Only the characteristics of meanness, envy, greed and competition eventually lead us out of the dark tunnel of scarcity.

Starting from a Hobbesian analysis it becomes clear that the tunnel of scarcity resembles some kind of cyclone in which men become caught, spinning around in rivalry with each other and creating in this process more and more needs and desires.

Scarcity as a social construction

A recent publication[9] speaks of the invention of scarcity in the 17th century. I prefer to avoid the term 'invention'; it suggests that someone just thought out and propagated scarcity at a given moment. In my opinion, the most that can be said is that modern economy invented the idea of an ever-present universal scarcity as the founding myth of modern society. In so far as the rise of scarcity is concerned I prefer to use the concept of social construction. In the 17th century Hobbes and Locke looked at their society and saw that something like scarcity was present in many human and social relations. In his 'Second Treatise' Locke systematized the way the upper classes in England were already trying to find a way out of scarcity, but this supposed way out, in the long run, only reinforced scarcity and made it omnipresent. By pursuing ever-more production and growth, the whole world of culture and nature was reduced to a field of scarce resources. Looking at the world in this way and above all acting this way, Western society, in a few centuries, succeeded in establishing the regime of scarcity in almost all spheres of social and personal life worldwide.

To put it bluntly, for several centuries by acting upon the assumption that nature is dead and worthless stuff that has to be managed by human labour and technology, we almost succeeded in making it dead and worthless. A Dutch proverb says that the landlord judges his guests from his own character and that he makes them behave in the way he expects them to. The same could be said, on a larger scale, of the social construction of scarcity. By defining everything as a scarce resource and acting this out, we are in the long run making it so. All the historical interventions of the economy in the cultural life of people, all the present interventions of development planners in traditional cultures, are turning nature's plenty, that Hobbes still knew of, into the present scarcity of resources on planet earth. And the big question we have to ask is whether many environmental efforts to fight scarcity are not in fact propagating it.

Survival

> You talk very little about life, you talk too much about survival. It is very important to remember that when the possibilities for life are over, the possibilities for survival start. And there are peoples here in Brazil, especially in the Amazon region, who still live, and these peoples that still live don't want to reach down to the level of survival.[10]

This reproach was made by one of the speakers from the floor on the occasion of a public hearing of the Brundtland Commission in São Paulo in October 1985 – probably the speaker was an Indian. At least his words echoed the well-known declaration of the North American Indian Chief Seattle of 1855. This statement also reflects the main opposition that exists between the continued existence of the white people and their lifestyle and indigenous peoples' own traditional way of life. From the economic point of view, the earth and all of nature become resources for what Hobbes called 'commodious living', for Chief Seattle and our Brazilian interlocutor this, however, means 'the end of life and the beginning of survival'.

The old Hobbesian and Baconian concept of survival, of trying to live as long and 'commodiously' as possible, is still central in most of our present environmental thinking. Since Locke the social and economic imperative has not changed: 'producing more with less' (the subtitle of chapter 8 of *Our Common Future*) is still supposedly the only answer to the problem of scarcity, of which 'The woman who cooks in an earthen pot over an open fire uses perhaps eight times more energy than an affluent neighbour with a gas stove and aluminium pans',[11] is one of the many examples provided by the World Commission on Environment and Development. Not once does the Commission suggest that the woman's mode of cooking or any other act is part of a cultural way of life that has a worth of its own. It is seen only as a purely economic act, directed at better survival.

Spaceship Earth

Another popular image closely connected to the concept of survival is that of spaceship earth. In the environmental movement this image is often used to drive home the point that we must move from the traditional notion of living 'on one earth' to the idea of inhabiting 'one world',[12] as the Brundtland Commission summarizes its Report. 'The security, wellbeing and survival of the planet depend' on the kind of changes that impress upon people the notion that we are all in the same (life-) boat, that we are all passengers of spaceship earth.

The image of spaceship earth, that is created from the idea of an all-pervading scarcity, contains some important implications. Firstly, as I have already hinted, the majority of the people in a spacecraft can only be passengers. Only the élite, 'the few', can be steersmen; the masses, 'the many', must simply put their fate in the hands of the leaders. The latest Club of Rome report goes a long way in this direction. An élite of scientists, as some kind of global steering committee, has to supersede traditional ways of politics which are now deemed an incompetent way to manage the present world crisis. Of course, Bacon and Hobbes could not conceive of the image of spaceship earth in their age; this can be done only in our age of space travel. Nevertheless, Bacon's scientists of Solomon's House closely resemble modern ideas about a global scientific steering committee; and Hobbes' political philosophy has been revitalized in important eco-philosophical contributions. Leviathan has been resurrected in a global form.

Secondly, it does not seem necessary to digress on the fact that in a spaceship the overriding objective is survival. Notwithstanding *Star Trek* and other films and television series about outer space, a space vehicle does not seem to be a suitable place for the development of a culturally acceptable good life.

Thirdly, the spaceship metaphor changes the staggering richness of nature into an aridly uniform environment. In a spacecraft it is impossible not to treat the environment as an aggregate of scarce resources. As I have already shown, this is precisely how *Our Common Future* argues. This is not to deny that we can occasionally find a faint suggestion that the extinction of traditional cultures that lived in harmony with their natural surroundings, as well as the extinction of innumerable species, are bad in and for themselves. But the main thrust of the argument is steadfastly the same: 'Species that are important for human welfare' should be conserved and 'the traditional rights to land' of indigenous and tribal peoples should be recognized, and also 'projects that open up an area to economic development' should be prepared. How the World Commission on Environment and Development thinks it is possible to square the circle (one page earlier they state: 'it is a terrible irony that as formal development reaches more deeply into rain forests, desert and other isolated environments, it tends to destroy the only cultures that have proved able to thrive in these environments') is never explained.[14]

Generally, the image of nature employed in much of the environmental discourse is entirely Lockean: nature is viewed as a scarce resource that must be strictly managed. Locke's assertion, of a hostile nature that forced people to wage war with each other in order to obtain scarce resources, reappears in the form of 'environmental stress as a source of conflict'. 'The deterioriation of the natural resource base and its capacity to support the population' seems to be the main underlying cause for war and conflict. Even the Hobbesean idea of security from the threat of the war of every person against every other is redefined from this perspective. 'The whole notion of security as traditionally understood . . . must be expanded to include the growing impacts of environmental stress – locally, nationally, regionally and globally',[15] states the Brundtland Commission. In the same vein the age-old promise linked to this idea remains essentially the same: peace and welfare are within reach when nature – the environment – is managed productively.

Growth without limits

This promise is finally highlighted in the idea of the necessity of ever-continuing economic growth. Since *Limits to Growth*, the 1972 Report of the Club of Rome, the notion of limits seems to have disappeared beyond the horizon of most of environmental policy. The only limits that, for instance, the Brundtland Commission can conceive of are 'limitations imposed by the present state of technology and social organization on environmental resources and by the ability of the biosphere to absorb the effects of human activities'. 'But', the Report immediately continues, 'technology and social organization can be both managed and improved to make way for a new era of economic growth.'[16] The Commission even foresees 'a five to tenfold increase in manufacturing output' deemed as necessary to raise the consumption of the developing countries to the present-day consumption level of the industrialized countries. Here, the question of squaring the circle could again be asked. But the reader is never told how this gigantic rise in industrial output could be realized in a sustainable way. Instead, the old economic promise that only in this way can we finally, and for the first time in world history, make an end to poverty, is constantly repeated. Missing in the analysis of *Our Common Future* and of a large part of environmental policy is the momentousness of the limitless rush forward that (Western) humanity began in the 17th century and of the driving forces behind it. Even persons and groups who propagate the necessity of limits often fail to see the propellent agents of growth and progress and the interconnectedness of the growth systems of which we all form part. Thomas Hobbes knew that scarcity originated from people and groups taking each other as models and in this way changing them into obstacles.

At present the Western way of living, with its built-in scarcity and devaluation of nature, seems to have become the model for the majority of people on earth. *Our Common Future*, with most environmental and developmental policy as a sequel, reinforces this tendency. Even if it were possible to raise the developing countries' level of consumption to the present Western industrialized countries' standards, this would not change the conflictual relations between rich and poor, mighty and powerless. The rush forward precipitated by the fear of scarcity, and the destruction of nature, would only be accelerated as the world's rich would continue to raise their own consumption levels. The search for limits must start with a recognition of this fear. Only when scarcity can be seen as a particular episode in modern history, instead of as a permanent condition, cultural limits, within which nature can become more than a resource for survival, are possible.

Finally, I would like to comment briefly on a recent remarkable study about the problem of sustainability in Holland, which demonstrates how hard it is to accept the idea of limits, intellectually as well as in practice. In autumn 1991 four people from the South were invited by the Alliance for Sustainable Development (the Dutch organization of NGOs working on environment, development, peace and security), to visit Holland and give their vision and perspective on a sustainable Netherlands. Mercio Gomes from Mexico, Chandra Niran of Indonesia, Sami Songanbele from Tanzania and Raji Vora from India travelled the country extensively for six weeks, talked with many representatives of the Dutch NGOs, the government, industry, the churches and universities and read the most important reports of the NGOs and the Ministries of Environment and Development on the subject of sustainability. The result, *A Vision from the South*,[17] deserves to be known in other Western countries as well as the Netherlands. This anthropological survey from quite other than the usual perspective (normally Western anthropologists study various groups and cultures in the South) sheds a sharp light on our modern limitless culture. As has often been the case in history, here also the vision of the outsiders may reveal the deepest and hidden foundations of a society.

One of the main self-imposed tasks of the four authors consisted in unravelling what they called the 'double-talk' of most of the people to whom they spoke. This double-talk they perceived most clearly in the concept of sustainable development itself and in the policies that purport to be working towards this goal of the Brundtland Commission. The concept was used by the persons interviewed and by the Dutch reports on the Commission 'as a guarantee against any serious change in outlook, international relationships, market structures or public policies'. The authors frequently came up against the deep abyss between the sometimes rather radical rhetoric of their Dutch interviewers and the meagre policy proposals resulting. The excuse for this is sought mainly in the necessity to keep or even improve the Western 'standard of living'. The idea of putting limits to economic growth seems impossible to accept for the vast majority of the Dutch. The Southern investigators correctly asserted that the category 'standard of living' is the anvil upon which all ideas of sustainability are tested 'and the altar at which sacrifices on the part of the masses of the Third World are invited and sanctified.' Behind this they discern precisely the same motive that I pointed at above. When we talk of 'standard of living', particularly when it means that the modern Western way of life is the standard, the category 'standard of life' becomes the most central function of power. What is known as 'progress' and 'development' has no intrinsic motivation – no motive force of its own. Power has been its motive force. It is the force of power which has propelled it and keeps it going. For this reason the authors were concerned to expose the relationship between power and progress on the one hand and between progress and the modernization of poverty on the other. Unless this analysis is undertaken in an impartial way we remain committed 'to the modern Western way of life in spite of our otherwise good intentions and emotional responses'.[18]

From their Southern perspective the authors also tried to unravel the double-talk about nature and environment. What they themselves perceive as nature is for the Dutch mainly environment, a 'conglomerate of statistical numbers and use values' . . . 'This narrow view of nature is translated into the whole way of life. Things are developed partially, even the human senses are developed partially, divorced from one another. It is said human beings naturally have six senses. For the Dutch it seems the most important is the optical sense. What is seen is very important. Almost everything is created for the look. The beautifully shaped and coloured flowers that have no smell; the big and spotless vegetables that have no taste; beautiful landscapes without internal harmony'.[19] In a technological way the Dutch are creating a façade of 'natural' beauty that is hiding the actual deterioration of what the authors recognize as nature.

In the interviews with government officials, even of the Ministry of Development, it became evident that none of them were really willing to jeopardize the Dutch life-style and position on the world market. In an interview at the Ministry of Agriculture, for example, on a question about the possibility of more Dutch agriculture turning to organic farming, the polite but negative answer was that high-tech solutions were more profitable, the overall objective of agricultural policy being to foster safe, competitive and sustainable practices. The use of the last concept in this context clearly showed the modernist and anti-Southern bias of it.

In the eyes of their visitors the Dutch people's hunger for more looks like a 'hopeless case of drug addiction. No matter how clearly you communicate to them that their behaviour is destructive to themselves and also to others, they cannot control it. They just keep on taking more and more, unless they are forcefully restrained'. The double-talk and the abyss between the awareness of global environmental problems on the part of Dutch politicians, NGO-activists and the public in general and their actual behaviour the four authors could explain only as due to this addiction to affluence. They even go as far as 'feeling great empathy with the Netherlands' in this respect. How hard it must be to convince yourself that less can be more satisfying when your whole life experience dictates that the more you have the more satisfied you can be'.[20]

In my more theoretical analysis above I have stressed the same point starting from the concept of scarcity. Most of the startling discoveries the four Southern anthropologists made about a modern Western society stress the importance of this concept for understanding this kind of society. Their conclusion that the main reason for the North's incapacity to limit growth and progress is connected with the unwillingness to change its life-style, reinforces my theoretical analyses. I can only agree with their conclusion: 'The more this issue is circled about and avoided, the more time is wasted in attaining sustainability'.

Notes

1. Francis Bacon (1955 [1627]) *New Atlantis*, in *Selected Writing of Francis Bacon*, New York, The Modern Library.

2. Ibid., p. 87.

3. Thomas Hobbes (1983 [1651]) *Leviathan*, London, Everyman's Library.

4. Ibid., chapter 11.

5. John Locke (1960 [1690]) *Two Treatises of Government*, Cambridge, Cambridge University Press.

6. Hannah Arendt (1951) *The Origins of Totalitarianism*, London, Harcourt Brace Jovanavich, p. 124.

7. Locke (1960 [1690]), p. 41.

8. John Maynard Keynes (1930) *Essays in Persuasion*, New York and London, W. W. Norton, pp. 365–7.

9. Nicholas Xenos (1989) *Scarcity and Modernity*, London and New York, Routledge.

10. World Commission on Environment and Development (1987) *Our Common Future*, Oxford, Oxford University Press, p. 40.

11. Ibid., p. 196.

12. Ibid., p. 1.

13. G. Hardin (1968) *The Tragedy of the Commons, Science*, pp. 1243–8; William Ophuls (1977) *Ecology and the Politics of Scarcity*, San Francisco, Freeman.

14. World Commission on Environment and Development (1987), pp. 15–16.

15. Ibid., p. 19.

16. Ibid., p. 8.

17. Mercio Gomes, Chandra Kirana, Sami Songanbele and Rajiv Vora (1992) *A Vision from the South*, Utrecht.

18. Ibid., pp. 38, 39, 40.

19. Ibid., pp. 95–7.

20. Ibid., pp. 106–8.

8.   Competing Notions of Biodiversity

Christine von Weizsäcker

A short introductory farce

Global and general terms are booming and numerical expression wins over
qualitative differentiation. Take the United Nations Conference on
Environment and Development (UNCED), which lived up to its informal
title 'the Earth Summit'. It was, indeed, a summit to 'sum it' all up. The very
general heading 'Climate and Energy' for instance made it possible to sum
up everything from woodstoves to nuclear power plants, from cow-farts to
car-fumes. Many men and women are able to see the difference between
woodstoves and nuclear power plants and many are able to smell the
difference between cow-farts and car-fumes. There is nothing special in that.
For doing the general sums, however, it needs specialists and experts with a
numerical zeal and a systematic forgetfulness for detail and qualitative
differences. Our old mathematics teacher did not allow us to add up apples
and pears. Only by inventing new comprehensive words like 'Fruit' could we
outwit our teacher's mathematical convention. Modern experts not only
have superior mathematical training and are very good at difficult sums, but
they also, by coining additional comprehensive terms for the debate,
increase the very demand for sums. So all ways 'to provide, to protect and to
save' nowadays seem to lead through the eye of the needle of global expertise
on 'Energy' and 'Climate'. Intricate, admirable and complex as these sums
may be, for the normal citizen they make life very simple and stories short.
You can do only three things with 'Energy': produce it; consume it; save it.
You can only do two things with 'Climate': you can stabilize it or you can
change it. So paradoxically, the grandiosity of all-embracing expert notions
seems to go hand-in-hand with a certain primitivity – or rather alienated
clumsiness – in the thoughts and actions of normal people, who,
surprisingly, have ceased to find this paradox surprising. They are prepared
for additional 'sums' of this type: how would you sum up elderberry and
bedbugs, cherry-trees and ducks, elephants and forget-me-nots, gnus and
humans, ibis and junipers, killer whales and love birds, marigolds and

nitrifying soil bacteria, oaks, panda bears and quails, rice and snails, termites, urchins, virus, warblers and zinnias? What is their common denominator?
These are words in the English language, one for each letter.
That is a too general and playful generalization.
They are God's creatures.
That is beside the point, and who knows anyway?
Some of them I eat, others I try to avoid, many I have never seen.
You are not summing up, and have failed the test.
They are objects of microbiology, botany and zoology.
These are old-fashioned branches of biology. Try again!
They all have genes, they all contain DNA.
Yes, you are not far from the mark.
They all add up to biodiversity.
Yes, there you are!
And biodiversity is the natural resource of biotechnology.
You have passed your test with honours.
To use it efficiently, sustainably and responsibly we need gene banks, intellectual property rights and ethics commissions.
Yes, only a deep-frozen, patented and ethically approved life form is a safe life form.

Why do we need a biodiversity alliance?

Now let us quit the farce and have a look at some good reasons why the biodiversity issue earns such widespread concern and support.

Biodiversity is quite new as a political catchword. Public attention has been gained only recently. In view of the wide attention given to the issue during the UNCED in 1992 it is quite surprising that a document as recent and as thorough as *The Global 2000 Report to the President*, published in 1980, contains only six pages on 'Changes in biological diversity'.[1] These important pages, hidden in the chapter on forestry, give a good, short summary of the research findings about an unprecedented loss of species: 'If present trends continue – as they certainly will in many areas – hundreds of thousands of species can be expected to be lost by the year 2000.' 'Extinctions projected for the coming decades will be largely human-generated and on a scale that renders natural extinction trivial by comparison.'[2] A substantial fraction of the expected 'extinction of between one-fifth and one-seventh of all species over the next two decades'[3] will occur in the tropics. This, by the way, means at least ten but perhaps up to 100 species lost per day.[4] This is sad indeed as, according to *Global 2000*, species could be termed 'the only strictly non-renewable resource'. The

Final Report of the Keystone Dialogue, which took place in Oslo in 1991, made the following appeal:

> We, the participants in the Keystone International Dialogue Series on Plant Genetic Resources, choose to speak now in a loud and clear voice, realising that while the world already has too many crises, it must take heed of yet another. Therefore, we call for a Global Initiative for the Security and Sustainable Use of Plant Genetic Resources. Why? Because we fear that the world's capacity to respond to change is being lost – all too quietly and all too quickly. We can hardly imagine a greater threat to the future well-being of the people in the world than the loss of genetic variability of plants.[5]

It is not at all surprising that the continuing loss of so much natural richness brings together conscientious, responsible and well-meaning people from many different walks of life, with different and sometimes nearly irreconcilable outlooks. Let us take a brief look at the huge variety of persons and groups assembled around this undoubtedly very urgent task:

– modern farmers, because supply of seeds is suddenly recognized as being very vulnerable.
– environmentalists, because they have a heart for whales and butterflies, mangroves and edelweiss.
– other environmentalists who want to provide suitable plants and microbes for the environmental rehabilitation of degraded land.
– religious people because they feel for their fellow-creatures and see it as their duty to defend the integrity of creation.
– development agencies because they want to provide sustainable higher yield crops for the poor and overpopulated areas of the world.
– new foundations which want to ensure that the necessary new crops are available when climate changes set in.
– human rights people who want to establish a legal right to a healthy and rich environment.
– plant breeders, who, in order to increase their options, need many well-recorded and well-organized accessions and samples of germplasm from gene banks.
– subsistence farmers, because they do not want to lose their traditional, low-input, appropriate and locally well-adapted landraces of crops.
– governments in the South, because they hope to earn royalties by selling the unique genetic traits present in their area.
– experienced bridge-builders between science and politics, because they feel a responsibility to share their knowledge and because they hope to make their warnings heard in time.

– young people who have an instinctive sympathy for wild things.
– biologists, who see species extinction as a fascinating problem in theoretical ecology and who expect a lot of interesting findings from the global field study on species loss on which humanity has unintentionally embarked.
– genetic engineers, because they see a crucial role and promising jobs for themselves in the technical aspects of the conservation and use of biodiversity.
– companies who hope for a greener image and more sustainable sales.
– older people who want their children, grandchildren and great-grandchildren to be able to see what they themselves feel happy to see.
– directors of national parks, zoos, botanical gardens and gene banks.
– politicians and diplomats, because there is work to be done on a legal and economic framework for the 'conservation and use' of biodiversity on the national and international levels: from the important question of funding to the questions of access, patenting, and breeders' and farmers' rights.

It makes sense to defend the richness and variety of living beings on this earth. It makes sense that it is defended by a rich diversity of men and women. It makes sense that they form an alliance for their common goals. But have they really undertaken the difficult task of identifying what these common goals are? This task would include recognizing and accepting the large differences among them in values, experiences, aims and hopes, and, on the basis of this knowledge, defining areas of fair co-operation. Urgency does not favour analysis and fairness. Globality does not favour non-scientists and non-economists. Our biodiversity problem is clearly urgent and global. This suggests that there may be an inherent serious imbalance of power in this alliance for biodiversity, an imbalance which give undue implicit advantages to certain of the policies and value-judgements.

In economic guise

It is really strange how long it took until our problem gained public attention. It has troubled scientists for more than half a century. In the 1920s and 1930s, a pioneer amongst the advocates of biological diversity, the famous and tragic agronomist and geneticist, Soviet Academician Nikolai Ivanovich Vavilov, later to become one of Stalin's victims, showed the importance of genetic diversity in plant breeding and developed a systematic action plan for collecting genetic material from the 'primary centres of origin' of crop plants. Wherever they were located, these centres were always characterized by 'very ancient agriculture, great ecological diversity (usually mountainous regions), and great human diversity in the sense of culturally distinct tribes with complex interacting histories'.[6] As early as 1932, during the 6th International Congress of Genetics held at Ithaca, USA, Vavilov also pointed out that:

[T]he growing needs of civilized man and the development of industry make the introduction of new plants necessary. The vast resources of wild species, especially in the tropics, have been practically untouched by investigation.[7]

It was and is probably due to a very realistic assessment of current value judgements and power structures then and now, 50 years later, that one tries to legitimize the conservation of biological diversity with the satisfaction of the 'growing needs of civilized man' and with a contribution to the 'development of industry', calling wild species a 'resource' relevant to research and to business. If one needs public attention, if one wants to point out that a problem is 'real', if one needs government funds or other funds of a similar magnitude for an action plan, this is probably the only way to get it nowadays. And so conservationists translate their concerns into economic wording:

. . . the potential value of this huge stock of biological capital . . . could be a rich, sustainable source of building material and fuel, as well as medicinal plants, specialty woods, nuts and fruits.[8]

Genetic resources are an asset and a tool to boost local, regional and national economies in all nations of the world; but their conservation is more certain if they provide jobs and incomes . . . Plant genetic resources have a key role in world trade. Increased agricultural production, not just in quantity but in diversity of crops, leads to improved standards of living, which in turn create increased demand for imports of both food and non-food items. This boosts world trade . . . In addition, plant genetic resources have a demonstrated ability to pay for their conservation many times over. The scale of this economic benefit is large enough to finance the cost of conserving other materials with as yet undiscovered useful qualities.[9]

Bearing these 'undiscovered useful qualities' in mind Merck & Co, a leading pharmaceutical company, recently signed an agreement with Costa Rica's National Institute of Biodiversity (INBio) and will receive samples from Costa Rica's rain forests for pharmaceutical testing and drug development. The Biodiversity–Biotechnology–Biobusiness link has been successfully established. For a world where economy is widely considered to be a synonym for reality, 'realistic' environmentalists have translated their concerns into economic wording in order to finally get public attention for the real dangers of the destruction of habitats, of the loss of species, and of genetic erosion within the species. Consequently, the Merck arrangement is seen by some prominent ecologists as a marked improvement and the best protection scheme realistically attainable.[10] So finally there seems to be nothing sinister or ridiculous either in an *Institute for Economic Botany* in the New York Botanical Garden, or in a sentence by an obviously honest and well-meaning Merck spokesman: 'We have therefore clearly heard the call to come to the rescue of biodiversity by exploring the medical potential of the tropical plant world.'[11] The large financial resources of industry have been tapped to secure biodiversity. This was done by offering the assets of biological diversity as a resource for industry. Is this a fair deal or a desperate last attempt?

Some points do not seem to be clarified yet. So, biodiversity is now an economic resource. But does it have all the proper qualities of an economic resource? Is it scarce? When a Danish bio-industrial group invited environmentalists in early 1992, probably 'because in the wake of the "Green Wave" environmentalists must be considered the primary target audience', the visitors were shown the most advanced fermenters. But at the same time residues of a nice old-fashioned view of a world that is rich and giving were handed around on glossy paper: 'Nature offers unlimited diversity'. This was surprising because one is used to find scarcity, not abundance, as the main theme of most modern scientific and industrial publications: 'Biological resources have limits.'[12] So, perhaps if you want to collect it, you call it an unlimited gift; if you want to sell it, you call it a scarce resource. The UNCED meeting in Rio, 1992, shifted the political focus on biodiversity. In 1972, during the UN Stockholm Conference on the Human Environment, the focus was still on the 'common heritage' aspect of biodiversity. In Rio, biodiversity established itself as a fully-fledged economic resource and commodity, endowed with the necessary element of scarcity. And in its wake biotechnology, which is frequently used as a euphemism for genetically-engineered products, will have gone one step further in establishing itself as the fully acknowledged, most efficient way to safeguard and to use, to conserve and to exploit biodiversity. The terms biotechnology and biodiversity already sound as if they were made for each other.

If this sounds too much like a historically compelling and logically conclusive train of events, let me counteract this impression by pointing out some elements in the discussion which compete with economic funda-mentalism, or at least retard its efficient application. Taking a closer look at the *Global 2000 Report*, you can find alien elements like '. . . natural wonders every bit as unique and beautiful as the Grand Canyon will be irreparably lost.'[13] Even in bureaucratic studies an 'irrational', rarely openly expressed, yet crucial driving force for many environmentalists and conservationists sometimes becomes visible. Not so very irrational, if we agree that '. . . our aesthetic sense is an early warning system for longterm dangers',[14] or if we accept beauty as a value in itself.

There is a strong religious element present, expressed for example in the engagement within the World Council of Churches (WCC) for the 'Integrity of Creation':

> We have contributed to the emergence of a consumerist and anthropomorphic worldview which denigrates both matter and the extra-human species.[15]

> With the industrial mode has come a worldview that looks on creation as manageable and at the disposal of human beings.[16]

Starting from these sentences it is not surprising that the WCC reached a rather critical assessment of some trends in biodiversity management.[17]

Set the fox to guard the chickens

Let us now have a closer look at some of the causes of the sad losses in biological diversity. Unlike the situation during the Cretacean turmoil, this time it is human activities that cause the disappearance of plant and animal richness. What are the causes most frequently named? The speeding up of environmental change, the destruction of wild habitats, human population explosion, economic growth, modern energy-intensive and monocultural agriculture, the degradation of land. All these are intricately linked to modern technology, modern economics and the present state of world-trade and international politics. Bluntly speaking, we are about to entrust the agents of destruction with the safeguarding of our riches. We are about to set the fox to mind the chickens. Yet, foxes and human beings should have the freedom to learn, to change and to mend their ways. Have modern science and technology, or modern economy mended their ways? It certainly has acquired a few new labels like 'environmentally-friendly', 'green', 'sustainable' which are stuck on to the machine. But has the machine been overhauled and changed? Is there at least an agreement on the destructive causes? Are the inventor and constructors of the machine aware of their misconceptions and misconstructions? Or are they all too hastily busy to conquer the market for remedies with the same machine that started the trouble?

There are some fundamental difficulties. One of these difficulties lies in the way in which variety, differentiation and co-evolution and ecosystems come about. They depend on geographical and biological barriers.[18] The description of Vavilov's centres of diversity as places with rich – that is, varied, often mountainous, small-patch – ecology, ancient agriculture, culturally distinct people with complex interacting histories, is in every single point contrary to promising sites for modern agriculture. Modern breeders and modern agriculturists, whose successes depend on collections of biodiversity, very often actively contribute to the destruction of those same sources from which they derive their successes. They use biodiversity, but they push it out of the fields, thus stopping the steady new generation of variety. Bearing in mind that these modern successes have usually been very short-lived and need a steady input of additional traits, this is a vicious, fundamentally non-sustainable circle indeed. Modern agriculture boasts of quick changes and efficient adaptations which, however, are of a type that adversely affects the very ability to change and adapt in the future.

If we remember how diversity is generated and presents itself, then even the term 'Global Ecology' carries a contradiction in itself. Ecology is always local, always unique and special, and so far has never depended on a central planning and management institution for its proper functioning. Classical biology showed some caution toward the use of one-dimensional, additive models for the assessment of plant and animal communities. In plant sociology, inventory lists were made, naming every single plant species together with estimates of 'the number of individuals and their relative contributions to ground cover'.[19] Researchers tried to link their results to those of historical geobotany, situating the species in space and time. In 1920 the zoologist August Friedrich Thienemann formulated two 'biozoenotic basic principles' using the correlation between environmental variability and the total sum of all animal species present in a given environment. This meant the abolition of the listing of species in favour of just giving the total sum. Yet, in 1976, many years older and wiser, the same August Friedrich Thienemann felt the need to point out that the principles he had formulated in his youth do not explain all biological communities, and that not only quantities but also qualities, including unique geographical and historical contexts have to be considered.[20] Somehow all this does not sound exactly like a theoretical basis befitting modern world trade. The new term 'biodiversity', however, has definitely lost the specificity of place, time and context and is based on a purely additive theoretical simplification. Species have become quantities instead of unique and irreplaceable qualities. This theoretical loss paves the way for the economic substitution of species, which in turn is very often a synonym for loss, this time a very practical one. Undoubtedly the economic and scientific foxes are some sort of specialists on chickens, but this is no reason to entrust them with keeping all of them.

A new round of the debt crisis?

Even a very simplistic description of the Debt Crisis will contain the following elements: the North is in need of a resource, and expects and plans an increase in future demand. This is often accompanied by the establishment of a new international expert élite closely linked to the centres of political power. Countries in the South are given loans to create the infrastructure which will allow the extraction of the resource and provide ample supply. The demand expands as predicted, yet the supply expands even more since many and competing poor countries have invested in the exploitation of the same resource. World market prices for the resource drop. So in a sense the poor countries of the South took up huge loans so that the prices of the resource for Northern countries could drop – due to ample supply. Unluckily the interest rates go up at the same time, due to deficits in the national budgets in the Northern and Southern countries alike – which also was clearly predicted by some people. Investment in the exploitation of a resource very often means an investment in the exploitation and destruction of natural habitats in the first place. Many analyses have shown that, in addition, debts are being paid for by very crudely 'selling nature'. An infrastructure of gross political and social injustice is thus linked to an 'infrastructure for the further loss of species'.

The resource 'biodiversity' may repeat elements of this pattern, although it does not as yet involve very high primary investments. Due to the 'infrastructure for the further loss of species', biodiversity is getting scarcer and scarcer. Due to the speeding up of cultural and environmental changes there is a growing need for the adaptability provided by biodiversity. So, a growing economic need is expressed by the North. A new biodiversity expert élite is being created. The scientifically and economically most powerful Northern countries will supply just enough funds for training the necessary compliant and loyal Southern scientific servants. They also will use this to stake their claims for the 'mining of biodiversity'. As soon as countries in the South realize the scientific, political and economic importance of biodiversity they may want to invest in the infrastructure for its extraction and this in most cases will mean loans. The demand will certainly grow, but the supply will grow even more quickly at first, because the remaining riches of the 'only strictly non-renewable resource' will be dumped on the market. If a sufficient number of Southern countries enter the race, royalties for genetic traits stemming from those countries – if reaching their countries of origin at all – will go down in price. On the other hand, once local people and local governments have lost control over local varieties and local species the thin line between good business and efficient blackmail will once again be crossed. It may not be possible for the North to continue to sell airports, pesticides, weapons and large dams to poor, heavily indebted and forewarned nations. Poor people once deprived of their 'biodiversity-subsistence' or 'species sovereignty' could still be drained of their last coins on a world market dealing in foods and medicines. And, therefore, we may have the Debt Crisis spiralling through a new equally indecent 'bio-round'. If again interest rates would have to be paid for by selling nature, further loss of species might be the final result of something that started as an attempt to 'conserve and to use' species. Being aware of this, it is little consolation that we already have some attempts at something I would like to call 'debt for patenting law swaps'. These are a recent perversion of the 'debt for nature swaps'. They are just an attempt at replacing old and inelegant debts by new and promising ones. Promising for whom? That is not difficult to guess.

Commons or commodities?

As we already have seen, biodiversity was used extensively in plant breeding. Traits of traditional varieties were newly combined and turned into 'miracle', 'high-yield' and 'high-response' breeders' products. This poses interesting questions as to the 'miraculous' quality of these products. Which is the greater miracle, higher yields for a few years or the lasting social redefinition of genetic traits? Local varieties were collected from wild places and from the fields of traditional farmers. They entered the gene banks as 'commons', inherited gifts for the community. They were given for free according to old rules of decency. In the gene bank, on the laboratory tables, in the experimental fields they acquire a new quality. They leave as 'market commodities'.[21] A miracle indeed!

Not long ago, conservationists talked grandly about *preserving a natural heritage of humankind held in trust for present and future generations* in all countries throughout the world.[22] Now it seems that they are only 'held in trust *for the use of present and future generations of research workers* in all countries throughout the world.'[23] It may be that the replacement of 'humanity' by 'research workers' is just a Freudian slip, it may however be that these researchers are 'those who, through fact-finding rituals, pretend not to choose our future but to make it safe.'[24] In the latter case this would be a stark step. And, one step further, we get trade related property rights (TRIPS) and patents on microbes, plants and animals. It is doubtful whether the hidden hand of economics will all of a sudden treat its environmental resources in a benign way. The *Global 2000 Report* presents some of the arguments in the 'commons–commodity controversy'. On the one hand, we can read: 'The difficulty – some would say, the impossibility – of managing common resources is well known.'[25] On the other we find:

A system of conservation based solely on economic self-interest is hopelessly lopsided. It tends to ignore, and thus eventually to eliminate, many elements in the land community that lack commercial value, but that are (as far as we know) essential to its healthy functioning. It assumes falsely, I think, that the economic parts of the biotic clock will function without the uneconomic parts.[26]

And a particularly disheartening piece of information is the following:

The higher the interest rate on money, the more difficult it is to conserve for the future. Or as economists put it: the higher the interest rate, the more heavily the purely rational man must discount the future.[27]

As a basis for preserving biodiversity the world market imbued with this special brand of 'pure rationality' does not seem to be a convincing tool. But if we turn to the 'commons' we find that they seem to lose their traditional vitality and strength once they are taken out of their traditional community and handed over to international management. The 'commons–commodity controversy' poses no minor debate for any person genuinely interested in the preservation of biological species. It is, however, being steadily resolved in a non-argumentative way: it is already possible to apply to Patent Offices for patents on life forms. In this legally protected ritual life forms can be turned into market 'commodities', if the applicant can prove that he came by them using a *unique and unprecedented scientific or technical procedure.* Patents are a non-monetary state subsidy. A complementary ritual and subsidy is not available: why don't we have offices where you could declare that a living being from now on belongs to itself and to the surrounding community and that from now on it is not accessible to 'the commodity forming mechanisms'? 'Latent Office' would be a nice name for such a place. It would be easy though, to prove that life forms came into existence *by a unique and unprecedented historical process.* And many people might like to hand in quite a few applications. But there are no such absurd and funny things as a 'Latent Offices' or other easy and globally available ways socially to define microbes, plants and animals as commons. There only are such absurd and funny things as 'Patent Offices'. Perhaps one has to leave the global level to get a fair chance for the commons in this controversy.

Beyond the naive biodiversity alliance

The following is certainly not meant to be an argument against searching for partners. The task has not become less demanding, and it can do with many different contributors. It is also not meant as an a priori exclusion for people of certain backgrounds. If – just to name an example – one were to exclude all those with vested interests (because they are biased) on the one hand, and all those with no training (because they are stupid and uniformed) on the other hand, almost nobody would be left. An alliance with open access for very heterogeneous people is very demanding: it can live with identified controversies, but it must not be blind to the different levels of power amongst the groups forming the alliance. Such blindness can make fools out of honest people of good will.

I think the discussion will have to become more *descriptive, differentiated, decent and diligent*. For such a '*4-D-Discussion*' it may be helpful to put aside the comprehensive terms from time to time and quit looking at 'Biodiversity' and 'Humanity'. Some stories can only be told when people have faces, and plants and animals have names.

Finally I want to point out three of the many trouble spots in the biodiversity alliance. These three – theoretical as they may sound – sometimes prove helpful in identifying and overcoming very practical difficulties.

Beware the 'hydra effect'!

In Greek mythology there is a nine-headed monster called Hydra. Whenever one of its heads is cut off, two new ones grow in its stead. Modern technology and its consequences often invoke the Greek myth: if one problem is solved, by the very process of solving it two new problems are generated. These are called either side-effects or counter-productivity according to different interpretational schools. If such a 'hydra effect' occurs, it is wise to assume that the extent of the problem and its implications have been underestimated and that the tools for problem solving are inadequate or incomplete. A correct interpretation of a 'hydra effect' leads to the insight that much wider insights and experience are needed. More and different people will have to be heard, certainly beyond the shallow style in which 'public acceptance' is usually promoted. As opposed to this it seems a stupid strategy to try to win against Hydra, simply by efficiently speeding up the process of hewing away the heads. This certainly means inviting no end of problems.

Resist the 'Atlas Syndrome'!

Again, in Greek mythology there is the giant Atlas. He carries the weight of the world, sustaining it on his shoulders. And as long as he does that, he cannot pick the golden apples.

The 'Atlas Syndrome' is a frequent modern affliction. It preferably attacks pleasant, well-trained and conscientious people. They undertake to develop global knowledge and feel a global responsibility. And the more lonely they get, and the more unbearable the weight of the global problem on their shoulders, the more righteous and admirable they feel. They tend to speak for those who cannot speak in person: the future generations and the environment. Is this type of 'global knowledge' possible or desirable? Is a qualified 'global responsibility' possible or desirable? Is anybody in a position to know what should be done globally? Is anybody able really to carry the global consequences, learn from all side-effects in every single village on earth, have global remedies? Global knowledge and global responsibility are in vogue. Nevertheless, if they are fashionable but impossible, it might be a good idea to resist the 'Atlas Syndrome'. Do not admire and trust the carriers of unrealistic, virtuous and virtual weights! Just imagine all the whales and elephants, ticks and fleas, baobabs and stinging nettles this person would have to carry in order to be a true 'Atlas of Biodiversity', then smile at this upside-down version of the world: basically we are not carriers, but rather we are being carried. So why should a person press his or her shoulders to the ground, pretend to steady the globe with supporting hands and – to make the picture perfect – stick their feet into the air, which is an airy footing indeed. And why do we revere such a clownish performance? Why not give it the laughter which is its due? Why not invite 'Atlas' to get up? This is what could be called a change of paradigm. The Non-Atlases have more versatility, the freedom to walk around, they can find good company and instead of lonely 'global responsibility' they can try to discuss and decide on appropriate responsibility, which makes responses possible.

Avoid the 'trap of tragic decisions'!

A tragic decision is one which is bad either way. There are quite a few of these decisions around: herbicide-resistant wheat or world hunger, jobs or environmental degradation, justice or peace, nuclear energy or global warming. These decisions are very unpleasant and difficult to make. The decision-makers need good advice. Therefore Ethics Commissions tend to increase in number like mushrooms after a warm autumn rain. Ethics Commissions in most cases mean that professors of biotechnology meet professors of ethics and thus try to respond to the necessity of a broad societal dialogue. They discuss and suggest the 'correct' hierarchy of values for political decision-makers which will help them in the gigantic and tragic decisions they will increasingly have to take. And our hearts bleed for the tragic heroes.

It certainly would also take an ethics professor to prepare a mother for the

130   *Confusion Over Sustainability*

tragic decision as to which one of two children she should save, if she finds herself with her two children in the middle of a deep lake. But mothers with more than one child rarely call in an ethics professor. If we ask how mothers usually succeed in raising more than one child, ethics specialists call this a surprising question and a call for inductive ethics.[28]

But how do mothers usually succeed? How do they avoid the 'trap of tragic decisions'? They hear from the villagers whether the captain of a certain boat drinks too much; they watch the sky for clouds; they have a close look at the boat; they make sure there are enough life-jackets; they teach their children to swim; they take a bus or walk around the lake; they sometimes even give up the idea of a trip to the other side of the lake altogether. Obviously they spend all their wits and energy on avoiding tragic decisions, not on preparing for them. They are not looking for unlimited and heroic alternatives, but for decent and easy ones. Successful and easy ways to avoid tragedy, perhaps this is what we call culture. It finds or builds ways which allow people to reconcile different aims and values. At first glance these ways may seem devious, primitive or without glamour. My deviations around the issue of 'biodiversity' were meant to be an invitation to take a second glance.

Notes

1. *The Global 2000 Report to the President – Entering the Twenty-first Century* (1980), Harmondsworth, pp. 327–32.
2. Ibid., pp. 327, 328.
3. Thomas E. Lovejoy, 'A Projection of Species Extinctions', in *The Global 2000 Report to the President*, pp. 328–31.
4. Ernst von Weizsäcker (1989) *Erdpolitik: Ökologische Realpolitik an der Schwelle zum Jahrhundert der Umwelt*, Darmstadt, p. 130 (English edition by Zed Books, 1993).
5. Keystone International Dialogue, 'Introduction', in *Final Report of the Keystone Dialogue*, Oslo, Norway, June 1991.
6. N. I. Vavilov (1926) *Studies on the Origin of Cultivated Plants*, Leningrad, Institute of Applied Botany and Plant Breeding.
7. Quoted from M. S. Swaminathan (1987) 'Genetic Conservation: microbes to man' at the 100th Anniversary of Academician N. I. Vavilov, Moscow, November 1987, (p. 1 of the conference report).
8. *The Global 2000 Report to the President* (1980), p. 329.
9. *Plant Genetic Resources – Vital for Global Development*, CGIAR Fact Sheet 3, Washington DC, 1991, pp. 1 and 2. This is part of a fact sheet collection entitled *Biodiversity and Plant Genetic Resources* prepared by the International Board for Plant Genetic Resources (IBPGR) on behalf of the Consultative Group on International Agricultural Research (CGIAR) as a contribution to

Competing Notions of Biodiversity 131

the debate on biodiversity for UNCED 1992. CGIAR was established in 1971 under joint sponsorship of the World Bank, FAO and UNDP.

10. Thomas E. Lovejoy (1992) 'Some Thoughts on Biological Diversity', *Special Network Supplement: reviews of Agenda 21*, A/CONF.151/PC/100/Add.20, *Independent Sectors Network '92*, No. IX. p. 2, Geneva, Centre For Our Common Future and the IFC.

11. Georg Albers-Schönberg (1991) 'Remarks on INBio at the Latin American Environment and Hemispheric Technological Cooperation Conference', Institute of the Americas, La Jolla, California, 17–19 November.

12. CGIAR Fact Sheet 1.

13. *The Global 2000 Report to the President* (1980), p. 331.

14. Georg Picht (1989) 'Die Wertordnung einer humanen Welt', in Lutz Franke (ed.), *Wir haben nur eine Erde*, Wissenschaftliche Buchgesellschaft, Darmstadt, pp. 9–18.

15. World Council of Churches (1988) *Justice, Peace and Integrity of Creation: programme report from Norway consultation*, Geneva, WCC, p. 23.

16. Ibid., p. 3.

17. World Council of Churches (1989) *Biotechnology: its challenges to the churches and the world*, Geneva, WCC.

18. Christine von Weizsäcker (1990) 'Error-friendliness and the Evolutionary Impact of Deliberate Releases of GMOs', in Dan Leskien and Joachim Spangenberg (eds.), *European Workshop on Law and Genetic Engineering – Proceedings*, Bonn, BBU-Verlag, pp. 42–6.

19. J. Braun-Blanquet (1928) *Pflanzensoziologie*, Wien, p. 865. Cited from Heinrich Walter, *Allgemeine Geobotanik*, Verlag Eugen Ulmer, Stuttgart, 1973.

20. August Friedrich Thienemann (1976) *Leben und Umwelt, Vom Gesamthaushalt der Natur*, Hamburg, Rowohlt Verlag, p. 44.

21. Christine von Weizsäcker (1991) 'Seed Options: four approaches to the *in situ* conservation of local crops', *Ecology + Farming*, No. 3, pp. 17–18.

22. Legal options formulated by FAO as cited in M. S. Swaminathan (1987) 'Wild Possibilities', *Nature*, Vol. 330.

23. CGIAR Fact Sheet 8, p. 2, IBPGR, Washington, 1991.

24. B. Wynne (1982) *Rationality and Ritual: the Windscale Inquiry and nuclear decisions in Britain*, British Society for the History of Science, London.

25. *The Global 2000 Report to the President* (1980), p. 332.

26. Aldo Leopold (1949) *A Sand County Almanac*, first published by Oxford University Press, cited in *The Global 2000 Report*, p. 332.

27. Garret Hardin (1979) 'Political Requirements for Preserving Our Common Heritage', in Council on Environmental Quality, *Wildlife and America*, pp. 310–16.

28. Ethics Panel of the Engelberg 1991 Forum, 'The Genetic Revolution – Impacts on Biology and Society', *Proceedings* in preparation; see comment by Stephan Wehowski, 'Die Ethik kommt immer zu spät', *Süddeutsche Zeitung*, München, 28–29 March 1991.

9.   The Shaky Ground of Sustainability

Donald Worster

The first thing to know when starting to climb a hill is where the summit is, and the second is that there are no completely painless ways to get there. Failing to know those things may lead one to take a deceptively easy path that never reaches the top but meanders off into a dead-end, frustrating the climber and wasting energy. The popular environmentalist slogan of 'sustainable development' threatens to become such a path. Though attractive at first view, it appeals particularly to people who are dismayed by the long arduous hike they see ahead of them or who don't really have a clear notion of what the principal goal of environmentalism ought to be. After much milling about in a confused and contentious mood, they have discovered what looks like a broad, easy path where all kinds of folk can walk along together, and they hurry toward it, unaware that it may be going in the wrong direction.

Back in the 1960s and 1970s, when contemporary environmentalism first emerged, the goal was more obvious and the route more clear before they became obscured by political compromising. The goal was to save the living world around us, millions of species of plants and animals, including humans, from destruction by our technology, population, and appetites. The only way to do that, it was easy enough to see, was to think the radical thought that there must be limits to growth in three areas – limits to population, limits to technology, and limits to appetite and greed. Underlying this insight was a growing awareness that the progressive, secular materialist philosophy on which modern life rests, indeed on which Western civilization has rested for the past 300 years, is deeply flawed and ultimately destructive to ourselves and the whole fabric of life on the planet. The only true, sure way to the environmentalist goal, therefore, was to challenge that philosophy fundamentally and find a new one based on material simplicity and spiritual richness.

I do not say that this conclusion was shared by everyone in those years who wore the label environmentalist, but it was obvious to the most thoughtful leaders that this was the path we had to take. Since it was so painfully difficult to make that turn, to go in a diametrically opposite direction from the way we had been going, however, many started looking for a less intimidating way. By the mid-1980s such an alternative, called 'sustainable development', had emerged. First it appeared in the *World Conservation Strategy* of the International Union for the Conservation of Nature (1980), then in the book, *Building a Sustainable Society*, by Lester R. Brown of Worldwatch Institute (1981), then in another book, *Gaia: An Atlas of Planet Management*, edited by Norman Myers (1984), and then most influentially in the so-called Brundtland Report, *Our Common Future* (1987). The appeal of this alternative lay in its international political acceptability and in its potential for broad coalition among many contending parties. As Richard Sandbrook, executive vice-president of the International Institute for Environment and Development, explained: 'It has not been too difficult to push the environment lobby of the North and the development lobby of the South together. And there is now in fact a blurring of the distinction between the two, so they are coming to have a common consensus around the theme of sustainable development.'[1]

Lots of lobbyists coming together, lots of blurring going on – inevitably, lots of shallow thinking resulted. The North and the South, we were told, could now make common cause without much difficulty. The capitalist and the socialist, the scientist and the economist, the impoverished masses and the urban élites could now all happily march together on a straight and easy path, if they did not ask too many potentially divisive questions about where they were going.

Like most popular slogans, sustainable development begins to wear thin after a while. Although it seems to have gained a wide acceptance, it has done so by sacrificing real substance. Worse yet, the slogan may turn out to be irredeemable for environmentalist use because it may inescapably compel us to adopt a narrow economic language, standard of judgement, and world view in approaching and utilizing the earth.

My own preference is for an environmentalism that talks about earth ethics and aesthetics rather than about resources and economics, that places priority on the survival of the living world of plants and animals on which our own survival depends, and that focuses on what nature's priceless beauty can add to our emotional well-being. I will return to that theme later, but first let us examine the shaky ground of sustainable development. So far we have not had a probing moral analysis of this slogan, despite all those books and reports mentioned above. Although I myself cannot offer any full analysis of it in so short a space, I do want to draw attention to the important subject of language and ask what is implied in that magic word of consensus, 'sustainability'.

Probing the slogan

The first and perhaps most difficult problem, one that seldom gets addressed, is the time frame that ought to be assumed. Is a sustainable society one that endures for a decade, a human lifetime, or a thousand years? It is not enough merely to say 'sustainable for a long time', or even 'for the next generation', if we want to establish targets for our institutions. On the other hand, no one really expects sustainable to mean 'forever'; that would be a utopian expectation that no society has ever achieved. The anthropologist Marvin Harris argues, in his provocative study of human culture, *Cannibals and Kings*, that all through both prehistory and history we can find only a few human societies that were able to sustain their technology, organization, economic patterns, and institutions for even a few centuries. Again and again, societies ran out of the critical resources on which they depended or they degraded their supporting environment to the point of crisis, requiring a revolutionary response. Whether due to population increase or environmental ignorance or excessive demands, they commonly ended by consuming their natural base. Harris goes so far as to argue that all the world's cultures have had their origin in that repeated failure of sustainability: a new culture emerged whenever people managed to get out of their resource trap and invent a new infrastructure, based on a different set of resources or a different approach to resource use. Thus, innovation, both technological and cultural, has been the outcome of ecological depletion, and without such depletion there would have been little cultural change over time. If at the outset of our history as a species we could have achieved a perfect sustainability, we would still be living in a hunting and gathering state; but then such an achievement would have required the strict adherence to a profoundly conservative social order, and probably an insufferably boring one, incapable of all the creativity as well as all the disasters of subsequent history.[2]

If we cannot expect to achieve a *perfect* sustainability that lasts forever, what then can we hope for and work toward? What *degree* of sustainability should we settle on? No one, to my knowledge, has yet made a definitive answer.

Besides suggesting no clear time frame, the ideal of sustainability presents us with a bewildering multiplicity of criteria, and we have to sort out which ones we want to emphasize before we can develop any specific programme of action. Among the dozens of possible sets of criteria, three or four have dominated public discussion of late, each based on a body of expertise, and they share little common ground.[3]

The field of economics, for example, has its own peculiar notion of what sustainability means. Economists focus on the point where societies achieve a critical take-off into long-term, continuous growth, investment, and profit in a market economy. The United States, for instance, reached that point around 1850, and has ever since been growing endlessly, despite a few recessions and depressions. By that standard any and all of the industrial societies are already sustainable, while the backward agrarian ones are not.[4]

Students of medicine and public health, on the other hand, have a different notion of the word; sustainability for them is a condition of individual physiological fitness, a condition to be measured by physicians and nutritionists. Thus, they focus on threats of water and air pollution or on food and water availability, or they talk about the threat of diminished genetic stock to the practice of medicine and the supply of pharmaceuticals. Despite the existence of many threats today, most health experts would say that human health has made great strides over the past few centuries in every part of the earth. By their criteria the human condition is far more sustainable today than it was in the past – a fact that explosive population growth and longer lifespans for most societies demonstrate. By the standard of physiological fitness people living in industrial societies are doing far better than our ancestors or our contemporaries in the non-industrial societies.

Still another group of experts, the political and social scientists, speak of 'sustainable institutions' and 'sustainable societies', which apparently refer to the ability of institutions or ruling groups to generate enough public support to renew themselves and hold on to power.[5] Sustainable societies are then simply those that are able to reproduce their political or social institutions; whether the institutions are benign or evil, compassionate or unjust, does not enter into the discussion. By this reasoning, the communist regimes of Eastern Europe and the Soviet Union have not proved to be sustainable and are being swept into the ashheaps of history.

These are all leading, important uses of the word found among various fields of expertise, and undoubtedly they all can be given very sophisticated (and far more precise than I have indicated) measurements. In contrast, we also have some simpler, more popular notions of the word. One of the clearest, most pithy, and least arcane definitions comes from Wendell Berry, the American writer and trenchant critic of all expertise. He called specifically for a more sustainable agriculture than we have today, by which he meant an agriculture that 'does not deplete soils or people'.[6] That phrase expresses, as so much of Berry's work does, an old-fashioned agrarian way of thinking, steeped in the folk history and local knowledge of his rural Kentucky neighbours. Like everything Berry writes, it has a concise, elemental ring, and the great virtue of recalling to our attention that people and the earth are interdependent, a fact that those specialized academic approaches by economists and the rest generally ignore.

In Berry's view the only truly sustainable societies have been small-scale agrarian ones; no modern industrial society could qualify. His own model, which is based on the livelihood and culture of the Jeffersonian yeoman farmer, must be seen as part of the economic past; it has virtually disappeared from modern American life. One might ask, as Berry's critics regularly do, whether he is offering us more of a myth than a reality: did such non-depleting rural communities ever really exist in the United States, or are they only idealizations or indulgences in a false nostalgia? But even if we accept Berry's distinction between 'sustainable agrarian' and 'unsustainable industrial', it is still not clear what the preconditions for sustainability, or the measurement of its success, would be. What meaning can we give to the idea of 'people depletion'? Is it a demographic or a cultural idea? And how much self-reliance or local community production does it require, and how much market exchange does it allow? For that matter, what is referred to in Berry's notion of soil depletion? Soil scientists point out that the United States has lost, on average, half of its topsoil since white, European settlement began; but then many of them go on to argue that such depletion is not a problem so long as we can substitute chemical fertilizers. Once more we are back in the muddle of whose expertise, language, and values are to define sustainability. Berry would answer, I suppose, that we should leave the definition to local people, but national and international policy makers will want something more objective than that.

All those definitions and criteria are floating around in the air today, confusing our language and thinking, demanding far more of a consensus of meaning before we can achieve any concerted programme of reform. To be sure, there is a widespread implication in the environmental literature I have cited that sustainability is at bottom an ecological concept: the goal of environmentalism should be to achieve 'ecological sustainability'. What that means is that the science of ecology is expected to cut through all the confusion and define sustainability for us; it should point out which practices are ecologically sustainable and which are not. Once again we are back in the business of looking for a set of expert, objective answers to guide policy. But how helpful really are those experts in ecology? Do they have a clear definition or set of criteria to offer? Do they even have a clear, coherent perception of nature to provide as a basis for international action?

How helpful are the experts?

Ecologists traditionally have approached nature as a series of overlapping but integrated biological systems, or ecosystems. In contrast to most economists, for whom nature is not a relevant category of analysis, they have insisted that those systems are not disorganized or useless but self-organizing and productive of many material benefits that we need. The role of ecologists then, as we have generally come to understand it, is one of revealing to laymen how those ecosystems, or their modifications into agro-ecosystems, undergo stress from human demands and of helping us determine the critical point when that stress is so severe that they collapse.

If we accept that expert tutoring, the ecological idea of sustainability becomes, quite simply, another measure of production, rivalling that of the economists: a measure of productivity in the economy of nature where we find such commodities as soils, forests, and fisheries, and a measure of the capacity of that economy to rebound from stresses, avoid collapse, and maintain output. Unfortunately, compared to economists, the ecologists have recently become very uncertain about their own advice. Their indices of stress and collapse are in dispute, and their expertise is in disarray.

A few decades ago ecologists commonly believed that nature, when left free of human interference, eventually reaches a balance or equilibrium state where production is at a steady rate. The origins of this idea go back deep into the recesses of human memory, deep into the past of every civilization before the modern. For Westerners in particular the idea of nature as a balanced order has ancient Greek, medieval Christian, and 18th-century rationalist antecedents, and it survived even the profound intellectual revolution wrought by Charles Darwin and the theory of evolution through natural selection. From the time of its emergence in the late 19th century the science of ecology echoed that longstanding faith in the essential orderliness of nature, and until recently almost all ecologists would have agreed that sustainability is a matter of accommodating the human economy to that constancy and orderliness. Now, that is no longer the case.[7]

During the first half of this century the dominant figure in Anglo-American ecology was an American, Frederick Clements, who came out of Nebraska and was a student of the native prairies of the mid-continent. Clements founded what has been called the dynamic or climax theory of vegetation, which holds that, although the organization of plant life is constantly changing on the earth, going through a process called succession, eventually harmony, stability, and order evolve in the landscape. That point was called the climax stage, and according to Clements, it would endure until some major disturbance occurred through a change in the climate. He compared the order of vegetation at that stage to a 'super-organism', suggesting that in terms of the integration of its parts, the coherence of the whole, the climax is like a single but highly complex organism. To disturb such an order is, in effect, to kill that organism.[8]

Throughout the geological history of the grasslands, the great killer had been drought and other abrupt shifts in climate. But in the late 19th and early 20th century another disturber of order entered: Euro-American farmers, armed with ploughs, destroying the tall-grass prairies and planting the land to wheat and corn. Then, during the 1930s, severe drought returned to the country and, in combination with extensive overploughing, created one of the worst environmental disasters in human history, the Dust Bowl of the Great Plains, a period of severe wind erosion, out-migration, and rural poverty. Clements and many of his followers were inclined to be critical of modern American agriculture, and indeed of much of modern economic development for being so destructive to the order of nature, and by extrapolation their ideal of a 'sustainable' life on the land was one that followed closely the model of the climax stage.

When the idea of the super-organismic climax began to seem a little far-fetched, ecologists replaced it with another concept of natural ecological order, the ecosystem. The ecosystem was a pattern of order in plant and animal assemblages that was based more on the study of physics than on analogies with the single living organism; in the ecosystem, energy and material flow in regular, orderly, efficient patterns. Human activity, warned ecologists like Eugene Odum much as Clements did before him, must conform to those patterns if we want to live in a harmonious, enduring relationship with nature.

Very recently, however, many ecologists have begun to question all those older ideas, theories, and metaphors, even to assert that nature is inherently *disorderly*. Some have tried to maintain that the ecosystem, like the climax stage, is a fiction that does not really describe the turbulence of the natural environment, or at least that such ideas are too vague or inflexible. Beginning around 1970 ecology went off in search of new ways to describe forests, grasslands, oceans, and all the other biomes of the planet, and the outcome is the emergence today of a more permissive ecology that rejects virtually all notions of balance and order, new or ancient, and portrays instead a nature that is far more lenient toward human activity than were Clements's or Odum's. We live in the midst of a nature that has been undergoing profound and constant change for as far back as we can look, scientists now argue with the aid of new scientific techniques; we confront a nature populated by rugged individualists, eager opportunists, and self-seekers. There is no integrated community in that nature, no enduring system of relationships; no deep interdependence. To be sure, the sun seems to come up regularly every day and in predictable spots; the four seasons come and go with a great deal of regularity. But pay no attention to all that, they say; look at the populations of plants and animals that live in any given area that we might call wild, pristine, or natural, and you will find no regularity, no constancy, no order there at all.[9]

Many of these ideas appear in a recent book entitled *Discordant Harmonies* (1990), which is self-described as 'a new ecology for the 21st century'. Here is how its author, Daniel Botkin, a leading California ecologist, sees the current situation in his science:

Until the past few years, the predominant theories in ecology either presumed or had as a necessary consequence a very strict concept of a highly structured, ordered, and regulated, steady-state ecological system. Scientists know now that this view is wrong at local and regional levels . . . that is, at the levels of population and ecosystems. Change now appears to be intrinsic and natural at many scales of time and space in the biosphere.

'Wherever we seek to find constancy' in nature, Botkin writes, 'we discover change.'[10]

The basis for this new ecology is a body of evidence that is essentially historical, including pollen samples, tree-rings, and animal population cycles, all of which show the world of nature to be in a constant flux, as unstable as the human scene where wars, assassinations, invasions, depressions, and social turmoil of every sort constitute the only normal condition we know.

For example, one can observe the history of a small, old-growth forest in New Jersey that was preserved from building development in the 1950s under the assumption that it was a surviving remnant of the mature climax forest, dominated by oaks and hickories, that once grew in the area. Scientists suppressed fire in the forest to keep it pristine and undisturbed. By the 1960s, however, they began to discover that maple trees were invading their preserve from the outside. If they suppressed all fires, if they tried to keep their forest 'natural', they were bound to fail. What then, they had to ask themselves, was the state of climax in this habitat? What could be called natural? What was the true order of nature?

Other evidence comes from pollen taken from pond and lake sediments all over North America, and indeed from all the major continents. They show that every area of the earth has experienced a wild variation in vegetation cover from year to year, from century to century, and from the glacial to the interglacial period. When the great ice sheets flowed over the North American continent, all the plants retreated south or into the lowlands – and it was not the orderly retreat of an organized, super-organismic community but a chaotic rout. Then when the glaciers retreated, leaving the land bare, the same plants made a ragged, chaotic invasion of their old ground. There was no organized return of whole communities.

Here is Botkin again:

Nature undisturbed by human influence seems more like a symphony whose harmonies arise from variation and change over every interval of time. We see a landscape that is always in flux, changing over many scales of time and space, changing with individual births and deaths, local disruptions and recoveries, larger scale responses to climate from one glacial age to another, and to the slower alterations of soils, and yet larger variations between glacial ages.[11]

But Botkin later makes a very telling amendment to that statement when he adds that 'nature's symphony' is more like several compositions being played at once in the same hall, 'each with its own pace and rhythm'. And then he comes to what is really the practical upshot of his ecology for policy makers, environmentalists, and developers: 'We are forced to choose among these [compositions], which we have barely begun to hear and understand.' Or one might say that after learning to hear all those discordances of nature, we humans must also assume the role of conducting the music. If there is to be any order in nature, it is our responsibility to achieve it. If there is to be any harmony, we must overcome the apparent discord. 'Nature in the 21st century,' this scientist concludes, 'will be a nature that we make.' Such a conclusion is where Botkin's science has been leading him all along: to a rejection of nature as a norm or standard for human civilization and to an assertion of a human right and need to give order and shape to nature. We are arriving, he proclaims, at a new view of Earth 'in which we are a part of a living and changing system whose changes we can accept, use, and control, to make the Earth a comfortable home, for each of us individually and for all of us collectively in our civilizations'. I believe that this new turn toward revisionism and relativism in ecological science is motivated, in part, by a desire to be less disapproving of economic development than environmentalists were in the 1960s and 1970s. Botkin criticizes that era for its radical, sometimes hostile, rejection of modern technology and progress. We need a science of ecology, he believes, that approaches development in a more 'constructive and positive manner.'[12]

A permissive ecology?

Those conclusions constitute what I would call a new permissiveness in ecoloy – far more permissive toward human desires than was the climax ecology of Frederick Clements and emphatically more permissive than the popular ecosystem ideas found among environmentalists of the 1960s and 1970s. This new ecology makes human wants and desires the primary test of what should be done with the earth. It denies that there is to be found in nature, past or present, any standard for, or even much of a limitation on, those desires. Botkin hints at this denial in the beginning of his book when he criticizes the environmentalism of the 1960s and 1970s as 'essentially a disapproving, and in this sense, negative movement, exposing the bad aspects of our civilization for our environment . . .' What we must do, he argues, is move away from that critical environmentalism toward a stance 'that combine[s] technology with our concern about our environment in a constructive and positive manner.'

This new turn in ecology presents several difficulties that I think the sustainable development advocates have not really acknowledged. In the first place, the whole idea of what is a normal 'yield' or 'output' from the natural economy becomes, if we follow Botkin's reasoning, far more ambiguous. Scientists once thought they could determine with relative ease the maximum sustained yield that a forest or fishery could achieve. They had only to determine the steady-state population in the ecosystem and then calculate how many fish could be caught each year without affecting the stock. They could take off the interest without touching the fixed capital. Botkin argues that it was just such assurance that led to over-fishing in the California sardine industry – and to the total collapse of that industry in the 1950s.[13]

But if the natural populations of fish and other organisms are in such continual flux that we cannot set maximum sustained yield targets, could we instead set up a more flexible standard of 'optimum yield', one that would allow a more general margin for error and fluctuations? That is where most ecological sustainability thinking rests today. Harvest commodities from nature, but do so at a lightly reduced level to avoid overstressing a system in stochastic change. Call it the safe optimum notion. But that formula does not really address the more basic challenge implicit in recent ecological thinking. What can sustainable use, let alone sustainable development, mean in a natural world subject to so much disturbance and chaotic turbulence? Our powers of prediction, say ecologists, are far more limited than we imagined. To many, our understanding of what is normal in nature now seems to be arbitrary and partial.

The only real guidance Botkin gives us, and this is likewise true of most ecologists today, is that slow rates of change in ecosystems are 'more natural', and therefore more desirable, than fast rates. 'We must be wary,' Botkin says, 'when we engineer nature at an unnatural rate and in novel ways.'[14] And that is all he really offers. But when we have to have more specific advice to manage this or that acre of land successfully, the ecologist is embarrassingly silent; he or she can hardly say any more what is 'unnatural' or what is 'novel' in light of the incredibly changeable record of the Earth's past.

In the much acclaimed partnership between the advocates of ecological sustainability and of development, who is going to lead whom? This is the all-important question to ask about the new path that so many want us to take. I fear that in that partnership it will be 'development' that makes most of the decisions, and 'sustainable' will come trotting along, smiling and genial, unable to assert any firm leadership, complaining only about the pace of travel. 'You must slow down, my friend, you are going too fast for me. This is a nice road to progress, but we must go along at a more "natural" speed.'

In the absence of any clear idea of what a healthy nature is, or how threats to that collective biological whole might impinge on us, we will end up relying on utilitarian, economic, and anthropocentric definitions of sustainability. That, it seems to me, is where the discussion is right now. Sustainability is, by and large, an economic concept on which economists are clear and ecologists are muddled. If you find that outcome unacceptable, as I do, then you must change the elementary terms of the discussion.

Flaws in the ideal

I find the following deep flaws in the sustainable development ideal:

First, it is based on the view that the natural world exists primarily to serve the material demands of the human species. Nature is nothing more than a pool of 'resources' to be exploited; it has no intrinsic meaning or value apart from the goods and services it furnishes people, rich or poor. The Brundtland Report makes this point clear on every page: the 'our' in its title refers to people exclusively, and the only moral issue it raises is the need to share what natural resources there are more equitably among our kind, among the present world population and among the generations to come. That is not by any means an unworthy goal, but it is not adequate to the challenge.

Second, sustainable development, though it acknowledges some kind of limit on those material demands, depends on the assumption that we can easily determine the carrying capacity of local regional ecosystems. Our knowledge is supposedly adequate to reveal the limits of nature and to exploit resources safely up to that level. In the face of new arguments suggesting how turbulent, complex, and unpredictable nature really is, that assumption seems highly optimistic. Furthermore, in light of the tendency of some leading ecologists to use such arguments to justify a more accommodating stance toward development, any heavy reliance on their ecological expertise seems doubly dangerous; they are experts who lack any agreement on what the limits are.

Third, the sustainability ideal rests on an uncritical, unexamined acceptance of the traditional world view of progressive, secular materialism. It regards that world view as completely benign so long as it can be made sustainable. The institutions associated with that world view, including those of capitalism, socialism, and industrialism, also escape all criticism, or close scrutiny. We are led to believe that sustainability can be achieved with all those institutions and their values intact.

Perhaps my objections can be fully answered by the advocates of the sustainable development slogan. I suspect, however, that their response will, in the end, rest on the argument that the idea is the only politically acceptable kind of environmentalism we can expect at this point. It is desirable simply because it represents the politics of compromise.

Having been so critical toward this easy, sloganeering alternative, I feel obliged to conclude with a few ideas of my own about what a real solution for the global crisis will require. I grant that it will be more difficult to achieve, but would argue that it is more revolutionary in impact and more morally advanced.

We must make our first priority in dealing with the earth the careful and strict preservation of the billion-year-old heritage achieved by the evolution of plant and animal life. We must preserve all the species, sub-species, varieties, communities, and ecosystems that we possibly can. We must not, through our actions, cause any more species to become extinct. To be sure, we cannot stop every death or extinction, since the death of living things is part of the inevitable workings of nature. But we can avoid adding to that fateful outcome. We can stop reversing the processes of evolution, as we are doing today. We can work to preserve as much genetic variety as possible. We can save endangered habitats and restore those needed to support that evolutionary heritage. We can and must do all this primarily because the living heritage of evolution has an intrinsic value that we have not created but only inherited and enjoyed. That heritage demands our respect, our sympathy, and our love.

Unquestionably, we have a right to use that heritage to improve our material condition, but only after taking, in every community, every nation, and every family, the strictest measures to preserve it from extinction and diminution.

To conserve that evolutionary heritage is to focus our attention backward on the long history of the struggle of life on this planet. In recent centuries we have had our eyes fixed almost exclusively on the future and the potential affluence it can offer our aspiring species. Now it is time to learn to look backward more of the time and, from an appreciation of that past, learn humility in the presence of an achievement that overshadows all our technology, all our wealth, all our ingenuity, and all our human aspirations.

To conserve that heritage is to put other values than economic ones first in our priorities: the value of natural beauty, the value of respectfulness in the presence of what we have not created, and above all the value of life itself, a phenomenon that even now, with all our intelligence, we cannot really explain.

To learn truly to cherish and conserve that heritage is the hardest road the human species can take. I do not even know, though I have plenty of doubts, whether it is realistic at this point, given the state of global politics, to expect most nations to be ready or willing to take it. But I do know that it is the right path, while following the ambiguities, compromises, and smooth words of sustainable development may lead us into quicksand.

Notes

1. Quoted in World Commission on Environment and Development (1987) *Our Common Future*, Oxford and New York, Oxford University Press, p. 64. See also R. Sandbrook (1982) *The Conservation and Development Programme for the UK: a response to the World Conservation Strategy* (1989) *Our Common Future: a Canadian response to the challenge of sustainable development*, Ottawa, Harmony Foundation of Canada; and Raymond F. Dasmann (1988) 'Toward a Biosphere Consciousness', in Donald Worster (ed.), *The Ends of the Earth: perspectives on modern environmental history*, New York, Cambridge University Press, pp. 281–5.

2. Marvin Harris (1977) *Cannibals and Kings: the origins of cultures*, New York, Random House.

3. I have found two books by Michael Redclift (1984 and 1987) useful here: *Development and the Environment Crisis: Red or Green Alternatives?* London, Methuen; and *Sustainable Development: Exploring the Contradictions*, London, Methuen. See also M. L'el'e Sharachchandram (1991) 'Sustainable Development: A Critical Review', *World Development*, Vol. 19, June, pp. 607–21. Also, several of the essays in the symposium, *History of Sustained-Yield Forestry* (edited by Harold K. Steen (1984), Durham, NC, Forest History Society), especially the following: Robert G. Lee, 'Sustained Yield and Social Order', pp. 90–100; Heinrich Rubner, 'Sustained-Yield Forestry in Europe and Its Crisis During the Era of Nazi Dictatorship', pp. 170–75; and Claus Wiebecke and W. Peters, 'Aspects of Sustained-Yield History: forest sustention as the principle of forestry – idea and reality', pp. 176–83.

4. Clem Tisdell (1988) 'Sustainable Development: differing perspectives of ecologists and economists and relevance to LDCs', *World Development*, Vol. 16, March, pp. 373–84.

5. Arthur A. Goldsmith and Derick W. Brinkerhoff define sustainability as a condition in which an institution's 'outputs are valued highly enough that inputs continue'. See their book (1990) *Institutional Sustainability in Agriculture and Rural Development: a global perspective*, New York, Praeger, pp. 13–14.

6. Wes Jackson, Wendell Berry, and Bruce Colman (eds.) (1984) *Meeting the Expectations of the Land: essays in sustainable agriculture and stewardship*, San Francisco, North Point Press, p. x.

7. An example of how these older ecological theories still influence the advocates of sustainable development is P. Bartelmus (1986) *Environment and Development*, London, Allen and Unwin, p. 44.

8. Donald Worster (1977) *Nature's Economy: a history of ecological ideas*, New York, Cambridge University Press, pp. 205–18.

9. I have discussed some of these trends in my article, 'The Ecology of Order and Chaos', *Environmental History Review*, Vol. 14, Spring/Summer 1990, pp. 1–18.

10. Daniel B. Botkin (1990) *Discordant Harmonies: a new ecology for the twenty-first century*, New York, Oxford University Press, pp. 10, 62.

11. Ibid., p. 62

12. Ibid., p. 6.

13. See also Arthur McEvoy (1986) *The Fisherman's Problem: ecology and law in California fisheries, 1850–1980*, New York, Cambridge University Press, pp. 6–7, 10, 150–1.

14. Botkin (1990), p. 190.

Part III
Against Environmental Management
on a Global Scale

10.   The Greening of the Global Reach

Vandana Shiva

The green movement grew out of local awareness and local efforts to resist environmental damage. The crisis of deforestation in the Himalaya was a concern first voiced by the local peasant women of Garhwa. The crisis of toxic hazards was first recognized by the affected residents of the Love Canal.

The pattern that emerged over the 1970s and 1980s was the recognition that major environmental threats were posed by globally powerful institutions, such as multinational corporations, and multilateral development banks such as the World Bank, whose operations reach every city, village, field and forest worldwide.

In recent years, the two decades of the green movement are being erased. The 'local' has disappeared from environmental concern. Suddenly, it seems, only 'global' environmental problems exist, and it is taken for granted that their solution can only be 'global'.

In this chapter I shall look more closely at what the concept of the 'global' conceals and projects, how it builds power relations around environmental issues, and how it transforms the environmental crisis from being a reason for change into a reason for strengthening the status quo.

The 'global' as a globalized local

Unlike what the term suggests, the global as it emerged in the discussions and debates around the UN Conference on Environment and Development (UNCED) – eventually held in June 1992 – was not about universal humanism or about a planetary consciousness. The life of all people, including the poor of the Third World, or the life of the planet, are not at the centre of concern in international negotiations on global environmental issues.

The 'global' in the dominant discourse is the political space in which a particular dominant local seeks global control, and frees itself of local, national and international restraints. The global does not represent the universal human interest, it represents a particular local and parochial interest which has been globalized through the scope of its reach. The seven most powerful countries, the G-7, dictate global affairs, but the interests that guide them remain narrow, local and parochial. The World Bank is not really a Bank that serves the interests of all the world's communities. It is a Bank where decisions are based on voting power weighted by the economic and political power of donors, and in this decision-making it is the communities who pay the real price and are the real donors (such as the tribals of Narmada Valley whose lives are being destroyed by a Bank-financed megadam) but have no say. The 'global' of today reflects a modern version of the global reach of the handful of British merchant adventurers who, as the East India Company, later, the British Empire raided and looted large areas of the world. Over the past 500 years of colonialism, whenever this global reach has been threatened by resistance, the language of opposition has been co-opted, redefined, and used to legitimize future control.

The independence movement against colonialism had revealed the poverty and deprivation caused by the economic drain from the colonies to the centres of economic power. The post-war world order which saw the emergence of independent political states in the South, also saw the emergence of the Bretton Woods institutions such as the World Bank and IMF which took over the language of underdevelopment and poverty, removed these independent political states' history, and made them the reason for a new bondage based on development financing and debt burdens.

The environment movement revealed the environmental and social costs generated by maldevelopment, conceived of and financed by such institutions as the World Bank. Now, however, the language of the environment is itself being taken over and made the reason for strengthening such 'global' institutions and increasing their global reach.

In addition to the legitimacy derived from co-opting the language of dissent is the legitimization that derives from a false notion that the globalized 'local' is some form of hierarchy that reflects geographical and democratic spread, and to which lower order hierarchies should somehow be subservient. Operationalizing undemocratic development projects was based on a similar false notion of 'national interest', and every local interest felt morally compelled to make sacrifices for what seemed the larger interest. It was this moral compulsion that led each community to make way for the construction of mega-dams in post-independence India. Only during the 1980s, when the different 'local' interests met nationwide, did they realize that what was projected as the 'national interest' was, in fact, the electoral interests of a handful of politicians financed by a handful of contractors, such as J.P. and Associates who benefit from the construction of all dams, such as Tehri and the Narmada Valley projects. Against the narrow and selfish interest that had been elevated to the status of 'national' interest, the collective effort of communities engaged in resistance against large dams began to emerge as the real though subjugated national interest.

In a similar way the World Bank's Tropical Forest Action Plan (TFAP) was projected as responding to a global concern about the destruction of tropical forests. When forest movements formed a worldwide coalition under the World Rainforest Movement, however, it became clear that TFAP reflected the narrow commercial interests of the World Bank and multinational forestry interests such as Shell, Jaako Poyry and others, and that the global community best equipped to save tropical forests were forest-dwellers themselves and farming communities dependent on forests.

Global environment or green imperialism?

Instead of extending environmental concern and action, the recent emergence of a focus on 'global' environmental problems has in fact narrowed the agenda.

The multiple environmental concerns that emerged from the grassroots, including the forest, and the water crises, toxic and nuclear hazards and so on have been marginalized. Thus the Global Environmental Facility (GEF) set up at the World Bank addresses only four environmental issues: (1) a reduction in greenhouse gas emissions; (2) protection of biodiversity; (3) a reduction in pollution of international waters; and (4) a reduction in ozone layer depletion.

The exclusion of other concerns from the global agenda is spurious, since, for example, the nuclear and chemical industries operate globally, and the problems they generate in every local situation are related to their global reach.

'Global environmental problems' have been so constructed as to conceal the fact that globalization of the local is responsible for destroying the environment which supports the subjugated local peoples. The construction becomes a political tool not only to free the dominant destructive forces operating worldwide from all responsibility but also to shift the blame and responsibility for all destruction on to the communities that have no global reach.

Consider the case of ozone depletion. CFCs, which are a primary cause of ozone depletion, are manufactured by a handful of transnationals, such as Dupont, with specific locally identifiable manufacturing plants. The rational mechanism to control CFC production and use was to control these plants. That such substances as CFCs are produced by particular companies in particular plants is totally ignored when ozone depletion becomes transformed into a 'global' environmental problem. The producers of CFCs are apparently blameless and the blame laid instead on the potential use of refrigerators and air-conditioners by millions of people in India and China. Through a shift from present to future, the North gains a new political space in which to control the South. 'Global' concerns thus create the moral base for green imperialism.

It also creates the economic base, since through conventions and protocols, the problem is reduced to technology and aid transfer. Dupont then becomes essential to the problem it has created, because it has patented CFC substitutes, for which a market must be found. The financial resources that go into the Montreal Protocol Fund for transfer of technology are in effect subsidies for Dupont and others, not for the Third World.

The erosion of biodiversity is another area in which control has been shifted from the South to the North through its identification as a global problem. Biodiversity erosion has occurred because of habitat destruction in diversity-rich areas, by dams, mines and highways financed by the World Bank for the benefit of transnational corporations (TNCs), and by replacing diversity-based agricultural and forest systems with monocultures of 'green revolution' wheat and rice and eucalyptus plantations, which were also supported and planned by the World Bank, in order to create markets for seed and chemical industries.

The most important step in biodiversity conservation is to control the World Bank's planned destruction of biodiversity. Instead, by treating biodiversity as a global resource, the World Bank emerges as its protector through the GEF (Global Environmental Facility), and the North demands free access to the South's biodiversity through the proposed Biodiversity Convention. But biodiversity is a resource over which local communities and nations have sovereign rights. Globalization becomes a political means to erode these sovereign rights, and means to shift control over and access to biological resources from the gene-rich South to the gene-poor North. The 'global environment' thus emerges as the principal weapon to facilitate the North's worldwide access to natural resources and raw materials on the one hand, and on the other, to enforce a worldwide sharing of the environmental costs it has generated, while retaining a monopoly on benefits reaped from the destruction it has wreaked on biological resources. The North's slogan at UNCED and the other global negotiation fora seems to be: 'What's yours is mine. What's mine is mine'.

The notion of 'global' facilitates this skewed view of a common future. The construction of the global environment narrows the South's options, while increasing the North's. Through its global reach, the North exists in the South, but the South exists only within itself, since it has no global reach. Thus the South can *only* exist locally, while *only* the North exists globally.

Solutions to the global environmental problems can come only from the global, that is, the North. Since the North has abundant industrial technology and capital, if it has to provide a solution to environmental problems, they must be reduced to a currency that the North dominates. The problem of ecology is transformed into a problem of technology transfer and finance. What is absent from the analysis is that the assumption that the South needs technology and finances from the North is a major cause of the environmental crisis, and a major reason for the drain of resources from South to North. While the governments of the South demand 'new and additional sources of finance' for the protection of the environment, they ignore the reverse transfer of $50 billion per year of capital from the poor South to the affluent North. The old order does not change through the environmental discussions, rather it becomes more deeply entrenched.

The problem of false causality

With the masking-out of the role of the globalized local in local environmental destruction worldwide, the multiple facets of destruction are treated as local causes of problems with global impact. Among the many simultaneously occurring impacts of maldevelopment and colonialism are: the rise of poverty; the increase of environmental degradation; the growth of population; polarization; and conflict between men and women, and between ethnic communities.

Extraction of surplus and the exploitation and destruction of resources have left people without livelihoods. Lacking access to resources for survival, the poor have been forced to generate economic security by having large families. The collapse of social cohesion and economic stability has provided the ground for ethnic conflict.

Instead of identifying the cause of these multifaceted problems as global domination of certain narrow interests of the North, however, these problems are selectively transformed from consequence to cause. Poverty and population are identified as *causes* of environmental degradation. Diversity is seeen as a defect and identified as a *cause* of ethnic conflict.

False causality is applied to explain false connections. Thus some UNCED documents went to the extent of pointing to population growth as a *cause* of the explosive growth in toxic chemicals. A problem caused by an irresponsible chemical industry is converted into a problem caused by fertility rates in the poor countries of the South. The 1991 cyclone in Bangladesh was similarly linked causally to the number of babies in Bangladesh.

The 'global' is not planetary

The visual image of planet earth used in the discourse on global ecology disguises the fact that at the ethical level the global as construct does not symbolize planetary consciousness. The global reach by narrow and selfish interests is not based on planetary or Gaian ethics. In fact, it abstracts the planet and peoples from the conscious mind, and puts global institutions in their place. The planet's security is invoked by the most rapacious and greedy institutions to destroy and kill the cultures which employ a planetary consciousness to guide their concrete daily actions. The ordinary Indian woman who worships the *tulsi* plant worships the cosmic as symbolized in the plant. The peasants who treat seeds as sacred, see in them the connection to the universe. Reflexive categories harmonize balance from planets to plants to people. In most sustainable traditional cultures, the great and the small have been linked so that limits, restraints, responsibilities are always transparent and cannot be externalized. The great exists in the small and hence every act has not only global but cosmic implications. To tread gently on the earth becomes the natural way to be. Demands in a planetary consciousness are made on the self, not on others.

The moral framework of the global reach, however, is quite the opposite. There are no reflexive relationships. The G-7 can demand a forest convention that imposes international obligations on the Third World to plant trees. But the Third World cannot demand that the industrialized countries reduce the use of fossil fuels and energy. All demands are externally dictated – one way – from North to South. The 'global' has been so structured, that the North (as the globalized local) has all rights and no responsibility, and the South has no rights, but all responsibility. 'Global ecology' at this level becomes a moralization of immorality. It is devoid of any ethics for planetary living; and based on concepts not of universal brotherhood but of universal bullying.

Democratizing 'global' institutions

The creation of new mechanisms for responding to the global ecological crisis was one of UNCED's agendas. Problematizing the 'global' through collective articulation of all local concerns and interests, in all their diversity, is the creative intervention in the global/local conflicts as they are emerging.

To democratize the 'global' is the next step. What at present exists as the global is not the democratic distillation of all local and national concerns worldwide, but the imposition of a narrow group of interests from a handful of nations on a world scale. But if genuine democracy is to exist at local and national levels it is essential for international interests to become democratized.

The roots of the ecological crisis at the institutional level lie in the alienation of the rights of local communities to actively participate in environmental decisions. The reversal of ecological decline involves strengthening local rights. *Every* local community equipped with rights and obligations, constitutes a new *global* order for environmental care.

The current trend in global discussions and negotiations, however, is to move rights further upwards towards more distant, non-local centralization in such agencies as the World Bank.

Multilateralism in a democratic set-up must mean a lateral expansion of decision-making based on the *protection* of local community rights where they exist, and the institutionalization of rights where they have been eroded. Two central planks of local environmental rights include: (1) the right to information; and (2) right to prior consent; that is, any activity with potential impact on the local environment should be subject to consent by the local people.

Basing an environmental order on globally institutionalized local rights also avoids the impracticable issue of representation and the terrible bungling resulting from international NGOs 'selecting' national NGOs to 'select' local NGOs to represent 'people' at global negotiations.

The 'global' must accede to the local, since the local exists with nature, while the 'global' exists only in offices of World Bank/IMF and headquarters of multinational corporations. The local is everywhere. The real ecological space of global ecology is to be found in the integration of all locals. The 'global' in global reach is a political, not an ecological space.

Institutionally, we should not be concerned about how to enable the last tribal to be present at World Bank decisions in Washington. What we need to ensure is that no World Bank decision affecting the tribals' resources is taken without their prior informed consent.

Whether the local as global and the global as local will exist in a way different from the imperialistic order of the last 500 years depends on this process of democratization. The imperialistic category of global is disempowering at the local level. Its coercive power comes from abolishing limits for the forces of domination and destruction and imposing restrictions on the forces of conservation.

The ecological category of global is an empowering one at the local level because it charges every act, every entity, with the largeness of the cosmic and the planetary and adds meaning to it. It is also empowering because precisely by embodying the planetary in the local, it creates conditions for local autonomy and local control.

An earth democracy cannot be realized as long as global domination is in the hands of undemocratic structures. Neither can it be realized on an anthropocentric basis – the rights of non-human nature cannot be ignored. And it cannot be realized if the need to ensure the survival of the planet is made the reason for denying the right to survival of those who today are poor and marginalized because they have borne the accumulated burden of centuries of subjugation.

11.   Resisting Green Globalism

Larry Lohmann

For generations, people have been ridiculing, undermining, subverting and deflecting the schemes of colonialists and developers. Machinery has been sabotaged, landlords and officials satirized and threatened, dams delayed, rallies held, experts' theories lampooned, loyalties shifted and bureaucratic defences tested in an endless flow of effort aimed at keeping outside forces at bay. Whether overt or subterranean, thwarted or beaten down, channelled into ideology or action, this resistance has been opportunistic, pragmatic and resourceful. Often using local traditions as an arsenal, perpetually being co-opted and defeated, it always cunningly finds fresh ground to fight from, some of it created by the very systems in opposition to which it must constantly transform and renew itself. Willing to adapt new developments to its own purposes, it is uncompromising when the bounds it has set are overstepped.[1]

This resistance has largely been a resistance to *incorporation*. Imagine the social universe as thousands of partly independent wholes – cultures, languages, practices of livelihood, theories, arts, sciences – each of which gives its constituent parts much of their significance. To a great extent, colonialism and development have consisted of attempts to break down these wholes and use the fragments, deprived of their old roles, to build up new wholes of potentially global scope. Farmland and forests have been removed from local fabrics of subsistence and converted to substrates for export cropping; rivers usurped to provide power for new urban sectors; and mangrove swamps razed to dig ponds to grow shrimp for export. The diversity of knowledge held by local people has been devalued, pulverized and supplanted by a handful of disciplines – Western science, economics and management – controlled by outsiders. By providing local leaders with an external power base, the state and private enterprise have undermined village checks and balances; by building roads and stimulating demand for cash goods, they have impelled villagers to seek an ever wider range of things to sell. Only in this way has it been possible to convert peasants into labour for the industrial economy, replace traditional with modern agriculture, and free up resources for the industrial economy. Similarly, only by atomizing tasks, redefining women as unproductive and separating workers from the moral authority, crafts and natural surroundings created by their communities, has it been possible to transform people into modern, universal individuals susceptible to management. And only by destroying local manufacturing, stimulating dependence and installing commercial export sectors by force has it been possible to open up local societies to global trade.[2]

The social wholes which have been dismantled in these ways have always been sources of meaning, dignity, and independence. But they have also been matters of livelihood, health, home and security. The same forest that serves as a burial place for ancestors is the source of streams feeding fields below, and the clan loyalty that assures a child a place in society also means that she/he will not starve. Resistance, whether it takes the form of blocking a logging road, surreptitiously siphoning off some of a landlord's grain, or burning a tree plantation, has often been indistinguishable from provision for survival. Small wonder that struggles against the effects of development often centre on precisely those values of well-being that development pretends to promote.

In recent years, a new kind of colonialism, a new kind of development, has begun to exert its disrupting influence. Élites worldwide have been shaken by environmental activism and by the prospects of global warming and depletion of biodiversity and of ozone. Northern leaders in particular, concerned about competition from a growing South for the resources and waste sinks they need to maintain their extravagant lifestyles, and seeking to create dependence on themselves for 'environmentally-friendly' technology, have called for global environmental management and 'sustainable' development.

Under this new globalist regime, integral local practices, particularly in the South, are to be broken down yet further in order to 'balance' a system whose goals remain determined mainly by the North. This time these goals are not simply to secure raw materials, cheap labour, markets and political control for the international economic system. They are also to supply environmental repair or caretaker services to mitigate the problems that system has itself created, and to attempt to preserve remaining local natural and moral knowledge by transforming it into a resource under the control of the North. Thus tree farms are to replace peasants' fields and fallows, in order to absorb carbon dioxide emitted by the industrial system; tropical forests and the knowledge of their inhabitants are to provide services to Northern industry, researchers and tourists; local commons are to be taken apart and reassembled into a fictitious 'global commons' and population control efforts are to be redoubled as a way of taking pressure off Northern-controlled resources. The possibility of instituting the reverse process, that is, dissecting and cannibalizing the so-called 'global' system to provide repair or caretaker services for thousands of local systems, is seldom raised. Few Northerners are proposing that Senegalese peasants be allowed to have a say in American energy consumption, or that Ecuadorian tribal peoples form groups to help protect German forests. Many Southern leaders, too, eager to extract a bit of compensation from the North for its past and present depredations, are willing to let it maintain control of the world's resources in return for more development aid or better terms of trade, thus acting over the heads of local people. Where such negotiation fails, 'resource wars' may well be supplemented by 'conservation wars' waged by North against South in the name of the 'global environmental good'.

Ordinary people's resistance to the effects of this new green globalism will accordingly be hard to distinguish from their efforts to defend the forests, fertile land, clean water and knowledge on which their livelihoods depend. Like development, green globalism undermines precisely the values it feigns to support. By integrating enclaves and erasing boundaries within large-scale economies and forms of knowledge, it obliterates the conditions which have made preservation of biological diversity possible – including the variations, not only in topography and natural history, but also in human history and culture, between one place and the next. It neglects the fact that, as one anthropologist puts it,

> [T]he environment itself is local; nature diversifies to make niches, enmeshing each locale in its own intricate web. Insofar as this holds, enduring human adaptations must also ultimately be quite local. Clearly, they require feedback and time to evolve.[3]

Among these adaptations are those institutions of the commons against which green globalism is carrying forward the war begun centuries ago by the market economy.[4]

Incorporation as translation

Green globalism appeals strongly to many Northern environmentalists, nevertheless, because it tries to translate all important 'environmental' practices and insights into a common, comfortably modern vocabulary. This globalism, being both geographical and intellectual, satisfies a deep-felt Western (and, probably, largely male-associated) need for containment and control. Hence the lack of criticism of the title of the Brundtland Commission's famous report *Our Common Future*; the pop wisdom that we should 'think globally but act locally'; the claims of 'bottom-up' environmental planners that we can all be 'empowered' by being incorporated into a 'shared vision of the wanted future'. Hence also environmental economics, which assumes that once views and values regarding nature are translated into prices, all possible conflicts concerning the use of forests, air, water, and land can be resolved by tacit consent using market bargaining.[5]

According to this vision, nature, human beings and sentences are characterized not by their roles in more or less self-contained, discrete communities or cultures but by their roles in single, universal, overarching systems. Conflicts which arise when one culture encounters another are regarded as either trivial or resolvable by translation into a master language in which all conflicts are resolvable according to criteria acceptable to all sides. In line with the shift in the dominant meaning of the word 'local' from the Middle-English-derived 'peculiar to a particular place or places' to the modern 'pertaining to a position in space', local areas themselves become mere spots on a universal grid.[6] Everyone everywhere is assumed to be playing, if only they knew it, roughly the same game.

This type of view, of course, is nothing new in Western thought. Plato was obsessed with the idea of commensurating all discourse no less than today's environmental economists.[7] The Enlightenment, too, hoped to find universally accepted criteria which could separate out the one agreed right answer to all questions that might arise. As Raimundo Panikkar complains,

Western culture apparently has no other way to reach peace of mind and heart – called, more academically, intelligibility – than by reducing everything to one single pattern with the claim to universal validity.[8]

But 'reducing everything to one single pattern' is more than just a way of achieving Western 'peace of mind'. It is also a means to, and a justification for, expropriation, domination and control. Colonialists use the assumption that their own language is universal to dismiss those who do not speak it as sub-human, irrational; in the words of Ashis Nandy, a 'fortress of resistance to be wiped out'. Developers use the same assumption to justify their claim that their own culture already contains everything worthwhile in others', that everyone else is just a junior version of themselves. And green globalists try to reinforce the dominance of a single industrial pattern, and perpetuate the foreign aid which spreads it, by demanding that 'developed countries' search for a 'new way of living and organizing economic activity and technologies which will be compatible with ecological harmony [and] *which all can emulate and strive to achieve.*'[9] Bureaucrats, meanwhile, need to get people to agree on a common language in order to organize them around a single end. Experts present their own language as universal to ensure an honoured place for their expertise. Economic advisers try to calibrate all values against a single yardstick in order to make 'trade-offs' involving the sacred and the irreplaceable look rational. Planners tame resisters and harness critics by wooing them away from their own society and assigning them places as creative officers or quality control inspectors in the planners' own systems. Shrewd managers, finally, instead of trying to homogenize diversity, turn it to advantage by resystematizing it, giving it a new Gestalt, converting it from *inter*-system diversity into *intra*-system diversity.[10] Why obliterate or ignore society's literature, after all, when you can translate it into English? Even the market, with its great pretensions to being self-regulating, relies on its ability to modernize non-market diversity. To a certain extent, it is compelled to try to encyst peasant societies and tropical forests and traditional values in order to forestall floods of refugees and environmental disruption. Cultural characteristics like family loyalty, proficiency in traditional medicine, or patron–clientage, meanwhile, become sources of 'comparative advantage' to be exploited, until they are finally worn away by the acid of the market, to create and satisfy world-market demands for such things as low-cost labour, trendy shampoos and prostitution.

Discrediting globalism

Globalism can be discredited in many ways. An attempt to discredit it at an abstract level may help show how and why it is being debunked by resistance at the level of everyday life.

One central idea that holds globalism together and makes it plausible is that because we can translate one language into another, there must therefore exist a neutral overarching global matrix which can assimilate all of them, leaving no messy loose ends of any interest to rational observers. One way of discrediting this idea is to look at languages, theories, cultures and other social practices on the model of games. Just as each move in chess makes chess sense only in the context of other possible moves, the significance of a string of noises in (say) Guarani cannot be comprehended without an understanding of a great many other Guarani sentences. Yet the context which gives a given Guarani sentence its sense is unlikely to be an exact analogue of the contexts which gives its Chinese or Spanish translations their sense. Just as there is no single global game which contains at once chess, volleyball and *go*, so there is no single system of thought which encompasses at once all three languages. To translate is to rip an alien word or action out of its context and try to put it into relation with a new one. This is always possible – one can always claim that a serve is the volleyball analogue of the chess move P–Q4 or that 'bored' is the English translation of the Thai *buea* – and there is obviously often a point to doing this, as dictionaries bear witness. But the more structurally disparate the games or languages concerned, the more wrenching the dislocation.[11]

This dislocation tends to result either in the translated word being regarded as quaint or perverse or in its being treated as a mere stand-in for a word in the home language. As Orwell remarked, a literal Newspeak translation of the American Declaration of Independence would be a mass of criminal thoughts ('crimethink'), while an idiomatic translation would be a 'panegyric on absolute government'. The point holds generally. No one can translate even as ordinary a Thai word as *naa-rak* into English, for example, without implicitly treating Thais, to some degree, as either successful or failed Westerners. (A literal translation, which entails applying some such word as 'lovely' to obedient dogs, docile children, tiny animals, cartoon characters, helpful adults, playful babies, and even clothing and ballpoint pens, sentimentalizes Thais, while an idiomatic one, by applying different English terms to each of the items above and thus neglecting the connections Thais see among *naa-rak* things, makes them seem to share Western tastes.) Try as they might, historians, anthropologists and economists cannot help but produce a 'Whiggish' story, one which is, to a certain extent, the 'ratification, if not the glorification', of the here and now as described in their native languages.[12] And similarly for any cultural artifact. Placed in isolation against an unfamiliar backdrop, a traditional community forest, a dance, or a car either will look somewhat silly or will have to be retooled to fit its new social surroundings. Where translation means remaining loyal to judgments and standards of adjudication which speakers of other languages may not share, it will not eliminate conflict. For those whose words are being translated – the framer of the Declaration of Independence or the native speaker of Thai – the risk is of becoming trapped in a double-bind situation in which one is 'deprived of means of arguing, and so becomes a victim'.[13]

Yet in political circumstances in which no single direction of translation dominates, and in which people are free to retreat into whatever language they want to live their lives in, this sort of risk need never become worrisome. On the contrary, it is likely to be one facet of a life of a certain degree and type of richness. Imagine, for example, tribes of roughly equal power inhabiting nearby areas. At home, in its native language, each tribe is free to indulge in the agreeable pastime of discussing the others' foibles in condescending terms. Each is free, moreover, to adopt the practices of neighbouring tribes – agricultural innovations or status-conferring writing systems, say – and twist them to its own purposes. Yet when meeting other tribes on common ground, whatever *lingua franca* all forge together is carefully hedged about so that everyone knows it applies only to certain matters. When venturing into another tribe's territory, moreover, each tribe knows to maintain watchfulness and self-deprecating reserve until, if it wants, it can enter into the other's language-game entirely. Understanding that its own ways of judging things are not shared by others, each tribe forbears to pronounce to others on how they should do things within their own borders. Each hesitates before applying the pronoun 'we' to people outside its local area; morality and language attain a specifically geographical dimension. None of this is an attempt on the part of the tribes to eliminate bias, become relativists, or otherwise step outside their own skins, but rather reflects an awareness of when it is (and is not) appropriate to cultivate an attitude of amused detachment about their own views (and their own bias). Not that any tribe always knows what will amuse others. But each must ready itself to be surprised in the most radical ways. The result is that each tribe is able to follow its own ways with a deepened sense of its own distinctiveness and to have the reality of those ways recognized by the others.

One of the most striking cultural features of colonialism, development and green globalism is the success all have had in doing away with their proponents' capacity for this sort of amusement and surprise (and, one might add, tragedy). As the power of élites has increased, so has their conviction that they have the *right* to use translations in any circumstances whatever. Whereas kingship and conquest were sanctioned by connections with the divinity, development and green globalism have been justified by positing a privileged relation between one particular language or theory and some external entity – nature, human nature, reason, 'the ecology' – which floats free of any particular society.

In globalism's moral economy, translations go in one direction only, and any sense of languages and theories being located in a tradition, landscape, or community, is lost. What Stephen Toulmin calls 'folly on the boundary' proliferates as Westerners assume that the theoretical models they use are automatically applicable to situations outside the ones in which they have evolved.[14] All sense of a *place* for ethnocentric behaviour, and with it all sense of bias itself, vanishes. Receptiveness and the vulnerability to the unexpected which comes with being accustomed to confronting radically different cultures through their own languages is replaced by a deadly earnestness about oneself as the carrier and expositor of universal human rationality. One is taught that one does not need to hear the words of the people of the world, since whatever they say that makes sense will automatically be distilled in the latest textbooks or in *Time* magazine, and that merely by being alive today, we have superseded the past and thus overcome any serious need to study it.

This sort of attitude, and the power which accompanies and fosters it, puts villagers, tribals, ethnobiologists, and all others with an attachment to local or particular social wholes in roughly the position the framers of the Declaration of Independence would be in if they were allowed to use only Newspeak. Consider environmental economics, one of the favoured languages of the new green globalists. When it tries to describe subsistence practices literally in its own terms, the result is nonsense; when it tries to describe them idiomatically, the result is so biased that those who have no chance of retranslating the description into their own language feel trapped. Asian peasants taking firewood, fodder and game meat from a forest in carefully regulated quantities to support themselves, for example, are accused of 'consuming', whereas a paper pulp firm razing the forest to plant eucalyptus trees, is praised as 'producing'. What economists describe as 'wasteland', similarly, may be to the peasant a source of food to eke out a livelihood, and what they call 'growth', 'intensivity', 'value', and 'diversification' may to the peasant be just the opposite.[15]

A similar thing happens when environmental economists try to give a monetary value to people's beliefs and values about the environment as a way of assimilating them into its world view. Many ecologists bridle at the translation of their concerns about pollution into demands that polluters pay, since in their terms no payment can be said to be 'equivalent' to a change in the course of evolution. Lay-people in both North and South, similarly, often refuse to say how much compensation they would accept for hydroelectric dams or polluted air, pointing out that for them the issue is one of political debate or other forms of cultural mediation, not for market bargaining.[16] The only way of 'translating' this refusal into economic language is to say that for these people, conservation has 'infinite' monetary value – an interpretation which is satisfactory neither to them nor to the economists.

Environmental economists reply that it can only be people's lack of understanding of economic language that makes them fail to acknowledge its universality. Since there are no 'conceptual' problems in treating economics as a global language, they insist, resistance will disappear when the 'practical' bugs are worked out of the translation machinery. One author, for instance, suggests that to refuse to give wilderness a monetary value and yet to recommend that it be preserved rather than developed

> . . . is to exhibit confusion and inconsistency. For to recommend preservation is simply to say that it has been in some way compared with development and found to be preferable. Cost-benefit analysis is a way of making the comparison explicit.[17]

The confusion, however, is all on the part of the economist. First, unless there are well-established practices of ranking two alternatives, it is difficult to see how even implicit comparisons between them could be made along a single yardstick. The sort of yardstick which environmental cost-benefit analysis requires has evolved in reality only within certain narrow techniques such as business accounting, in which goals have been artificially and ruthlessly simplified for a special purpose (in this case, deriving a bottom-line monetary figure) within a larger enterprise. Second, even where such a yardstick has evolved, people may not always want it to be used to make decisions. To demand preservation may merely be to value social relations and obey moral imperatives that have developed in historical circumstances distinct from those which have resulted in the modern market. It does not follow from the fact that people choose wilderness over development that they have implicitly or explicitly compared the two along a single scale any more than it follows from the fact that courts make judgments that they have followed a set formula for doing so. Ultimately, the only way of making sense of environmental economics would be simply to *replace* people's beliefs, desires and values with consumer preferences – a course of social transformation which would provoke no less resistance than current attempts at translation.[18]

Possibilities of alliance

> . . . a serious effort to define ourselves among different others – others neither distanced as Martians, discredited as Primitives, nor disarmed as universal Everypersons, bent like us on sex and survival – involves quite genuine perils, not the least of which are intellectual entropy and moral paralysis. The double perception that ours is but one voice among many and that, as it is the only one we have, we must needs speak with it, is very difficult to maintain. . . . But however that may be, there is, so it seems to me, no choice.[19]

Resistance to incorporation is thus likely to be unending. Is it also necessarily isolated? Are there are any prospects for an alliance among globalism's opponents which is not itself another globalism? Can different groups join with others in furthering the interests of each without positing once again an oppressive common project or privileged common language?

The example of the tribes sketched above hints that the answer may be yes. The tribes probably would see it in their own interest to defend the space in which each can maintain its distinctness. But the example also suggests how thoroughly an affirmative answer has to be qualified. The making of the kind of alliances in question cannot be separated either from participation in specific groups' concrete struggles to depose Northern economies and theories from their dominant position, or from those groups' equally concrete strivings to achieve political equality among themselves. It also cannot be separated from the attempt to clear away the confusions with which would-be anti-global alliances are so often burdened.

One such confusion is between intracultural models of 'democracy' and 'free exchange', which presuppose overarching, all-inclusive common languages and norms of conflict-resolution (parliamentary democracy, sports tournaments, 'normal' science as conducted in the pages of *Nature*), and models of intercultural democracy and free exchange which do not presuppose such languages or methods. Another such confusion is that between 'relativism' and the approach of the tribes described above, who have doubts about the vocabularies they use, because they have been impressed by others, yet who realize that argument phrased in their present vocabularies 'can neither underwrite nor dissolve those doubts'.[20] No one can withdraw from judgment altogether into some 'neutral' position. Such a position, in so far as it could be described at all, would require its own language or system and thus would have its own biases. An attitude which pretends to regard everyone's ways and theories with equal irony or humour is also incoherent, for parallel reasons.

Another such confusion is the claim that 'equal exchange' or 'combination or compromise of views' is possible between groups with radically different languages. Even the shortest exchange between two people with different systems of thought must be conducted in the terms of one or the other system, and the person whose system is not being used runs the risk of being dominated. There is no 'compromise' between Bellarmine and Galileo, Spanish and Chinese, or the worship of the Indian smallpox-goddess Sitala and the state-backed apparatus of vaccination. In practice, any attempt at combination will result in one of the sides' being absorbed into the other. Either Spanish vocabulary must become Chinese loan-words or vice-versa; either the technique of vaccination has to be absorbed into the worship of Sitala or the worship of Sitala will be swamped by the 'political and cultural entailments' of vaccination.[21] Nor are academic ecology, religion, economics and traditional knowledge going to be merging soon in a seamless unity of universal science, any more than Chinese and Spanish, Islam and Presbyterianism, or chess and volleyball are going to grow together. By the same token, 'certifying' selected village practices on Western scientific grounds generally carries an implicit challenge to the systems of justification which exist in village culture and tends to dominate no less than would the dismissal of those practices as 'superstitious'.

A final confusion is the idea that learning and appreciating many languages and ways reduces or eliminates ethnocentricity and scientism. This is false. While the ability to join in others' ways can make people more bemused by their own positions in cultural space, it cannot get rid of those positions. It merely makes diversity and intercultural conflicts internal by introducing in individuals multiple centres of consciousness and loyalty among which they can switch at will. It does not get rid of individuals' biases, but gives them new ones: Hanunoo bias, Quechua bias, microbiological bias, consumerist bias and so on.

People seeking anti-global alliances are likely simply to have to drop the idea that there are going to be any interesting neutral criteria of rationality or democracy embedded in any particular local language or system and instead content themelves with adopting certain ethnocentric virtues of inquiry: watchfulness, curiosity, tolerance, patience, humour and open-mindedness.[22] That means defending an intercultural space which is not a language nor a system nor an attitude, but rather a readiness, such as that found in the West in literary criticism or art history, to let incommensurable points of view alone, to be receptive as well as active, to move back and forth among separate social wholes seen as 'reciprocal commentaries, mutually deepening . . . one upon another, the one lighting what the other darkens.'[23] It means a willingness to join, when requested, *ad hoc* unions to fight interference, expropriation and disruption. It means emphasizing 'ungrounded solidarity'[24] with those who are different rather than trying to incorporate them in new strategies for global change. All this may be impossible. But it would be wrong to want more.

Notes

1. James C. Scott (1985) *Weapons of the Weak*, New Haven, Yale University Press, and (1976) *The Moral Economy of the Peasant*, New Haven, Yale University Press; Philip Hirsch and Larry Lohmann (1989) 'The Contemporary Politics of Environment in Thailand', *Asian Survey*, Vol. 29, No. 4, April, pp. 439–51; Citizens' Clearinghouse on Toxic Waste (1984) *Love Canal: a chronology of events that shaped a movement*, Falls Church, VA, CCHW.

2. Karl Polanyi (1945) *The Great Transformation*, London, Victor Gollancz; Ivan Illich (1981) *Shadow Work*, London, Marion Boyars; Frédérique Apffel Marglin and Stephen A. Marglin (eds) (1990) *Dominating Knowledge: development, culture and resistance*, Oxford, Clarendon Press.

3. Richard A. O'Connor (1989) 'From Fertility to Order, Paternalism to Profits: the Thai city's impact on the culture–environment interface', in Siam Society (ed.), *Culture and Environment in Thailand*, Bangkok, Siam Society, pp. 393–414.

4. Richard B. Norgaard (1987) 'The Rise of the Global Exchange Economy and the Loss of Biological Diversity', in Edward O. Wilson (ed.), *Biodiversity*, Washington, National Academy Press; Cary Fowler and Pat Mooney (1990) *Shattering*, Tucson, University of Arizona Press; Miguel A. Altieri (1991) 'Traditional Farming in Latin America', *Ecologist*, Vol. 21, No. 2, March–April, pp. 97–100; Robert Wade (1989) *Village Republics*, Cambridge, Cambridge University Press; Fikret Berkes (ed.) (1989) *Common Property Resources*, London, Belhaven; Bonnie McCay and J. A. Acheson (1988) *The Question of the Commons*, Tucson, University of Arizona Press; Louise Fortmann et al. (eds) (1988) *Whose Trees?*, Boulder, University of Colorado Press; Samaj Parivartana Samudaya et al. (1988) *Whither the Commons?*, New Delhi, SPS; Ramachandra Guha (1989) *The Unquiet Woods*, Oxford, Oxford University Press; Vandana

Shiva (1990) *Staying Alive*, New Delhi and London, Kali for Women and Zed Books; Larry Lohmann (1991) 'Who Defends Biological Diversity?', *Ecologist*, Vol. 21, No. 2.

5. World Commission on Environment and Development (1987) *Our Common Future*, New York, Oxford University Press; Jeffrey A. McNeely (1990) 'What Value for Wildlife?', *IUCN Bulletin*, December, p. 15; David W. Pearce (1976) *Environmental Economics*, London, Macmillan, p. 1; J. T. Winpenny (1991) *Values for the Environment*, London, Her Majesty's Stationery Office, p. 2; World Bank (1990) *The World Bank and the Environment*, Washington, World Bank; Mark Sagoff (1990) *The Economy of the Earth*, Cambridge, Cambridge University Press.

6. *Shorter Oxford English Dictionary* (1973) Oxford, Oxford University Press.

7. *Euthyphro* 7B-D.

8. Raimundo Panikkar (1987) 'The Invisible Harmony: a universal theory of religion or a cosmic confidence in reality?' in Leonard Swidler (ed.) *Toward a Universal Theology of Religion*, Maryknoll, NY, Orbis Books, p. 120.

9. Chakravathi Raghavan (1991) 'UNCED Meet Highlights North–South Divide', *Third World Resurgence*, No. 10, p. 16; *Crosscurrents*, 26–28 March.

10. William Ray Arney (1991) *Experts in the Age of Systems*, Albuquerque, University of New Mexico Press.

11. Ludwig Wittgenstein (1953) *Philosophical Investigations*, Cambridge, Cambridge University Press; Wilfred Sellars (1963) 'Some Reflections on Language Games', in *Science, Perception and Reality*, London, Routledge & Kegan Paul, pp. 321–58; Raimundo Panikkar (1982) 'Crosscultural Economics', *Interculture*, Vol. 77, pp. 26–36.

12. Herbert Butterfield (1981) *The Whig Interpretation of History*, Oxford, Oxford University Press.

13. Jean-François Lyotard (1983) *Le Différend*, Paris, Editions Minuit, pp. 24–5, quoted in Richard Rorty (1991a) *Objectivity, Relativism and Truth*, Cambridge, Cambridge University Press, p. 216. See W. V. O. Quine (1960) *Word and Object*, Cambridge, MA, MIT Press, chapter 2, and (1968) *Ontological Relativity*, Chicago, University of Chicago Press; Richard Rorty (1972) 'Indeterminacy of Translation and of Truth', *Synthese*, Vol. 23, pp. 443–62; Donald Davidson (1984) *Inquiries into Truth and Interpretation*, Oxford, Oxford University Press.

14. Quoted in Norgaard (1987).

15. Vandana Shiva 'Biodiversity Conservation: the Northern bias', *Third World Resurgence*, No. 13, pp. 26–7.

16. Sagoff (1990); Juan Martinez-Alier (1990) *Ecological Economics*, Oxford, Blackwell.

17. Michael Common (1988) *Resource and Environmental Economics*, London, Longman, p. 306. See Jean-Philippe Barde and David W. Pearce (eds) (1991) *Valuing the Environment*, London, Earthscan, pp. 7–8; David W. Pearce et al. (1989) *Blueprint for a Green Economy*, London, Earthscan, pp. 53–6; David W. Pearce (ed.) (1991) *Blueprint 2*, London, Earthscan, pp. 4–6.

18. David Wiggins (1975–6) 'Deliberation and Practical Reason', *Proceedings of the Aristotelian Society*, Vol. 76, pp. 221–40, and (1978–9) 'Weakness of Will, Commensurability, and the Objects of Deliberation and Desire', *Proceedings of the Aristotelian Society*, Vol. 79, pp. 251–77; Martha C. Nussbaum (1986) *The*

Fragility of Goodness, Cambridge, Cambridge University Press; Karl Marx (1982) *Capital*, Vol. 1, London, Penguin, pp. 125–77; Martinez-Alier (1990) p. 5; I. M. F. Little (1950) *A Critique of Welfare Economics*, Oxford, Oxford University Press, p. 270; Peter Self (1970) *Econocrats and the Policy Process*, London, Macmillan.

19. Clifford Geertz (1983) 'Local Knowledge: fact and law in comparative perspective', in *Local Knowledge*, New York, Harper Torchbooks, p. 234.

20. Richard Rorty (1990) *Contingency, Irony and Solidarity*, Cambridge, Cambridge University Press, p. 73.

21. Frédérique Apffel Marglin, 'Smallpox in Two Systems of Knowledge', in Apffel Marglin and Marglin (1990).

22. Richard Rorty (1991b) 'Science as Solidarity', in *Objectivity, Relativism and Truth*, Cambridge, Cambridge University Press, pp. 35–45.

23. Geertz (1983), p. 233.

24. Rorty (1990), p. xiii.

12. The Fallacy of Ecomessianism: Observations from Latin America

Eduardo Gudynas

Today it is widely acknowledged that the severe environmental problems we face are closely linked to social problems. The 1992 UN Conference on Environment and Development (UNCED) placed the environment firmly on the development agenda, and environmentalists, once regarded as severe critics of the development process, are now asked by governments, businessmen and citizens alike, to provide solutions to the problems it has created. It is assumed that the measures proposed by environmentalists, when implemented throughout the whole of society, will prove to be effective.

One of the more recent and threatening phenomena in this context is the emergence of messianic positions. This 'ecomessianism' seems to be typified by inordinate faith and certainty, that is without reason or proof, that environmental and ecological ideas can serve as agents of change.

In this regard two observations can be made. First, some environmentalists believe that they are entrusted with a mandate to save not only human life, but all forms of life on the planet; they are deeply inbued with a sense of justice toward all living creatures. Second, within the environmental movement – especially some Northern groups – there are organizations or individuals who believe that they have the knowledge and the human and financial resources which entitle them to lead the environmental movement, and hence all of society, on the only true road to Earth's salvation.

The ideas, concepts and values and the measures proposed are all linked to a new discourse: the 'ecocratic' discourse – in which 'eco' stands for ecology, and 'cratic' refers to the Greek *cratos*, that is, power and authority. Today, this ecocratic discourse embraces a wide series of issues: from the extinction of species to pollution, from agrochemicals to the greenhouse effect, and so on. It should also be noted that this mode of discourse is held not only by environmentalists, but also typifies current thinking among such influential institutions as, for example, the World Bank or the European Economic Community (EC). This is matter for concern.[1]

Distorted images

Many of the North's environmental organizations have distorted images of the South's environmental problems, including those affecting ecosystems and local communities. In some cases, their views are so reductionist as to nullify all possible alternatives. For example, in the North, the main ecological problem in Latin America is commonly identified as 'deforestation', and the image that springs to mind is of the Amazon rainforest. This view has led to Latin America being seen solely in terms of the Amazon rainforest. Such distorted images can be found even in what are regarded as competent and reliable sources, such as the World Resources Report of 1990–91, edited by the World Resources Institute. In that Report, the identification of another area of environmental concern – the Andean mountains – slightly extends the region.

Such literature thus largely ignores other major ecosystems (such as Patagonia in Argentina, Llanos in Venezuela, for example) thereby furthering the reductionist view in so far as the implication is that no environmental problems exist outside those ecosystems considered.

But scientific evidence tends to contradict such a reductionist view: for example, the highest deforestation rates are to be found in the Paraguayan sub-tropical forest (4.7 per cent compared to 0.4 per cent in the Amazon forest). Deforestation occurring in the cold woodlands (southern Chile, Argentina) could be an even greater disaster, as the eco-systems' surface is small and regeneration rates are low.

Another aspect is the interaction between these distorted images and the media. Journalists tend to select the more dramatic and simplistic images to offer the public at large, as exemplified by headlines such as 'The Amazon rainforest: the lungs of the earth'. Here again, vegetation experts have shown that the temperate boreal forests, or any other ecosystem comprised of green plants, are as much a 'lung' as the Amazon rainforest. Nevertheless, these distorted images tend to engender widespread belief among concerned people, environmentalists, politicians, and so on that the Amazon is a key ecosystem, not only at the local level, but worldwide.

In this context, the apparent ignorance or trivialization of environmental problems in areas transformed by men, such as agricultural land or urban settlements, should be noted. Latin America's environmental problems tend to be reduced to wilderness-related ones, while the impacts of, say, cattle-ranching or those affecting millions of people living in mushrooming megalopoli, are seemingly disregarded. Possibly these problems receive scant attention from Northern organizations because of the social dimensions involved, and the potentially serious political conflicts which could be linked to them.

The scientific superiority complex

There are shared responsibilities for this situation. While targetting journalists, politicians and laypersons, the role of scientists should not be overlooked. Whether from the North or the South, scientists are part of the group who believe themselves to be charged with a mandate, and possess the knowledge, to determine the viable management of nature. Human beings' relationship to nature is divorced from any political connotation and presented as a strictly scientific and technical problem. Therefore, only those trained in specific fields can determine how to conserve or use wilderness, natural resources or any other attribute of the environment.

The statements of D. H. Janzen, a well-known ecologist working on conservation measures in Central America, exemplify this view:

> The tropical ecologist has a clear mandate to be a prominent guide . . . Ecologists are specialists at understanding interactions between complex units and their environments; the future of tropical ecology lies, above all, in the interface between humanity and the tropical nature that humanity has corralled. It is this generation of ecologists who will determine whether the tropical agroscape is to be populated only by humans and their mutualists, commensals, and parasites, or whether it will also contain some islands of the greater nature – the nature that spawned humans yet has been vanquished by them.[2]

Some environmentalists invoke scientific evidence as the only basis upon which to propose specific solutions and measures. This kind of belief, rooted in a number of scientific disciplines (the environmental sciences), may easily lead to the deluded notion that scientific knowledge is superior to all others; Western knowledge in particular always being considered superior to grassroots knowledge.

While disregarding the fact that even among scientists there are extremely diverse positions – and that there is no agreement on such facts as the actual extent of the Amazon rainforest, the rate of deforestation, potential for recovery and so on – it is often forgotten that grassroots' knowledge, that is of farmers, indigenous peoples, and marginalized urban communities, is also very rich and complex in so far as relations between human beings and nature are concerned.

So this superior stance in relation to scientific knowledge is another manifestation of a messianic posture. By weakening public and open discussion on how society as a whole should manage its natural resources, and how to share the benefits accruing therefrom, the paradox is reached whereby environmental postures minimize the political dimensions involved, and produce ecocratic discourses which inhibit a discussion about its propositions, hidden contradictions and absence of alternatives.

Hidden links

The distorted images underlying messianic views are also supported by links that are usually hidden or ignored by the public at large, yet they are influential in the decision-making process. For example, in the heated debt-for-nature swaps debate, an influential document (published in 1989)[3] was presented as a Latin American view on the issue. A closer look, however, reveals that some sections are almost identical to an article published in the *Journal of Environmental Affairs* in 1989.[4] Neither paper makes reference to the other. The problem is not one of priority, but rather where and by whom such ideas are generated and why this issue was not properly addressed. Sooner or later these linkages are discovered, and serve only to create suspicion in the South, undermining the solidarity essential for the international environmental movement.

Another important dimension in distorting images is language. International journals, magazines, books, and so on, are usually published in English. For example, Spanish and Portuguese literature describing environmental problems and ecosystems are rarely circulated in the North. Access to this literature is usually mediated by a Northern academic centre that classifies, analyses and summarizes information from the South and publishes the results in English, when it is made available to the Northern groups.

The North's pedagogic tendency

This tendency is demonstrated by the North attempting to teach the South how to attain sustainable development. But, for example, there are no Latin American networks advising how to deal with, say, Canadian and US Pacific forests.

The problem here is not with the intentions: these are usually good. The basic effect, however, is a transfer of Northern perceptions and potential solutions to the South. This is not a dialogue. Furthermore, since the Northern positions, as we have seen, are the result of distorted images, there should at least be some discussion on the proposed solutions.

But the reality is different. Messianic and pedagogic stances can contribute to an increase of international constraints on development policies as a result of the Northern environmental perspective. The environmental conditionalities now linked to multilateral development bank loans exemplify this. This may be seen as positive, because it obliges Southern governments to follow some minimal environmental measures, but it also opens the way to political intervention in internal affairs. This in turn can invoke reactions like that of the Indian environmentalist Guha

(1989), who stated that the 'wholesale transfer of a movement culturally rooted in US conservation history can only result in the social uprooting of human populations in other parts of the globe'.[5]

The metaphysics of globality

Distorted images tend to lead to a focus on global problems, and the regional and local ones directly linked to them. This presentation of global problems is in itself reductionist and displays a messianic tendency: the apocalyptic scenarios, where no one is safe, where rising water levels or ultra-violet radiation can affect anyone in the near future. Understandably, the public begins to feel the need for 'ecological' responses to these 'ecological' problems.

Let us come back to the distorted image of the depletion of the Amazon rainforest as Latin America's main environmental problem. This is also seen as a global problem. In fact, such key ecosystems are identified as the common heritage of humankind. The fact that it is a global concern then becomes the rationale that justifies the right of every nation to participate in decisions on how such areas should be managed.

The establishment of 'global' environmental problems has a radical exclusive characteristic: all regional and local Latin American problems are now of secondary importance compared to the global ones. Furthermore, there is an intrinsic contradiction in considering these 'global' problems. Why are only environmental problems 'global'? It is now widely acknowledged that environmental problems are the result of multi-dimensional causes: why then analyse them separately? The adjective 'global' is thus imbued with a metaphysical quality: it is more a matter of faith than fact.

Features of the ecocratic discourse

Ecocratic discourses, linked with the aforementioned messianic tendencies, are now extending their influence beyond the governments of industrialized countries to the South's governments and environmental organizations. Examples of this can be found in the Tropical Forest Action Plan, the second World Conservation Strategy, UNCED's Biodiversity Convention and some of the climate change debates.

In this context, some scholars are of the opinion that the growing interest of citizens in the environment is largely due to a new discourse of the environmentalists. Actually, my opinion is that the contrary is so: I think that in essence, the environmental discourse is very similar to that in the early 1970s, at the time of the first UN Environmental Conference in Stockholm; the main ideas, objectives and outlook have been maintained. It is true that new issues have been raised, in particular those related to biodiversity, genetic resources and the like. The ethical dimensions of the problems are also increasingly emphasized; and it is interesting to note that some of these new issues originally emerged from outside the environmental movement (for example, that of the depletion of genetic resources).

But if the essence of the discourse is the same, what has changed in the past 20 years? The foremost fact is that society now perceives them differently: the same discourses are producing 'truth effects', that is, they are seen to contain true and valid statements that should be followed not only by the single individual but by the whole of society.

The common belief of the 1960s and 1970s – that environmentalists were a bunch of eccentric radicals – has died away. Today, important sectors of society, both North and South, recognize that the environmental discourse invokes ideas of common justice and welfare. Furthermore, the discourse is no longer of a radical and oppositional nature; it has in fact been adopted by the very sectors which had been criticized in the past. Concern for the environment now extends across all society and inevitably it reproduces the diverse and often contradictory aspects of any society or nation. This feature is particularly striking in times of great public apathy and lack of grassroots mobilization.

As mentioned above, the environmental discourse now offers not only a diagnosis of current problems, but also offers measures on how to deal with them. There is in this context an underestimated effect of power: an ethical basis and legitimacy are given to set up new norms and institutions in our societies. Today, we further witness that this discourse is also championed by non-environmentalists. Thus, the already heterogeneous nature of the environmental movement – and its exponents, each with a different proposal to attain the needed measures – is 'enriched' by the arrival of a wide panoply of new actors, such as businessmen and politicians, who also present environmental concerns as a main part of their proposals. This confusion does not allow the environmental discourse to identify the specific steps needed to set up effective norms or institutions. It does, however, provide the needed consensus that 'new' and 'environmental' institutions are indeed legitimately needed, and that the ecomessiahs are entitled to set them up. Unawares, therefore, the messianic eco-discourse contains very clear political consequences.

The new policy of conservation

This new scenario opens the way to an environmentalism imbued with a neo-liberal atmosphere. In other words, the ideology of progress need not be abandoned, rather, the necessity of nature conservation is presented as an integral part of economic growth, instead of in opposition to it. Natural resources that in the past were outside the market are now internalized; economics now embraces what had been left out. Societal interactions are reduced to economic and market transactions, environmental management is put in the hands of private interests. A new brand of environmentalist is born, who, while still interested in nature, has abandoned all concerns for solidarity and social justice.

The ecocratic discourse thus presents a framework for conservation which invests in the potential economic value of natural resources. Wilderness is now seen as a consortium of banks (gene banks, seed banks, and so on); fees will have to be charged for the use of such banks, and so on. Paradoxically, human beings may become a problem in such an interpretation of wilderness; they may interfere with natural ecological processes. In any event indigenous populations must be removed.

This is where sustainable development becomes sustainable economic growth, where a new ecological wisdom becomes the tool to open a new era of welfare and growth. A messianic posture, rooted in the positivist belief that science is superior to other forms of knowledge, based on the reductionist vision of society as synonymous to market, basically anti-utopian, where the balance of power and domination remains unchanged. The whole UNCED process, in which governments repeated *ad nauseam* that ecology is part of their objective for growth, the establishment of a Business Council for Sustainable Development and the like are eloquent examples.

Shared responsibilities, shared actions

It is not my intention to present Northern governments and environmental movements as the 'new' problem, thus reviving old polemics about ecological imperialism. My objective is to show that both in the South and in the North, the environmental movement is a heterogeneous and complex thing, and that governments are slowly entering the environmental dimension, without, however, abandoning their basic postulates. A new danger has thus arisen, whereby the environmental movement has provided the old credo of 'economic growth at any price' with a new look: 'economic growth with a sense of limits'. The ecocratic discourse legitimizes policies which can affect all society and nature as well, while conferring upon ecomessiahs the right to become the new agents of change.

The environmental movement should not be trapped into making a superficial assessment of this phenomenon, nor should it consider all

Northern governments to be cynics, or all Southern governments to be the champions of nature's protection. This drama is not played out in black and white, but encompasses varying shades of grey. So, if it is true that Northern governments impose conditionalities on natural resources in the South that they themselves were unable to protect in the North, this does not mean that, for example, Latin America should not take seriously its current problems and shield itself from the global issues as a way to flee its responsibilities for industry, deforestation, pollution, and so on. On the contrary, the South should develop its own agenda, in fact as many agendas as possible, and consequently respect the agendas of others, seeking joint efforts and actions as a new sign of international solidarity.

To fend off the danger inherent in ecomessianic postures, the environmental movement should call upon one of its vital features and strengths: self-criticism, and the capacity to look for basic ethical stances. Whether in the North or in the South, this criticism should focus on all forms of power, wherever messianic and authoritarian expressions are in evidence towards humanity or towards nature. A new relationship to nature involves a new relationship among people. Power, which immobilizes and corrupts, is also a major ecological disaster, which must be fought everywhere, even among those of us in the environmental movement. In this struggle, all actions must be shared, because the responsibilities are shared: whatever the result, our failure or our success will affect us all.

Notes

1. My source of data is derived from a study on the interrelationships of Northern environmental organizations (governmental and non-governmental) with the non-governmental organizations in Latin America. Part of the study focused on the relationships of US organizations with those in Latin America, and later I obtained further data on European organizations. My data base is about 1,500 organizations in Latin America, most of them related to networks on environment and development (ELCI), conservation (IUCN, CIPFE), social ecology (CLAES), theology and ecology (CIPFE), and alternative agriculture (IFOAM). I have had contacts and interviews with all major environmental organizations and institutions in the USA and many of those in Europe.

2. D. H. Janzen (1986) 'The Future of Tropical Ecology', *Ann. Rev. Ecol. Syst.*, Vol. 17, pp. 305–24.

3. L. R. Sevilla L. and Q. A. Umaña (1989) *Por qué canjear deuda por la Naturaleza*, Washington, Nature Conservancy, WRI and WWF; M. Simons (1988) 'Vast Amazon Fires, Man-made, Linked to Global Warming', *New York Times*, 12 August.

4. D. Page (1989) 'Debt-for-nature swaps: experience gained, lessons learned', *Journal of Environmental Affairs*, Vol. 1, pp. 275–88.

5. R. Guha (1989) 'Radical American environmentalism and wilderness preservation: a Third World critique', *Environmental Ethics*, Vol. 11, pp. 71–83.

References

T. L. Anderson and D. L. Leal (1991) *Free Market Environmentalism*, Boulder, Westview Press.

E. Gudynas (1990), 'The Search for an Ethic of Sustainable Development in Latin America', in J. R. Engel and J. G. Engel (eds), *Ethics of Environment and Development*, London, Belhaven Press.

E. Gudynas (1992) 'Una extrane pareja: los ambientalistas y el estado en América Latina', *Ecologia Politica*, Vol. 3, pp. 51–64.

S. Schmidheiny (1992) *Changing Course: a global business perspective on development and the environment*, Massachusetts, MIT Press.

WRI (1990) *World Resources 1990–91*, New York, Oxford University Press.

13.   'Gaia': The Globalitarian Temptation

Interview with Guy Beney*

For some time now, you have warned us about the 'global-ecologist danger'. You even wrote 'It is no longer the moment to call oneself an ecologist.' Is this pure provocation?

BENEY: This obviously does not mean that at the local level one should not save a river or an ecosystem, and so on. Nor that urgent global issues at the planetary level (the greenhouse effect . . .) should not be addressed. But we must see that ecologism, up until now a necessary counter-culture, has been transformed due to pressures by populations and political powers demanding increasingly radical eco-technocratic measures. Therein lies a potential totalitarian danger, and even more specifically, a 'globalitarian'[1] one.

When the dream becomes reality it must become integrated into institutions, must it not? We've always known that ecology was global. What have you against the global?

BENEY: Of course the global pressures are there and are even imminent. The programmes for managing the planet (for example Global Change, Rio 92, . . .) are therefore necessary. But have we really understood that these programmes will grow and even accelerate the already heavy burden of an omnipresent techno-science? Here they come, the scientists, the eco-technocrats (we can speak of even 'geocrats') promoted to the status of experts capable of foreseeing and managing crises in the global society.

The first concern is – what of democracy? These experts who join knowledge and power are at the same time both judge and judged, and they are from the West much more than from the Third World. They are the ones who will impose their choices on their populations and on their elected representatives who lack transdisciplinary knowledge and skills. Are we condemned to a benevolent tyranny of an élite in order to save us from catastrophe?

The second concern is – what of human rights? The new decision-makers

---

*   First published in French in *Actuel*, December 1991.

will tend to impose not only their methods, but also their ways of thinking about the world and man. Man risks having his own rights threatened by the 'rights' of nature. The social space could easily be engulfed by the new triumphant science: biology. For with the concept of global ecology we are no longer merely individuals but indeed a genus, in co-evolution with millions of other living species, all embarked on space vessel Earth. Will we soon need to justify our presence on board in an ecological sense?

But don't you think that desertification or the disappearance of millions of animals and vegetable species is extremely serious for us all?

BENEY: Of course, but we must not, in the name of preservation of biodiversity do damage to the other essential *human* biodiversity. It is true that the latter pertains only to one species, but until now the humanistic traditions – of course, pre-scientific – have told us that each one of these individuals is invaluable.

In my opinion this is the major problem of the 21st century: *the fundamental conflict between global ecologism and universal humanism*, and even more deeply between two radically opposed interpretations of both the universe and of man. On the global scale, it might be interpreted as *the alternative between Nature and the South*, either we preserve the 'health' of the Earth (the great biochemical equilibriums), or we let the megacities of the South assume full possession of their rights (of development, and so on).

Well, let us suppose that it becomes possible to envisage justice for the South. Would that, in your opinion, be incompatible with the politics of ecology?

BENEY: Theoretically, it is compatible but at such a high price (a world tax, the loss of economic competitiveness, a decline in the standard of living, and so on) that it is feared that most people in the North would baulk at paying the price. The usual ambiguity when addressing the global ecological problem is to talk about man in general, or even to criticize the excesses of the North. However, the real issues between men (including competition, dominance, processes of inertia, transition of paradigm) remain unspoken. This will result in the heaviest burden of ecological measures being laid on the populations of the South.

Let's be clear. We in the North, have seen the light, the 'planetary consciousness', and have discovered its environmental constraints. These constraints, by the way, have been caused mainly by us. Now without delay we intend to transform this handicap into a new challenge. Liberal economics relishes this, it even thrives on this. It is already becoming green (see relations between UNEP and ICC, for example), ensuring its survival and its development. It will motivate the whole Northern population towards the new and noble cause of 'sustainable development'. As to being equitable . . .

'Global consciousness' is changing, geopolitically, into a competitive and even selective edge for the people of the North. Our instinct for survival is now awakened by a sense of urgency, and this new ecobusiness is already offering its services. In this context the North could therefore be tempted to reduce, and have the means to reduce, in every sense of the word, the last recalcitrant actor: the populations of the South. We would therefore focus, above all, on those who, in our utilitarian eyes, have no other objective but to survive by continuing to pick away at *their* environment – *our* common heritage. All this, and meanwhile our futurologists are dreaming of outer space, of 'virtual reality', of Earth as a garden . . .

In sum, the South is a problem. The ecologization of world society appears therefore as the latest version of Western development dynamics, the survival of which must be maintained at all costs. In its new form, it could well reveal itself as an efficient planetary 'Mr Clean'.

For a lot of people, however, ecology is the only way out for the Third World. We can imagine food crops based on adaptations of traditional methods, independent of the multinational agro-business corporations.

BENEY: Well, that's failing to recognize the entire dynamics of the history of domination which shows that these solutions are no longer 'natural'. They can only exist as a counter-measure to 'The Westernization of the World' (to use the pertinent expression by Serge Latouche.) Thus the difficulty in using these solutions.

What is 'natural' today, however, aside from the demographic growth of the South, is spontaneous organization on a planetary scale, that is, the techno-economic development of the North. Witness, therefore, the recent victory of capitalism over communism. Further, what is the object of scientific ecology if not the forced inter-devouring (interdependency between predators and preys, food chain, parasitism, and so on), both regulatory and organizing (evolutive complexification) at work in the biosphere for the last three billion years. Of course authors like Lynn Margulis, or even Murray Bookchin, emphasize 'co-operation', 'mutualism' or 'symbiosis' (such as that existing in a lichen organism composed of fungus and alga in association). But beyond all else, these behaviours are strategies for survival. So, is there really co-operation or is it enslavement? Think about the 'symbiosis' which was the triangular market during the 16th to 19th centuries: European merchants/African slaves/American plantation settlers . . . a magnificent eco-development for that period, too long 'sustainable'. All that with the planetary blessings of the sea currents and 'alizés' ('tradewinds')! Geodynamics is amoral, and men who 'naturally' tend to follow it may become immoral.

The 'genius' of the West is merely to flee towards the exterior (further frontiers), to surf a max on the spontaneous processes of organization – to the extent that in a few centuries the West has become the principal planetary wave. Economics and ecology, both of which touch the living, are Siamese twins coming from the local ('eco' = habitat). Having been thrust against the global, here we find them obliged to fuse. The theoreticians of 'bioeconomics' (Nicholas Georgescu-Roegen, René Passet, for instance) are delighted. The other side of the coin is that the current fashion of 'everything-eco' (one speaks of 'global', 'general', 'deep', 'of mind', ecologies . . .) risks being the Trojan horse of a new 'enslavement' and a mask for an undermining of traditional humanisms. We may pass from a vision of humanity *and* its environment to a vision of humanity *in*, and from now on, *for* the biospheric dynamics.

But in order to understand this, one must first tackle the dangerously efficient super-theory of systemics, and more generally, the new paradigm of theories of self-organization.[2] Roughly, these sciences look at the biosphere as an increasingly complex progression moving from matter to the living, the society, the technical, and so on. By so doing, systemics dissolves the classic distinction between nature and the artificial within the notion of the 'system'. Everything becomes a system, from a galaxy to a company, from a cell to the planet, and so on. In this new framework, 'eco' definition moves from being a cultural habitat to a wild system, and the Western dynamics is revealed as the techno-natural pursuit of biological evolution.

And that dynamics is supposed to continue on the level of human society and the economy. Thus, either a naivete or a shrewdness is demonstrated by terms such as eco-socialism, eco-humanism or eco-sophism, terms which we make up and broadcast in order to quickly integrate the New Eco-deal into human society.

We can therefore understand better the danger in attempting to project the techno-scientific universe, and especially the bio-organical, onto the human world on a planetary scale. Someone like Joel de Rosñay views us already as 'planetary cells' or 'enzymes'. Imagine, the humanists didn't even baulk, and of course the 'Christian' followers of Teilhard even less so. How fascinating it is to participate in the organization of the great planetary organism, of a 'Global Leviathan' . . .

Of course! We have the fascinating Gaia hypothesis by James Lovelock, in which man ceases to live cut off from nature, and is, on the contrary, fully participating in its evolution. That's great.

BENEY: If it were only just a scientific hypothesis one could have some sympathy for it. However, already by its very name (the great Greek mother-goddess), it immerses us in the archaic and biotic myth. Therefore this ascent of a biospheric vitality, this Gaia paganism all seem to me to present a number of ingredients (vital urgencies, defending sacred land, saving the global, an organicist sense of history . . .) which may react and turn virulent, at any time in the future.

'Earth is a living entity.' Does this hypothesis seem scientifically questionable to you?

BENEY: Well, it certainly makes one think. However, it does not allow for its own refutability, a condition (according to Karl Popper) of scientific integrity. Without going into detail, I think one has to distinguish two complementary notions. First, the 'Geostat', or the natural homeostasis of the Earth. This is the global self-regulation which James Lovelock describes by citing the fact that the biosphere by itself maintains oxygen, CO_2, and so on at constant and optimal levels. But even more importantly and at the root of the process is the fact that 'Geopoiesis', the planetary self-organization, has been working for more than four billion years. The fact that the biosphere creates itself, in some ways, and is constantly increasing its own complexity is a profound trend which Lynn Margulis describes.

What have you against this planetary self-organization?

BENEY: Most people prefer to look at Gaia from the conservative angle (Geostat), but they ignore the wild side of the 'Goddess' (Geopoiesis) . . . So in order to really understand the political and ethical aspects of this organizational fresco we must unveil the dark side of self-organization and descend to the level of energy to make the following statement: roughly, from time immemorial, and on every scale, 'islands of order' organize themselves through the backwash and eddies of their environment, bringing 'order out of disorder'. One can imagine the price which is paid in the process.

Let us recall the old thermodynamic concept that 'everything is decaying, the universe is moving towards its maximum entropy'. An ultra pessimistic view that one finds also in Beckett and in Levi-Strauss. It was certainly a despairing view, at least in appearance, but everyone was in the same state and we would decay all together. The 1970s brought a complete change with Ilya Prigogine's Nobel Prize work as well as the work of others which showed that, in certain open systems, 'islands of order' can organize themselves locally, contrary to the general tendency.

How does it work? At the cost of an enormous amount of energy. These islands of order structure themselves using their own environment, which they dissipate, thus the name 'dissipative structures'. We can successively call them: the *Earth*, immersed in the solar flux; *life*, which takes its nourishment from the entire sphere of terrestrial energy; *animal*, which lives off plants or herbivorous animals; *Homo sapiens*, who above all since the neolithic era, either cuts himself off from his environment or systematically exploits it; the *West* and its followers; which have generalized the hunter-gatherer-exploiter approach to resources and populations of the globe . . .

That's the point you wanted to make . . .

BENEY: Wait: from within this organizing series – where we see the energetic continuity of the natural, human and artificial realms – the process is going on. The last-born is the 'connected West', organized in networks, which forces new 'techno-ecological niches' (informatics, robotics, 'artificial life',[3] for example). The process is inflating speculative bubbles . . . burst into financial cracks. It is already being prepared to delve into the human genome and the virtual world, or to develop artificial biospheres[4] – with a view to colonizing Mars or Titan . . .

So much of this we have viewed with real enthusiasm. But don't you think that this has reinspired the scientific view of the world, after the disenchantment?

BENEY: The problem is that energy dynamics in itself is amoral. Little by little, this techno-natural pressure is replacing manual man, and even disqualifying humanism. Mother Nature, with which Michel Serres invites us to have an illusory 'contract', shows herself as a horrible stepmother. Her history is one in which she has several times destroyed the great majority of living species through unforgettable catastrophes.

An example of this is the 'invention' of oxygen, this supertoxic polluter for the first inhabitants of the biosphere . . . but from which came the animals which live by breathing this gas. Another is the extinction in the Cretaceous period which eliminated the dinosaurs . . . but left the small mammals running under their feet in order to undertake their slow dominion over the biosphere. Some authors, such as the Gaia partisan Peter Russel, think that the rapid success of the prolific and industrious human species may lead to a new comparable global catastrophe. Should we follow them and let nature (which nonetheless has become techno-nature) have its way (*laisser faire*), merely in order to have better adapted human beings (as regards to their number and mind) to the new ecodeal?

The emergent paradigm of 'order out of disorder' – the famous 'organizing chaos', or 'creative destruction' – puts us in front of the following dilemma: *between energetics*: to live is to self-organize by degrading-exploiting-excluding (according to the situation) the other (for example, to breathe, eat, develop); *and ethics*: to be human is to care for the other who is suffering. But instead of helping us to think about this existential drama, a great number of theoreticians of the self-organization and of complexity avidly followed by the politicians, the business world and the media, present us with the new paradigm as if it ought to re-enchant the world ('New Alliance').[5] It is presented as a salvation for this global crisis.

This is the attitude of someone like Prigogine, happy to deliver us, he thinks, from thermodynamic pessimism, and who openly preaches 'chaos and enthusiasm' (*Science et Technologie*, Oct. 1989).

A notable yet recent exception: a veritable cry by biotheoretician and philosopher Henri Atlan in his last book, *Tout, non, peut-être*,[6] in which he denounces 'the transformation of ecology into an ideology of the 21st century, a totalitarianism more terrifying than those totalitarian regimes of the 20th century in that this risks being planetary in scope'. But he doesn't go far enough in the analysis of this emergent 'globalitarism'.

But after all, you have people like Rifkin in the US, Jacquard or Testard in France, who are sounding the alarm on subjects related to 'bioethics'.

BENEY: Whatever the interest and good intentions of such initiatives, they are far from the real issue: the *energetic* analysis of organizing processes. Therein lies the iron law of wages, which is *the principle* (of Fermat, Maupertuis, John Stuart Mill . . .) of *natural economy*: the least amount of action or effort. This is the Graal of the strong and the Baal of the weak. All the genius of life – and the West – is to nourish itself from this. What matters is the 'connectedness' (or 'connectics') – anything which will reduce distances, delays, energy costs, and increase speed, information, productivity.

The notion of the 'planetary brain' belongs to this trend. By itself, isn't it the height of the socialist ideal? A vision in which all humans collaborate together in the same organism?

BENEY: Propagating this notion without criticism is above all irresponsible. Not because this 'global brain' isn't in the process of developing – it is in fact the last 'little island' of organization! It is through this huge 'techno-brain' that we develop networks of communication (informatics, telecommunications, indeed, but also in the future the fusion of these with bio-technologies). It is there that the empire of 'connectics', with all its impulsiveness, extends itself.

This 'Global Brain' is, in fact, on a planetary dimension. You find televisions in Calcutta railway stations, the telephone in Lagos, computers in São Paulo. But, the core and the command of this brain proceed from three gigantic socio-econo-technical 'ganglions' – the Japanese, European, North American 'gigapoles' (billions of interconnections) – all in the Northern hemisphere.[7] And underlying this? The techno-economic 'trading posts' of the West. Because the South, entangled in its battles between an imposed westernization and a defence of its own traditions – fighting for its first rights and thwarted by its plagues (famine, AIDS, . . .), the South does not have the time to develop its 'techno-neurons'.

Is biological comparison valid?

BENEY: It should even be explored further. For example, the energetic aspect. A brain has a weight and volume relatively small compared to the entire organism which is the 'sustainer'. But the brain has a metabolism which is higher. The same relationship exists between North and South. A 'Northerner' can consume several hundred times the energy of a 'Southerner'. On the other hand, physiologically, the brain has to remain separate from its 'sustaining' body through a specific barrier called 'hemato-encephalic barrier'. During the embryonic development, this barrier co-evolves with the nervous substance being formed.

Here we must introduce a property of the self-organizing systems, which Francisco Varela[8] analysed and named 'operational closure': the vell (membrane), the organism (skin), social man (languages, standards, among others), all the big complex systems were able to organize themselves only because of their specific barrier. The latter simultaneously structures and protects the systems and above all gives them their identity. So, during this new evolutionary stage through which we are now living, the planetary brain must co-evolve with its own barrier which roughly corresponds to the increasing breach between those who are 'in' and those who are 'out', hence especially between North and South.

Here we find again the geopolitical division between North and South, described by Jean-Cristophe Rufin in his book L'Empire et les Nouveaux Barbares?[9]

BENEY: Yes, but this time from an analysis of the global eco(non)-technocratic dynamics. In effect, the famous '*limes*' – the frontier which protected the Roman empire – in fact, the principal organizational pole of each period – against the barbarians separates henceforth a unifying North from a shattered South left to its own devices. This breach risks becoming greater since it is co-evolving with the identity and functions of the West, which through its planetary brain, is obsessed with its insular 'giga-techno-bubble' (SDI programme, Global watching system, and so on) as if it unconsciously wanted to pursue the improbable incarnation of some 'Techno-eden'.

In summary, you would say that on the scale of the globe a 'Big Body' is being organized . . .?

In this emerging context, 'development' has a completely renewed meaning. In the eyes of certain eco-technocrats, this process is *not just* yesterday's debate on 'liberal' economic reductionism destroying the traditional cultures all over the globe, but *in addition* it appears as the embryonic-like development of a planetary 'organism' and even 'entity'. A techno-natural 'Global Golem' is being built up through the Northern activity – or, if we are pessimistic, a Leviathan or a Big Alien . . .

This process, according to the geocrats, must not be hindered or delayed because it is perceived as *the sense of the Earth*, the fruit of the whole life evolution, and thus of the billions and billions of lives that have ever animated the biosphere. Hence, it is no longer the moment to criticize 'development' but, through its last 'green' and 'sustainable' version, to fulfil its mission. 'Real Teilhardianism' is on the move.

But perhaps it is time for the South to decolonize itself once and for all?

BENEY: Rufin and Latouche[10] underestimate the global ecological pressures. From now on, no one will escape the planetary management. Look at the UNCED in Rio, the West will not let those populations situated beyond the *limes* remain outside its eco-control. Because, whether they know it or not, those populations and their environments are part of the physiology (Lovelock's 'geophysiology') of the planetary body.

Thus, there could be a great temptation for the North – as the 'ecopolit' of the globe – to limit the rights of the masses of the megacities in the South to grow and use their environment as they please. 'Earth first!' The new global deal puts the South in a stranglehold between the centuries-long global Western techno-economical and cultural pressure and percolation,[11] and the new global eco-control under process. Feeling the rise of a new social ('geo-') Darwinism (survival of the fittest), some populations of the South might think that in order to survive they must cross the frontier which the North is hastily reinforcing for fear of this 'invasion'. Already, Europe (agreement at Schengen) and the US (Mexican-country as a 'canal-lock') are being transformed into fortresses . . . like the Japanese islands.

Thus, the new – 'geobiotic'[12] – sense of history, at the heart of global ecologism, combined with the emerging planetary idolatry ('Gaia') is revealed as an ideology of winners, and the 'New Alliance' it proclaims as a pre-humanist regression. It is not surprising that we are seeing a turn to the right in the ecologist movement. Will it go as far as a return to Haeckel or Spencer? It could justify the miseries of massive unemployment, poverty and so on, as disasters that planetary integration processes invariably induce, leading us to legitimize them as the natural price to be paid if 'we' ('our children', 'our grandchildren') want to remain in the evolutionary run and pursue the unique value recognized in the biosphere by eco-technocrats: global autopoiesis.

So, to applaud the new paradigm, one must be quite oblivious, and more particularly, feel assured of being on the right side of 'geobiotic' history! Nonetheless, a 'Third Millenary' social trend is already rising, as a spontaneous, multi-ambiguous collusion between: 1) inescapable *global emergencies* that are indeed awakening 'global consciousness' . . . but above all, our instinct of survival; 2) the rise of the *'new paradigm'* viewed as salutary (for the Geostat . . . hence for the Geopóiesis); 3) the adaptative techno-scientist *revival of the Mother-Earth cult* (from natural passive virgin icon, seen from outer space, to active techno-matriarchal 'pregnancy' idol – 'gynecologism'); 4) and finally, the *transnational, worldly entrepreneurial dynamics*, which gathers together and diffuses all the above three tendencies for their own benefit. When we realize that a number of those taking part are socialists, Christians, those caring about ethics, or mystics (the New Age movement), we can appreciate the power of illusion that the instinct to survive – or its regeneration – can have.

Amongst the authors you criticize, is there not a hope that the planetary brain could lead to an 'awakening' in humankind?

BENEY: A lot of them play on the ambiguity of the word 'awakening'. For some of them it is the 'planetary consciousness', the real one, the mystic dream of the transcendental meditator Peter Russel, or of a Teilhardian such as Joel de Rosnay, who moreover, is inspired by the school called *neo-connectionism*. The cerebral development having been accomplished, it's the planet itself which would awaken and begin to think. Imagine the mythical force behind such ideas: the myriad of sufferings and deaths – the history of the Earth is steeped in it – at last justified by the problematical psychic 'tilt' of Gaia. Because of this, the list risks being even longer . . .

A word also on the artificial Biospheres. In my opinion the Biosphere 2 project is perverse because it brings, at least at an imaginary level, a technical solution (an airlock, a safety valve) to global problems. Instead of all of us really being 'in the same boat' and trying together to 'manage the Earth like good fathers', some risk going further with a remake of Noah's Ark and the Mayflower: leave a corrupted Earth for better worlds . . .

In sum, you understand that in this global context, 'eco-socialism', 'eco-citizenship', 'eco-humanism' – all this is not very serious. Think, for instance, about the following quotes, in which the 'globalitarian temptation' of a techno-natural selection of human beings is revealed. Remember, according to this 'macroscopic' view, by changing the level of organization we get the following equations: a neuron = an individual, and the individual = the planet. Next century could be globally turbulent . . .

Little globalitarian anthology

- The people plague . . . Humans on the Earth behave in some ways like a pathogenic micro-organism, or like the cells of a tumour or neoplasm . . . As a vast collective, the human species is now so numerous as to constitute a serious . . . planetary disease, *Disseminated Primatemia*, the superabundance of humans . . .

  James Lovelock, *Gaia: The Practical Science of Planetary Medicine*, London, Gaia Books, 1991, pp. 153, 155, 156, 199.

- Earth is indeed the best of all worlds for those who are adapted to it . . . City life reinforces and strengthens the heresy of humanism, that narcissistic devotion to human interests alone . . . Our humanist concerns about the poor of the inner cities of the Third World, and our near-obscene obsession with death, suffering, and pain as if these were evil in themselves – these thoughts divert the mind from our gross and excessive domination of the natural world.

  James Lovelock, *The Ages of Gaia*, New York, W. W. Norton & Company, 1988, pp. 33, 210, 211.

- What should we do to eliminate suffering and disease? It's a wonderful idea but perhaps not altogether a beneficial one in the long run. If we try to implement it we may jeopardize the future of our species. It's terrible to have to say this. World population must be stabilized and to do that we must eliminate 350,000 people per day. This is so horrible to contemplate that we shouldn't even say it. But the general situation in which we are involved is lamentable.

  Jacques-Yves Cousteau, *The UNESCO Courrier*, Nov. 1991, p. 13.

- On the planet, we are living the era of network expansion (telephone, cable, telecommunication satellites, etc.) . . . We are the neurons of the Earth: the cells of a brain in formation at the dimensions of the planet . . . The neuronal network . . . develops according to a process of 'redundant proliferation' during certain phases of life, then stabilisation and selection . . . Neurons die, but this hecatomb is a normal part of the individual development. To learn is to eliminate.

  Joël de Rosnay, *Le Cerveau planétaire*, Paris, Olivier Orban, 1984, pp. 11, 22.

- Nature is like a gigantic brain, which must be chaotic to fulfil its functions.

  Ilya Prigogine, Paris, Sorbonne, 1991.

- As the communication links within humanity increase, we will eventually reach a time when the billions of information exchanges shuttling through the networks at any one time create similar patterns of coherence in the global brain as are found in the human brain. Gaia would then awaken and become her equivalent of conscious . . . It does indeed seem possible that we alive today could witness the emergence of a true high-synergy society – a healthy social super-organism. If so, we may truly be one of the most privileged generations ever to have lived . . . From the perspective of dissipative systems theory crises can be seen as the catalysts pushing humanity onto a new evolutionary level. If humanity successfully adapts to the crises it may break through to a higher level of organisation. But if it fails to adapt it may, if the crises are severe enough, breakdown and collapse completely.

  Peter Russel, *The Awakening Earth – The global brain*, Ark Ed., 1982, p. 86, 180, 206.

- Life is a wave. . . . The preferred . . . definition of life is the genetic one: 'a system capable of evolution by natural selection'. . . . No one denies that life is a struggle to exist. We are always too many. . . . If the surface of the Earth behaves as a physiological system, unfettered human growth may elicit a retaliatory response against the ecologically offending party. . . . It may be an ecological fact that crowded organisms *become* superorganisms acting at new, higher levels of organization. . . . Rapidly growing populations either transform or collapse . . . technology is part of the evolutionary process itself. Technology is *natural*. . . . A disturbing possibility is that future life [on Earth] may exist only inside ecological enclosures, each a kind of biologically miniaturized world. . . . It is [with reproducing biospheres] propagation by, of, and for the Earth, *through* humanity. . . . Tamed humankind, you might say. The baby earths [are] born . . . from the humble motivation of sheer necessity. . . . For the first time we recognize our cosmic role as midwives aiding in gestation, delivery, and development of a new form of life. . . . Our destiny is to traverse the universe – and that is exactly what we are doing, right now.

  Dorion Sagan, *Biospheres – Metamorphosis of Planet Earth*, New York, MacGraw Hill Publishing Co. 1990; Arkana, 1991, pp. 7, 9, 16, 25, 43, 68, 71, 112, 117, 158, 174, 184.

> • This has always been the way of the world. If stress is severe enough, only tolerant organisms survive . . . Darwinian natural selection is the ultimate ancient Gaian feedback system upon which all the newer technological and behavioral ones are based . . . If catastrophe strikes, as it regularly has in life's history, some options will no longer be viable. But their expiration, in the form of death or extinction, makes the biosphere as a whole stronger, more complex, and more resilient. (This of course has nothing whatever to do with human progress or well-being . . .) . . . whether people carry the primeval environment of the ancient microcosm into space or die trying, life does seem tempted in this direction [to leave the Earth and conquer space]. And life, so far, has resisted everything but temptation.
>
> Lynn Margulis and Dorion Sagan, *Microcosmos – Four billion years of evolution from our bacterial ancestors*, New York, Summit Books, 1986, pp. 263–5.

So what would you do?

BENEY: Each one is brought back to himself and the following *energy/ethic dilemma*, which is difficult to internalize: the theoreticians of self-organization have really uncovered some important spontaneous processes. However, they are somewhat wrong on the ethical plane. All of this energetic dynamics is amoral, even if there are secondhand phenomena of co-operation. What can we do? One phenomenon is worth our attention: that which the scientific historian, Patrick Tort, has named 'reversive effect'.[13] Globally, it is a process of progressive reversing of the selective efficiency during biological evolution: at first, the natural selection process acts alone; throughout the ages (millions of years) this process is distorted (like a Moebius ring) and hindered by the emergent anxiety to defend the weakest – first, the motherly protection of babies and even, with time, those left behind.

Some examples?

BENEY: A shewolf which gives milk to a little one of another species, a dolphin helping an injured fellow creature (or even a person) to remain on the surface in order to breathe, or elephants supporting an old female in the herd who is dying. Little by little this 'reversive effect' reveals itself in the animal world and is especially prevalent with mammals. Darwin himself, who was not so 'darwinist' as certain people would like to think, had already identified this tendency as the progressive beginning of anti-selective social instincts.

A natural law which the Nazis would not have appreciated, since they claimed that the defence of the weak was a Judeo–Christian invention.

BENEY: Whereas in fact, the reversive effect seems to be the global consequence of a battle during millions of years among a myriad of sensitive beings which continues through social man. In the final analysis it is nature itself, which from within refuses to remain a brute force, an inflexible horrible stepmother. So, a certain ethical behaviour – caring for the other – existed long before the arrival of human beings.

The mistake with those who popularize the evolutionary fresco (the last 'Great Story' about our origins) is that too little focus is given to this natural and innermost tendency of evolution. All the new idols – complexity, autonomy, self-organization, co-evolution, symbiosis, the planetary dynamic, and so on – are those which these authors seek to bring to the fore. What a pity if they were to appear to future generations as the Gobineau of eco-fascism which risks rising up out of the 'Global Age'.

But don't you also fall into this scientism by looking for biological roots to the ethical?

BENEY: Fortunately, one doesn't need to know the reversive effect in order to be ethical. However, focusing on this effect helps to avoid idolizing the organizing force and reduces the risk 'eco'. This *progressive* 'energy/ethic' *reversal*, even if it is not devoid of all perverse effects, appears as the only thing of value at work within the biosphere.

In concrete terms, how is the reversive effect manifested today?

BENEY: It seems to me that its evident incarnation is in those associations and non-governmental organizations (NGOs) created out of compassion in the face of misery and whose networks are everywhere: partnerships with populations of the Third and Fourth worlds, assistance to the injured, the handicapped, and to refugees, aid to the dying – including those campaigns against the use of animals in laboratories, and so on. One can detect it also in the attempt to establish the right to humanitarian assistance, or a world citizen's income, or a declaration of humankind's duties towards any suffering being, be it human or animal.

In sum, in the face of rising 'globalitarian temptation' of the eco-technocratic Northern powers, this is no time to naively call oneself an ecologist without *personally* digging into the root meaning of 'eco'. As Simone Weil said, 'One must know how to change camps – just like justice, that fugitive from the victor's camp.' The new ecologist can only be 'reversive', ethical, by exercising an extreme vigilance towards the greening of powers and the new scientist ideologies – too 'natural' to be human. He or she must be attentive to the rejected people – and especially to those of 'outer-*limes*'. We can assume that this attention will carry a heavy price. The volunteers to the Third and Fourth Worlds and certain marginals – NGOs or not – daily pay that price. Thanks to their efforts helping more than hindering, the irrepressible Westernization of the world still merits the name of civilization. Laico-planetary version of the ethical reversal: the *complexity* of the global analysis brings us back to the *perplexity* of one's own intimate 'energy/ethic' choice: to whom and for what am I going to give my energy?

Notes

1. See: Guy Bèney, 'Gaïa: de l'hypothèse au mythe', *Lettre Science-Culture du GRIT*, Nos. 26, 27, 28, 30–31, 32, 35, 36–37, 1987–88; *Futuribles*, June 1990; Contribution to the *Rapport au ministre de la recherche et de la technologie*, Paris, GRET, 1992, 'La Citoyenneté au risque de l'écologisme global', *IFDA-dossiers*, No. 79, 1990; *Revue du MAUSS* (Ed. La Découverte), No. 8, 1990; 'La montée des Géocrates', in *La Terre outragée*, Ed. Autrement, 1992; 'La Tentation globalitaire', *Dossier du Nouvel Observateur*, June 1992.
2. Works by H. Atlan, G. Bateson, J. P. Dupuy, E. Jantsch, L. Margulis, H. Maturana, E. Morin, I. Prigogine, H. Reeves, F. Varela, etc.
3. See, for example, the First European Colloquium on Artificial Life, ECAL 91, organized by F. Varela and held in Paris on 11–13 December 1991.
4. Dorion Sagan (1990) *Biospheres – Metamorphosis of Planet Earth*, Mac-Graw Hill Publishing Co.
5. Ilya Prigogine and Isabelle Stengers (1979) *La Nouvelle Alliance*, Paris, Gallimard.
6. Henri Atlan (1991) *Tout, non, peut-être*, Paris, Seuil.
7. See the recent alliance (July 1992) for a 'creative triangle' between Toshiba, Siemens, and IBM, in order successfully to leapfrog towards the new generation of 256 megabyte chips.
8. Francisco J. Varela (1987) *Principles of Biological Autonomy*, Holland, Elsevier.
9. Jean-Christophe Rufin (1991) *L'empire et les nouveaux barbares*, Paris, J.-C. Lattès.
10. J.-C. Rufin and Serge Latouche (1991) *Les Naufragés de la planète*, Paris, La Découverte.
11. For instance, according to the agronomist Marcel Mazoyer, within two centuries (20th and 21st) two billion peasant farmers will have been uprooted by competition in the world market (gains of productivity having increased a thousandfold!) and forced to swell the suburbs of the megapoles (in T. Gaudin (ed.) (1990) *2100*, Paris, Payot (French Ministry of Research and Technology report).
12. 'Geo', as the planetary global reference, 'bio' as the whole biological evolution, 'tics' as the pursuit of the evolutionary trend of complexification through technical activity by mankind ('informatics', 'productics', 'connectics', 'biotics', procreatics', etc.).
13. See the colloquium 'Darwinisme et société', Paris, 4–6 June 1991.

Part IV
Ecology from Below

14. Sacred Groves
Regenerating the Body, the Land, the Community

Frédérique Apffel Marglin
with Purna Chandra Mishra

> When nature is separated out from the activities of men, it even ceases to
> be nature in any full and effective sense. Men come to project onto nature
> their own unacknowledged activities and consequences. Or nature is split
> into unrelated parts: coal-bearing from heather-bearing; downwind from
> upwind. The real split, perhaps, is in men themselves: men seeing
> themselves as producers and consumers.

Raymond Williams[1]

Ever since the publication of the Brundtland report the buzz word has been
'sustainable development'. Sustainable development dominated the discussions at the UNCED conference on development and the environment. The
establishment view of this concept amounts to a judicious mix between an
updated version of Progressive Conservation and Wilderness Thinking, the
two most popular environmental movements in the US. Progressive
Conservation, the movement begun at the turn of the century in the US, is
the forerunner of the concept of 'sustainable development'. It arose in
response to the environmental ravages wrecked by *laissez-faire* capitalism
and is closely identified with scientific forestry and water resource
management. The movement advocates the rational utilization of natural
resources and has meant the rule of experts as well as centralization; it is
located in the US Forest Service and the Bureau of Reclamation. Scientific
Forestry and water management engineering were both used in the service
of the rational utilization of natural resources. Today this outlook has been
generalized to all agricultural and industrial activities under the rubric of
'sustainable development'. The rule of expert knowledge means bringing
ever-new portions of nature under human dominion for increased
production of a sustained yield of marketable resources.

The other face of US environmentalism, Wilderness Thinking, has as its
mission to preserve 'wild' nature from the ever-expanding and colonizing
thrust of development. Wilderness Thinking arose in opposition to such

conservationist sentiments as those expressed by John Widshoe, advisor to the Bureau of Reclamation: 'The destiny of man is to possess the whole earth and the destiny of the earth is to be subject to man'.[2] The Wilderness movement has spawned movements such as Earth First! and Deep Ecology. It sees itself as the champion of unspoiled, wild nature threatened by the increasing encroachment of development. Wilderness Thinking sees human intervention in nature as inherently destructive and is therefore fundamentally hostile to subsistence agriculture and to pastoralism. The export of Wilderness Thinking to the Third World, in the form of Wildlife Parks and Nature Reserves, has had disastrous consequences for local communities.[3] Wilderness Thinking separates the spiritual from the material and livelihood from nature. Although it is opposed to development and Progressive Conservation on the issue of the domination of nature by 'man', Wilderness Thinking shares with it both the disconnecting of society from nature and a profound aversion to peasant and tribal ways of life. In Ramachandra Guha's words:

> Progressive Conservation places society above ecology (Nature must follow the dictates of Man), in Wilderness Thinking ecology is placed over society (Man must follow the dictates of Nature). Peasant culture, by embedding ecology in society, transcends both these perspectives. (Op. Cit.)

The network of sacred groves in such countries as India has since time immemorial been the locus and symbol of a way of life in which humans are embedded in nature and in which the highest levels of biological diversity are found where humans interact with nature. The sacred grove and what it represents escape the either/or logic of both Progressive Conservation (along with 'sustainable development') and Wilderness Thinking.

In coastal Orissa, on India's eastern seaboard, rice cultivators have farmed the land for at least two millennia and the land continues to give forth generously. The sacred grove is the keystone in a way of life that has maintained such astounding sustainability. Far from being a mini nature preserve, the sacred grove is both locus and sign of the regeneration of body, land, and community. It stands for the integration of the human community in nature. The practices that regenerate body, land, and community are periodic, following the rhythms of the seasons and of women's bodies. The sacred grove, with its shrine to the local embodiment of the Great Goddess, is the permanent material sign of these periodic processes of regeneration. It is because of the existence of the Goddess in her sacred grove that the body, the land and the community can be integrated into a single process. It is through the Goddess in her sacred grove that the body is embedded in the land and the community in nature. In the following pages I shall attempt to make clear the keystone role of the Goddess in her sacred grove in these practices of regeneration.

Land

Purna Chandra Mishra and I first came to the sacred grove of Goddess Haracandi in June 1987 on the occasion of her annual festival.[4] At the summer solstice this otherwise deserted place is a bustling centre of activity during the four days of the celebration of the Goddess's annual menstruation, called Raja Parba (the festival of the menses). Haracandi has her temple at the top of a wooded hill rising out of the flat alluvial plain criss-crossed by the bunds and channels of rice fields. On the first day we noticed that no farmers were to be seen in the fields ploughing with their bullocks, as they usually were. As the hill came into view we left the fields entering casuarina pine groves that led to a grove of tall, ancient tamarind and neem trees on the steeper slopes of the hill.[5] In the steaming heat of June, entering the shady grove of stately trees with a sea breeze blowing on our skin we felt immediately refreshed. Mid-June marks the end of the hot, dry season and the beginning of the monsoon rains when the summer crops (*kharif*) are planted. At the top of the hill we climbed the steps to Haracandi's temple to pay our respects. Coming out of her sanctuary high on the hill we had a breathtaking view of the wild land between where we stood and the sea shore some two kilometres away. In the other direction, we saw the fields and the small villages lying inland. The wooded hill stands at the edge of the cultivated land, set apart from farmers' settlements, overlooking a grove of casuarina trees and a river meandering into the sea. During the festival of the menses of the Goddess, people from some 60 villages in a 20 km radius around the sacred grove come in bullock carts, on foot, bicycles, buses and scooters.

Purna Chandra and I asked men and women why they came to this festival and what it was all about. Dibulata Devi, a mother of four, spoke to us in her village where we visited her later. Women celebrate the festival in the villages, while the men set up tents among the trees in the sacred grove for the four days of the festival:

> This festival is almost like our menstruation; in this festival we do not bleed but we follow the same rules as during our menses. We sleep apart from our husbands. We do no work, no cooking, no cutting of anything, no grinding of grains or spices. In this festival the Goddess is at her menses and we follow all these rules of menstruation as we are of the same kind as Her. She is a woman and we all are women; we are Her partible form (*ansa*). We do no work; we play on swings; we play cards;

we decorate ourselves; we walk with friends and sing together. This reminds us of our menarche festival when everyone keeps us happy. Now we make ourselves happy during Raja. People also love us when we take care of our bodies, when we rest and our minds become gentle and sweet. With these qualities we love men, and creation becomes possible and we get strong and healthy children.

Rajana Palai, a 55 year old farmer said:

We come during this time of Raja to spend four days when She is bleeding. If we worship Her at this time She will give us good crops and cause many things in nature to grow. She is Prakriti. Another big reason we come here now is that she is at her periods which is good for each and everyone. This means that She will give forth. When She is pleased it means She will take good care of us. She is a mother and will do everything for us. We come here leaving the women in the village. We consider our women to be the representatives of the Goddess. They are female and they are Her partible form (*anśa*). We think they also are at their periods, really not, but symbolically. We feel that the Mother bleeds through them, so it is incumbent upon us that we should please them and not have them work for us but rather have free time and play.

We also spoke with old Bhikari Parida:

Women are Prakriti, the creative energy (*srusti shakti*) and we are Purusa and come here to worship the greater energy (*adishakti*), the Mother (*Ma*) . . . Women are reflections of the Mother and of the Earth (*pruthibi*). The Mother, the Earth and women are the same thing in different forms . . . During the menses of the Earth women do no work; they play and sing with their friends. The sole reason is for them to rest, just like during their monthly periods when they do no work and must not be disturbed, they should not be touched, they are then untouchable. When the Goddess is bleeding we also stop all work in the fields, and not only we farmers but all other men: blacksmiths, carpenters, potters, washermen, barbers, etc . . . The young women celebrate Raja because they are the centre of creation. We like to make them happy.

In these words we are told that the Goddess is the Mother, the earth, Prakriti and so are the women, in partible form. Another way of putting it is that women are small parts of the Earth Goddess. The Goddess menstruates annually at the articulation of the hot and the rainy seasons, a time known as *ritu*, which is also another word for menses.[6] The hot, dry season, from April to June following the harvest of the winter crops, is the fallow period; the earth is parched dry and cracked and nothing grows.

The trees and all the things that grow wild in the Earth Goddess's sacred grove must never be cut, never cultivated by human hands. The sacred grove stands apart from the cultivated fields and the settlements of the villagers; it is the Goddess's own place: Her trees, Her plants, Her wild animals. The festival of the menses, Her great feast day, is the only festival which all villagers celebrate together; it is also the only time of the year when a large fair takes place. It is, however, clear from the words of the villagers that the Goddess does not only represent wild nature – the sacred grove – but that she is also the crops, the food the men grow and the women process. They worship Her so that they will have bountiful harvests and be free of famine, drought and disease.

During their monthly periods the villages women stay apart, rest, and are not to be disturbed. They neither cook, cut nor grind anything. They stay apart from their husbands, that is, they do not have intercourse. If any man touched or disturbed a woman during her menses great calamities would befall him. Similarly, if anyone disturbs the sacred grove by cutting down a tree, killing a wild animal, or cultivating any plants, great calamities would befall that person. The sacred grove, like menstruating women, must not be disturbed; like them it is set apart from the normal human activities of village and field.

Body

In cultivation, ploughing and planting are likened to intercourse and insemination; the woman is the field in which the man plants his seed. The injunction against intercourse during the festival of the menses, as during women's monthly periods, parallels the injunction against cultivating in the fields during the four days of the festival. The injunction against disturbing or touching women during their menses corresponds to the injunction against disturbing anything in the sacred grove. That is the Goddess's place of rest, of regeneration, where Her body remains permanently undisturbed, untouched.[7] But only during the four days of the festival are the fields left untouched so they can rest. Women are productive in the household, in generation, except during their monthly periods, these represent their sacred groves, where their bodies regenerate themselves so that the energy for creation can replenish itself. Men must keep the sacred grove inviolate, keep women happy particularly during their menses, and please the Goddess during Her menses, all of which is the same thing. If all this is done, well-being will result, but if not all sorts of afflictions will befall humankind.

The villagers spoke about this by telling us what happened to Draupadi, the heroine of the great Indian epic, the Mahabharata. Sisulata, sister-in-law of Dibulata, said that:

during Raja Parba, Haracandi is Draupadi. She is the wife of the Pandava brothers. One wife, five husbands. When the Pandava brothers came back to their mother after the wedding they told her 'We have brought a fruit,' and she said: 'Let the five brothers share it equally.' Since the mother told the five brothers to share equally, five husbands came to one woman.

At the sacred grove we spoke with a young washerman, Ramachandra Nayak, about Draupadi, after we had learned that during the festival Haracandi was identified with her. The following reproduces part of the conversation:

RN:　　Draupadi who was queen of the Pandavas was at her periods and Duhśasana [one of the Kaurava brothers, enemies of the Pandavas] at the order of Duryodhana [elder brother of the Kauravas] gave her mental and physical pain and insulted her, irritating her to the maximum. She became very angry and a spirit moved her and as a result of her curse the whole lineage of the Kauravas was destroyed because of this sin.

FAM:　*What sin?*

RN:　　She was disturbed during her *ritu* (menses); she was taken by the hair and the result was that everything was destroyed; blood was shed.

PCM:　*Do your observances during this festival mean that you give rest to mother earth?*

RN:　　Yes. If we do not allow her to rest during her menses, the result will not be good. Our works will not be fruitful. That's why our women are given lots of rest since they are the representatives of Mother Earth.

PCM:　*What would happen if we do as the Kauravas did and disturb the earth?*

RN:　　We will get afflictions.

FAM:　*What kind of afflictions?*

RN:　　Everything will be spoiled. If you plough, it will not give results. That is why we give rest to women during their menses. If they rest it will be good for them. They do not work; they are untouchable; we do not disturb them. So the Mother Goddess should take rest at this time.

The inviolate nature of the sacred grove is the concrete sign reminding humans of the need to give rest to the land and to women so as to regenerate life's creative energies. The sacred grove is also the place where the community of farmers regenerates itself. Let us listen to the men who come to camp for four days in the sacred grove about what they do during that time.

Community

We spoke with 55-year-old Raghaba Sahu, leader of the tent housing the men from Candiput village:

> I called a meeting before the festival and we all agreed to contribute 80 rupees per household . . . We are poor and we know we have to spend money here for four days. But we like to come here to worship our Goddess. Only one man per household comes. If the father comes the son won't, but it rotates every year so that in time every man can come. Everybody in the family knows the amount of the contribution; it's the same for everyone in the village to create a good feeling among everyone. They are our treasuries, we deposit everything in their hand. They remind us to give the contribution in time; they like to keep up the prestige of our families. The money goes into the village fund. We have a village project, begun by the Orissa government, of cultivating shrimps in the village pond. The profit from the sale goes into the village fund and we are all happy to spend that money here in the festival. We bought with that project's profits four rams to offer to the Goddess; it costs us a little over 2,000 rupees. Because of the village fund it is possible for us to have a good feast everyday up to the end of the festival.

Rajana Palai told us about feasting in the sacred grove and the leader's task of distributing the food equally among everyone:

> Distribution of the food is very important and I take great care with it. I know who will eat what and how much – that is my sixth sense. I balance everything between the rich and the poor, the younger boys, the grown men and the old ones. I am very careful about that. I eat only after everyone has been fed and is fully satisfied. Especially when the meat curry is served I forget about the face of anyone and only look at their leaf plates, serve them, and go to the next in the line from first to last. Everyday, four times I have to do this to keep my villagers happy – that is why they trust me.

Banambar Baraa, a youngish man from Handiali village, spoke about relationships between men of different villages at the festival:

> Coming to the place of the Mother at this fair we forget everything, all our problems, our individual responsibilities. We feel that we are all the children of Mother Haracandi and that we are all the same. Except for the fact that we eat with our fellow villagers, we do not feel as if we belong to one particular village. Here all the men feel as brothers since She is the

Mother and we have come here to receive Her blessings. There is no feeling of inferior or superior. There is competition – we play cards, we have song fests – but there is no quarrel among us; we do not lose our tempers. Even if there is some quarrel between some people or between some villages, we carefully manage it so as to resolve it and forget our quarrels. We do not allow such disturbances to develop and destroy the peace and beauty of the festival. If there is peace then She becomes peaceful and gives us peace. When She is *shanti* then She does everything good for us. Whether we get food or not is not the most important thing, but we need peace (*shanti*). We try to do constructive things; we don't want to bring any harm or destruction. We do not show our individual greatness or express our power and dignity. We try to keep peace and order in this sacred place. Nobody has bought this land to become master over another; the sacred grove belongs to everybody. With all the tents in it it looks like one big village, the tents are the houses and we all are the children of the Mother. The Mother's temple is our village temple.

Siddheswara Nayaka, the 40-year-old leader of the tent from Nandapur village, gave another reason why co-operation and harmonious relations between co-villagers and men of different villages was necessary:

We feel that this tent is our home during four days and we are members of the same household. So there is no feeling about 'this is mine and this is another's.' Our tent leader treats everyone equally and shares the tasks among us, like cutting vegetables, fetching fuel and water etc . . . Everyone takes responsibility for his task very seriously. No one goes away from the tent before completing his duties. If one were to do this, it would anger the tent leader and he might report this to the village headman. Villagers feel very bad about any sort of allegation brought by the tent leader, they feel that the reputation of the village will be damaged. Preserving the reputation and prestige of the village is extremely important because if it is ruined nobody will want to give their daughters in marriage to our village and no villagers will want to take our daughters. Our image will be spoiled, then our life deserts us. So we co-operate . . . After finishing our duties in the tent we visit other tents. Our relatives and in-laws all come from this area of Brahmagiri [the market town in this area of 60 villages where the sacred grove is located]. We talk about many things; about cultivation, fertilizing the land, water problems. Sometimes we meet persons who are very knowledgeable in agriculture or about ayurvedic medicinal plants and leaves to cure many kinds of diseases. We also often discuss possibilities of marriages between grown sons and daughters and about the money involved. Meeting so many friends and relatives from other villagers is a very big pleasure for us.

For the men of these villages the festival of the Earth Goddess's menses is not an impromptu affair but a carefully planned mobilization of village resources, a duty as well as a pleasure for all men past childhood; and a major political and social event. Deciding upon and then collecting contributions from every household in the village is the beginning of a carefully thought out and carried out process of creating solidarity, equality, and conviviality. Villages are often multi-caste – the cultivator caste being the most numerous – and all hierarchy is put aside for the duration of the festival.[8] Everyone, as we have seen, contributes equally and profits from the village fund to pay for the sacrificial animals to be offered to the Goddess and then eaten by the men. The food is prepared and cooked by the villagers and carefully distributed by the tent leader. In feasting the men share equally in the collective resources of the village and simultaneously create solidarity.

Relations between men of different villages are handled with as much care and forethought as relations between co-villagers. Any conflicts that erupt or simmer are quickly resolved. The sacred grove becomes one big village and all men there behave as brothers – the children of the Goddess. Peace and harmony are essential since conflicts and disharmony would displease the Goddess and She would withhold Her blessings. Peace gives Her peace, so that She becomes peace and gives Her blessings; anger in the community means the anger of the Goddess and that spells disaster.

The regeneration of the community goes beyond fostering solidarity, equality and conviviality. Villagers co-operate, do not quarrel, and jealously preserve the reputation of their village in order to contribute to the regeneration of people. For a village to lose its good name, as we have seen, would mean that no one would give or take daughters from that village, and this would spell the death of the community. The 60 or so villages of the area around the town of Brahmagiri are united by marriage exchanges. Men marry women from other villages, therefore daughters leave their natal village upon marriage. The festival is a major occasion for finding out who is marriageable and for evaluating the worth of a village as a potential home for one's daughter and as the place of one's future in-laws.

The sacred grove is where community is regenerated, through concrete experiences of feasting, singing, playing and talking. This regeneration is accomplished with extreme deliberation and forethought, carefully planned for and carried out. As Banambar Barala told us, no one owns the sacred grove; it belongs to every one; it is common land, the land of the Goddess. Just as the Goddess, and women too, must be undisturbed and pleased during their menses, the sacred grove as the material embodiment of this state is the locus where all the male villagers live in common. In this communal state, this unified household, they treat each other as brothers, undisturbed by quarrels and dissension. And it is in that very harmony that marriage exchanges, the first step towards village regeneration, are first discussed.

The deliberation with which villagers plan, organize, and carry out their participation in this festival matches the deliberation and care with which all people of the Brahmagiri area preserve and respect the sacred grove. There is no need for forest guards or environmental police (as they exist in my home town) or fences to enforce the inviolate character of the sacred grove. The people themselves know that the sacred grove is the very safeguard of their well-being and the locus of the regeneration of the land, the body and the community. To cultivate or to cut trees there is the equivalent of rape, an abomination and great insult to the Goddess fraught with dire consequences for human beings.[9]

The sacred grove is not a nature reserve or a wilderness park. Those are creations of the consumption phase of industrial capitalism in opposition to and in conflict with the ethos of co-operation with nature for increased production. The sacred grove on the hill of Haracandi overlooks, on its western flank, rice fields and villages. It is preserved by the people in these villages, not because it represents the antithesis of their productive activities but because it safeguards their livelihoods and their continued existence. It would be a mistake to oppose the sacred grove to productive activities as nature is opposed to culture. The sacred grove is the permanent sign of women's periodic flow of blood and of the earth's seasonality; in the felicitous local language the sacred grove represents the *ritu* of women and of the earth. Appropriately enough it is the locus of a *ritu*-al where men regenerate their communities.

Among the peasants of coastal Orissa, culture and society are embedded in nature, and the spiritual is embedded in the material. No amount of planning for sustainable development can bring about an ecological way of life. For this, rediscovering the sacred groves and the practices that have preserved them (if in reduced form) in the face of colonial legislation is a surer path. The model of the wildlife reserve has been transplanted to the South at great cost to the communities which live in and from the forests. Even in the United States the present government is in the process of deregulating access to state and national reserves for timber and other developments in order to stimulate a flagging economy. The sacred grove can not only be the regenerating principle for the local communities, but for forests in India in general. When the commons of local communities are still protected by the Goddess, nature's diversity is preserved. These pockets of biodiversity can be used for the regeneration of forest cover in general. The sacred grove, in its principle of embedding the body and the community in nature, could also perhaps become a model for the North.

Notes

1. (1972) 'Ideas of Nature', in J. Benthall (ed.), *Ecology: the shaping enquiry*, London, Longman, p. 160.

2. Quoted in Ramachandra Guha (1993) 'Two Phases of American Environmentalism: a critical history', in F. Apffel Marglin and S. A. Marglin (eds) (n.d.) *Decolonizing Knowledge: from development to dialogue* (forthcoming).

3. In the article mentioned above by Ramachandra Guha, he gives the example of the Keoldeo Ghana bird sanctuary in India where in 1982 police fired and killed local villagers exercising traditional grazing rights. There is also the example of the Ik of Uganda made (in)famous by anthropologist Collin Turnbull (*The Mountain People*, New York, Touchstone Books, 1972); the Ik's hunting grounds in the Kidepo valley in northeast Uganda were turned into a wildlife sanctuary from which they were excluded; this action led to their dying of starvation.

4. Purna Chandra Mishra lives in Puri, Orissa and he and I have collaborated in field research ever since 1975. I returned to the sacred grove and participated in the festival in June 1990; I also spent some time during the 1990 festival in one of the villages celebrating with the women there. Purna Chandra Mishra has returned to the festival in June 1991 and sent me detailed written reports.

5. The casuarina is an evergreen pine-like tree that originated in Australia. It was introduced in India some 30 to 40 years ago. The sacred grove of Haracandi now only covers some half a square kilometre on the hill itself. It used to have an additional 40 acres which was totally deforested and which the present-day priests of Haracandi have replanted in casuarina pine. The deforestation was caused by colonial forest policy: 'The forest settlements which followed the Indian Forest Act of 1878 resulted in the takeover of the *kans* [sacred grove] as state property. . . . The forest resources thus went out of community control. The minor forests became common property resource open to larger numbers of people. The general scarcity of biomass for the peasantry resulted in unregulated exploitation' (M. D. Subash Chandran and Madhav Gadgil (1991), 'Kans: safety forests of Uttara Kannada' ms. p. 15.

6. The Sanskrit (and Oriya) word 'ritu' is the same root as the English word 'ritual'. On this see my chapter 'Woman's Blood: challenging the discourse of development', in Apffel Marglin and Marglin (n.d.).

7. Chandran and Gadgil (1991), both biologists, see the sacred groves of India as the sites for the potential regeneration of forests in India since they are repositories of biodiversity.

8. With the exception of the brahmins, the priestly caste, the only caste that does not celebrate this festival.

9. The work of the Sanskrit scholar Alf Hiltebeitel on the Sanskrit Mahabharata has shown that Draupadi's hair and her garment represent the forest and plant cover of the earth and that Draupadi herself is the symbol of the earth. Duhśasana's disturbing her during her menses is the equivalent of a rape and spells the denudation of the earth, famine, drought and the death of the lineage (A. Hiltebeitel, 'Draupadi's Garment', *Indo-Iranian Journal*, No. 22, 1980, pp. 98–112 and 'Draupadi's Hair', *Perusartha*, Vol. 5, 1981, pp. 179–214.

15.   Village Contradictions in Africa

Yash Tandon

Introduction

This chapter comprises several seemingly disjointed pieces of information about certain 'happenings' in Africa, the significance of which it is preferable for the readers themselves to analyse. Having been nurtured in an essentially top-down pedagogy of learning whereby the author's interpretations assume the authority of law, we have come to realize that the author's is only one possible interpretation of events – even those that he/she sets out to narrate – and indeed, may not be the most insightful interpretation.

Having said this, we shall, towards the end of this chapter, try to draw our own conclusions from these stories (events, episodes), for after all, the selection was made by us, and so we cannot really escape an obligation to analyse them. But we claim no better understanding of what import these stories convey than any other observer of the African scene.

First, are four cases of people's efforts in the villages of Southern and Eastern Africa to survive against the background of the continent's worst drought in nearly a century. Then follow two cases of 'ecological development': one, the global strategy 'to save the elephant' by imposing an international ban on the export of ivory; and the other, the switch by commercial farmers in Southern Africa from food production to ostrich farming and game ranching. We follow this up with two cases of alternative strategies offered by those who are looking for ways out of the predicament that Africa faces.

Village vitalities

The Dande people in Zimbabwe wake up from deep colonial slumber
In the Dande Valley in the north of Zimbabwe, close to the borders of Zambia and Mozambique, some people are rediscovering a lost science.

They are falling back on traditional foods and medicines to survive and to fight back the regime of dispossession imposed on them by recent (that is, colonial) history. Deprived of access to their natural resources (wild life, forests and fish) the people were forced either to flee from the Valley and sell their labour-power to neighbouring white commercial farms and mines, or to stay in the Valley and eke out a precarious existence. Today the bulk of the people are still caught up in the vagaries of commodity economy. But a small minority, mostly women, have gone back into history and dug out past knowledge of traditional foods that has kept them going during hard times.

Historically, there were only occasional hard times, mostly during drought. Even then, the wild life, of which they had plenty, provided the survival buffer. Now, since the white man came, hard times are an everyday affair. The bulk of the people have nothing to live on except charity either from donor NGOs from Europe, or from the state in the form of 'food for work', a wasteful and artificially created 'solution' to a primarily historical and structural problem.

So hard times are now pushing people to fall back on their traditional resources for survival. Among the foods they have rediscovered are *mupama*, *guruhwu* and *mhanda* (all used as substitutes for maize), *manyanya* (used instead of onions), *musangwi* (seeds boiled for relish), *karemberembe* (baobab leaves cooked with okra) and *mawuyu* (like fruits, which when dried make good porridge), *masawu* (like berries from which they make a strong alcoholic drink), *musiga*, *hakwa*, *katunguru* and *bwabwa* (all traditional fruits). These hitherto neglected foods and fruits are now coming back into the consumption (but not yet production) cycle.

People are also becoming conscious of the fact that it is not God-given that all good things of life are meant only for the white man, as they were made to believe in 100 years of colonial indoctrination. This awakening has both a positive and a negative aspect. An attitude of contentment is giving way to one of greed; a philosophical and contemplative life of casual ease is giving way to one aimed at material acquisition. Development is thus equated with material consumption and accumulation of 'the good things of life'. At the same time, the awakening has generated a newly-won sense of 'equality' with the white man. At times, this expresses itself in the desire to emulate; at other times as acts of defiance.

In the Zambezi Valley, both the negative and the positive aspects of this new consciousness manifest themselves. Colonial psychology has instilled an attitude (backed by legislation) that all the wild life and fish in the Valley were meant only for the white man. Local people were prohibited to hunt or to fish using the traditional methods. These means of traditional livelihood were criminalized. Harsh punishments were meted out to those caught 'poaching' (an invention of the white man, though when he does it, he is said to be engaged in 'sport'). Even the independent government has idolized the tourists who come to hunt and fish in the Valley because 'he brings in foreign exchange'. So the legal prohibition against hunting and traditional means of fishing continues to exist.

The people, however, no longer accept this colonial dispensation. Therefore they fish secretly, using traditional methods, and hunt animals at night. If caught they become criminals by law, which means people resort to 'criminal' activities to survive. They are made to feel guilty for simply wanting to survive. Public guilt, however, is in conflict with private morality. The whole psychology, the whole being, is in revolt. However, this act of subversion (which is the same thing as self-reliance) is for the minority who dare to defy the law. For the bulk of the people it is easier, and safer too, to simply become passive recipients of 'hand-outs' from Western NGOs, who call them 'lazy', and who by their act of 'charity' even further depress the spirit and dignity of the people. But for the daring few, it is time to resist. It is time to reclaim control over the lost resources and to rediscover old knowledge.

Thus a new spirit seems to be awakening the people (some of them) of the Dande Valley. It is still in the fringes of society, but it is there.

No new phenomenon emerges, however, without giving rise to its opposite. So the spirit of revolt in some arouses the opposite spirit of conservatism in others. Those in power – the 'modernizers' and the collaborators of the system – feel their interests threatened. They have the support of the state and of 'development' capital, which wants to come in the Valley to explore for oil and uranium, and to build luxury chalets for the tourists to come to hunt and fish. Development, the simple defiant folk of Dande Valley have discovered, is no simple economistic issue; it is, at its root, a question of power.

They have also discovered that when they threaten power at the local level its tentacles go all the way from the Valley to the big shots in power in government. That is as far as they have been able to see as yet. They have still to discover that the tentacles go beyond the seat of government in Harare to the centres of finance capital all the way to the World Bank which has told the government that all 'development' projects in the Valley must be 'bankable', and supported by feasibility studies done by 'recognized' consultants. The ecologically destructive work of the European Economic Community (EEC) and the UN Food and Agriculture Organization (FAO) 'development consultants' and 'agro-experts' in the Valley is, however, another story for another occasion.

Thusano Lefatsheng rediscovers indigenous veld products in the semi-arid areas of Botswana
Botswana with 600,372 sq.km. has two-thirds more land than Zimbabwe

with 390,580 sq.km., and yet only two per cent of its land is arable. Eighty per cent of the population of about one-and-a-half million live on the eastern strip along the railway line. The centre and south-west is covered by the desert steppe of the Kalahari basin, whilst the Okavango River basin in the north-east has a tropical climate.

The Tswana people are natural pastoralists. Before the advent of colonialism, every Tswana had cattle, and in the arable areas also oxen to plough the land. With colonialism came settlers (mainly *Afrikaner*), and mining corporations (mainly British). Foreign mining capital controlled all the diamonds and iron, copper and nickel deposits. The commercialization of beef production, especially its export to EEC countries, has led to land concentration mostly in the hands of the *Afrikaner* and a few rich African farmers. Over 60 per cent of the rural population are dispossessed of their lands and cattle. By the 1980s, more than 25 per cent of the population had gone to the cities in search of employment.

Naturally, a community which, in the precolonial times, knew how to survive in the natural economy of land and cattle, is now confronted by the sheer problem of survival. In the post-independence period, major land reform and the national repossession of the mineral wealth are precluded by the power and interest of the landowning oligarchy and international corporate capital. Therefore the dispossessed people in the rural areas have no choice but to use whatever resources the veld has to offer them in order to survive. Furthermore, in the strongly patriarchal society, women find themselves even further marginalized at the household level.

It is against this background that a group of women, faced with the perennial problem of food security, formed themselves into a non-governmental organization (NGO) – *Thusano Lefatsheng* – in 1984. They were always aware that veld products, specifically indigenous food and medicinal plants, were not only drought-resistant, but also underexploited. So *Thusano Lefatsheng* organized a small research farm called *Thusego*, and began testing veld crops, such as the Morula fruit, Morula kernels, Morama tubers and Morama beans. They also found that the Kalahari Devil's Claw, a well-known medicinal plant, could be cultivated and processed to provide a self-reliant means to treating some of the common ailments.

The *Thusano Lefatsheng* have found that these veld crops are well-adapted to the harsh and variable climate of Botswana, and therefore that the benefits they get from harvesting and marketing these crops in terms of food, employment and income are less vulnerable to inclement weather, and thus a more sustainable source of food security. They also found that since men were not interested in these 'inferior' veld crops, they could generate cash income for themselves without it being appropriated by their husbands. So around these indigenous crops, the group organized a range of activities, including production, harvesting, purchasing, processing and marketing.

The group has thus succeeded in providing significant employment opportunities for rural women through its harvesting and processing activities. By 1989, 1,500 harvesters and ten processors, mostly women from very poor areas, were involved in these activities. At the research farm they are now researching into the traditional methods for ecologically-sound harvesting techniques, and protection of wild vegetation through development of successful cultivation techniques. *Thusano Lefatsheng* has thus developed a profitable and sustainable farming system whereby traditional crops, new crops, medicinal plants, trees and livestock are integrated to provide a stable ecological system.

In the meantime, the 'catchment area' for beef for EEC countries continues to expand and claim the best lands and the best cattle. A handful of people get rich; the bulk get poorer. And the EEC countries bring in 'humanitarian' aid through their NGOs to bail out the poor 'and the lazy'. And they talk incessantly, unashamedly and without any sense of contradiction in regard to what they are doing, of 'sustainable development' when daily they undermine the efforts of the people to sustain themselves.

The women of VDF show the way in Zambia

The Village Development Foundation (VDF) is a development NGO based in Mungwi, 27 km. from the Provincial capital of Northern Province, Kasama, which is some 980 km. from Lusaka. It borders Tanzania in the east and Zaire in the west.

Before colonialism, the Northern Province (formerly Bembaland) was part of the Bemba Kingdom, which was a highly organized state, with a paramount chief who had divine and religious power over the whole of Bembaland, but no direct control over the junior chiefs. The junior chiefs and councillors ruled over a group of villages. In every village was a headman appointed by the chiefs. The Bemba practised shifting cultivation called '*chitemene*'. They also fished, hunted and engaged in blacksmithing and skilled handicrafts, as well as environmental conservation. People used practically every kind of material found in the area; wild life, skins, iron, ivory, forest wood, tree roots, clay and grass.

When colonialism 'integrated' the Bemba economy into the colonial economy, it not only killed the local economy, but also took away large numbers of young people to work in the copper mines. Added to this, the two World Wars saw large numbers of Bemba youth being taken to help the colonialists; very few returned after the wars. Agriculture was killed deliberately, with a view to creating labour availability for the copper mines – the colonialist's chief interest.

Now hard times have descended. Copper prices have plummeted. Young men are returning to the villages jobless. But they have no idea of how to do agricultural work. The 'culture of agriculture' was killed over two generations ago. The government farms out land to white farmers who come from Zimbabwe to grow wheat and feed-grass for cattle.

The women of VDF took the initiative. In the village of Ngulula they formed a 'Research Club' to analyse their situation, and to find practical ways to empower themselves. In April 1991, the Ngulula Club started to grow potatoes using compost manure which they made themselves. They managed to raise 8,000 Kwacha from the sale. They are making more compost, and growing more potatoes and have also learned how to secure seeds from the previous crop. This may seem surprising to those who do not know Zambia. Their grandmothers knew all these things in the past. But in Zambia all this past knowledge died during the colonial period when people simply used to wait for those who had gone to the copper mines to send money home with which to buy even imported potatoes.

Moreover, to counteract the commercial seed company who advise people to buy hybrid seeds, the Club is showing others how to save and test the seeds from the previous crop. 'We place them in water, those which sink are fertile while those which float are infertile.' The yields from the seeds tested in this manner are high, and there is no great variation in the quality of the potatoes. 'The percentage of germination is higher than the hybrid seeds, as we found in our research, and no greater amounts of seeds will be used at planting.' The Club advises that the seeds should not be stored for more than one year, for otherwise the germination will be poor. Also their research has shown that seeds stored mixed with ashes will greatly increase their life span.

The women can see light at the end of the tunnel. They say it is fun to do your own research, and they are becoming enthusiastic about doing things by themselves. Now the Ngulula Club has started to do research on soya beans. 'We shall report to you about this another day,' they say. The Club has opened an account with the Zambian National Commercial Bank – for the first time in the women's lives; they are still shy to approach the Bank to withdraw money and to write cheques. The VDF is helping them to gain self-confidence. 'Is this not what development is all about,' they ask, 'our ability to do things by ourselves?'

Ukwile and Msia in Tanzania practise Low External Input Agriculture (LEIA)
Ukwile and Msia are two villages in South-Western Tanzania, one in the District of Mbozi and the other in the Ileje District. At both villages people are engaged in Low External Input Agriculture (LEIA) – that is agricultural practices aimed at maximizing the use both of local knowledge of the people as well as local resources, and minimizing the use of external inputs.

People are experimenting with the use of *utupa (Trifosea Vogelli)*, a local tree known to the people as a pesticide in the control of pests in maize production and storage. People in the area have traditionally used leaves from this tree and made them into a liquid solution for application to the crops. The people are now experimenting with converting the leaves into a powder form since it is easier to store the pesticide in dust form. They also plant *acacia albida* (a local tree) and sun-hemp to fix nitrogen in the soil.

They make alternative implements, such as wooden wheel-barrows, and doors and windows for village houses and stores. They make tiles for roofing out of cement fortified with sisal, a widely grown crop in Tanzania, and these tiles cost 40 per cent less than corrugated iron sheets. Even the mould for the tiles is locally made. Tractors are replaced by ox-mechanization. There are trial and demonstration plots on which to carry out their experiments, and to demonstrate the use of these alternative methods of agricultural production to the population around the villages. They make improved grain storage models out of local materials and, where successful, people are encouraged to build similar ones in their homesteads. At Ileje, in addition to the above, they research into indigenous varieties of trees and bushes (for example, *nzigati*) whose knowledge, with the people, was dying out. Local *nganga* and older people are consulted to identify these trees, and knowledge resurrected for growing and propagating these indigenous varieties.

But the villagers are not having an easy time. Three kinds of forces are arraigned against them. One is the EEC and NGOs such as Global 2000, which are insisting on chemicalization of agriculture ('to increase yield'). These institutions distribute fertilizers to the farmers free of charge, in order to keep them within the 'chemical ambit'. Secondly, there is pressure from the better-off 'progressive' farmers who are wedded to High External Input Agriculture (HEIA). Finally, the results from LEIA are slow. LEIA needs time to show its cost-effectiveness and environmental compatibility. But people have been made to believe that 'development' means high yields and fast results. They are in a hurry, as if running to catch a train to some urgent destination.

There are thus active forces at work which find the 'alternative' model of development a threat to their interests. In other words, the struggle for alternative development strategies is not purely a struggle about 'appropriate technology'. There are active social forces (both local and international) at work to frustrate alternative and sustainable models of development.

It is a battle. The people have to be taught the 'real' science of agricultural production, say the LEIA practitioners of Ukwile and Msia. They hold workshops for the people around. Agriculture, they try to show, is not just about obtaining 'high yields'; it is also about conserving the soil. Soil consists of two distinct layers; a topsoil 'humus' that supports microbes and higher plant and animal life, and a surface layer of almost lifeless bedrock. The peasants nod in agreement, they know all this already. But, they ask, what is wrong in applying fertilizers to the soil?

Fertilizers, the LEIA practitioners explain, cause microbes to grow. These microbes feed on humus, breaking it down faster than they would without fertilizers, also enabling the crops to grow faster. But with no humus to hold the soil, it is washed away, and you have to use more and more fertilizers to give the soil artificial nutrients, and the cycle continues. The energy cost of a unit of food thus goes up. To be sure, you get more yield per acre of land, but more and more of it goes to the companies to pay for the fertilizers. So you may grow more and earn less. You are now working for the corporations. That is the immediate effect. But the more important long-term effect is that you have lost control over your soil. The land may belong to you, but that soil is no longer yours. By using chemical fertilizers, you have surrendered control over the soil to the corporations.

Also, they argue, chemical fertilizers contribute to the effects of drought. Because they suck out the natural nutrients from the soil, chemical fertilizers parch the soil of its moisture. That is the reason why when you use these fertilizers, you must also use more water. Therefore, in times of drought its effects are more damaging than it would have been had you avoided chemical fertilizers in the first place.

Thus, the contradictions of 'sustainable development' play out their eternal war dance on the soil of Africa, with the corporations wearing their macabre mask of fertilizers and pesticides pushing people to 'hurry, hurry, hurry' to some dubious destination called 'development', and the ordinary people (the more enlightened among them) urging the rest to pause and reflect on what they are doing and where they think they are going.

Western doublespeak on 'sustainable development'

The story of the elephant

The Western countries' ban imposed on the export of ivory from Africa has fuelled a fierce debate in Southern Africa on what 'sustainable development' is all about. The ban was initially recommended by the London-based Ivory Trade Review Group (ITRG), which claims to be acting for IUCN's African Elephant and Rhino Specialist Group. The group recommended banning the ivory trade to counter declines in elephant populations in Africa caused by heavy poaching. This was subsequently endorsed by both Worldwide Fund for Nature (WWF) and the International Union for Conservation of Nature (IUCN).

The world ivory trade is regulated by the Convention on International Trade in Endangered Species (Cites). Under Cites trade in animals and animal products is controlled depending on the degree of threat to the survival of the species concerned. Those listed under Appendix I are species on the 'brink of extinction' and trade in their products is totally prohibited; Appendix II lists animals which can be traded under stringent controls; and animals under Appendix III are endangered in some countries and not in others.

Until 1989, that is until ITRG's recommendation, elephants were under Appendix II. At a Cites meeting in Tokyo in March 1992, Zimbabwe and other Southern African countries tried, unsuccessfully, to prevent elephants being shifted from Appendix II to Appendix I. The effect is that the Southern African countries can now no longer trade in ivory because the elephant is defined as on the 'brink of extinction'.

The effects of this ban are immediately felt in Southern Africa. In the Kariba District of Zimbabwe alone, there is an estimated population of 2,500 elephants, growing at a rate of five per cent per annum. They are prodigious herbivores, devastating acres of woodlands and pillaging neighbouring farmlands belonging to poor African farmers who are already having a hard time surviving.

So the Nyaminyami Wildlife Management Trust has a programme for managing the elephants, among other animals. They have decided to put two per cent of the herd (54, in 1989) to productive use, half for an international safari quota, and the other half (including some rogue elephants) for a cropping quota. The meat (60 tons) goes to feed the population, the trophies bring in an income of US$100,000, and the ivory is left to be sold on the market – but, now, where?

'Most of the world's "developed" countries have no idea of the meaning of "sustainable" and instead get hysterical about whales, seals, rhinos and elephants,' says Simon Metcalfe, Interim General Manager of the Nyaminyami Wildlife Management Trust. 'Zimbabwe long ago learnt the difference between a windfall and a sustainable return from biological capital we live on. We are setting an example in elephant management and should not be steered off course by failures in East Africa' (*Financial Gazette*, Harare, 21 July 1989).

Indeed, the ban on ivory was triggered by IRTG based on the East African experience, and without consultation with the governments in Southern Africa. Now the total ban imposed at the Cites meeting in March 1992 threatens to destabilize the controlled management of ivory trade. Legal ivory was fetching a price of Z$350 a kilo at local auctions; now, in the illegal market, some say the price has more than doubled.

Once again, there is a conflict between public guilt and private morality, this time at international and national levels. At the international level, the sale of ivory is criminalized by an unthinking (and hysterical) largely Western public opinion. At the national level, sustainable development, for both ecological and economic reasons, demands that Zimbabwe occasionally culls its overpopulated herd of elephants, secures meat for the population, and markets the ivory for sale to help defray the cost of conserving wildlife.

It takes annually around US$200 per sq.km. of territory to protect elephants. With five million sq.kms. of elephant territory in Africa, it costs US$1 billion to protect them 'for posterity' – to use the Brundtlandian phrase. Where this money is to come from is a question neither Cites nor UNCED in Brazil bothered to put on their Western-dominated agenda.

The story of the ostrich and the impala

Whilst nobody in Europe wants to eat elephant meat, they have suddenly become gluttons for ostrich meat. Ostrich exports fetch enormous prices in Europe. At the same time, tourists from Europe (even ordinary tourists) are beginning to get a kick out of hunting impalas and warthogs in Africa. And so the commercial farmers in Zimbabwe (mostly white) are turning cattle ranches into ostrich farms or game ranches for hunting.

Speaking at a World Bank workshop on Wildlife Resource Management in Harare in September 1989, Robinson Gapare, Chairman of the Zimbabwe Communal Farmers Association, said: 'In the eyes of the peasant farmer, who is terribly hungry for land, it is senseless to set aside prime land for wildlife production.' He said that most of the revenue generated from wild life is spent on luxury services and none is ploughed back into agriculture.

> Today . . . communal farmers in marginal areas face everyday risks of being shot, punished, ridiculed and blamed for the extinction of wildlife population because of their traditional subsistence hunting. In reality, it is the international demand for exotic wildlife products, ensured on lucrative illegal trade . . . rather than subsistence hunting, (that) has been the root cause of the dwindling populations (of wildlife). (*Financial Gazette*, 29 September 1989)

This is happening at a time when it is general knowledge that the semi-arid lands into which the African population was herded during the colonial period do not have the 'carrying capacity'. Because of this, there is an environmental catastrophe that the European mind cannot even begin to imagine. Rivers that only a few years ago were teeming with hippos and crocodiles are now completely dry. In some rural areas up to 90 per cent of the population engage in gold-panning just to survive, causing massive river siltation. The fragile ecology is weathered and broken through overuse of the soil and through deforestation. And yet every effort to try to solve the land question in Zimbabwe brings shouts from the World Bank and the EEC in defence of 'private property'.

Alternative strategies of development

AZTREC* invokes the Spirit Medium for ecological stewardship

Every culture has its own cosmology. The 'culture of modernist development' (if it is right to call it that) has a uni-generational cosmology. Only the present generation matters; the dead are interred with their bones, and the unborn are irrelevant. It took the Brundtland Commission in 1987 to tell the present generation to think of 'sustainable' development in terms of leaving behind a habitable world for posterity.

Furthermore, in the modernist cosmology, nature is just a 'thing' to exploit. You can cut down forests, churn the soil upside down to extract gold and asbestos from it, divert rivers for commercial irrigation, and lop off mountain tops to build TV antennae and golf courses. You can hunt down wild life for their trophies and push them into 'game' parks, and you can chemicalize the soil for the sake of 'high yields', thus exterminating the rich fauna, birds, reptiles and insects and disturb their natural eco-rhythm. When you have thus carried out your eco-carnage, you can 'quick-fix' the damage. You can add chemical fertilizers to the soil whose natural humus you have already killed. You can grow eucalyptus trees where forests have been cleared in the name of maximizing the production of biomass in the quickest possible time whilst ignoring its effects on ground water. You can stop the further destruction of the ozone layer by using 'ozone friendly' refrigerators and hairsprays. And so on.

In the (traditional) African religion on the other hand, the dead, the living and the unborn are all relevant to the present. The spirits of the dead continue to take part in the lives of the present generation and inhabit the unborn. As for nature, it is not set apart from humanity, it is part of humanity. The spirits live in trees and in mountains; you cannot just chop down any tree you fancy, or desecrate sacred mountains.

One of the most enduring features of Shona culture in Zimbabwe is the institution of the spirit mediums, through which ancestors, when they feel the need to communicate with the living, decide to speak. When a medium, a man or a woman, is possessed of the ancestral spirit, they say *svikiro inobatwa nemidzimu*. The *midzimu* (ancestral spirit) then speaks through his or her medium. Thus it was that the *chimurenga* (liberation war) that the people of Zimbabwe fought against the illegal regime of Smith was fought not only by the living but also by the spirits of the dead. The most important of these were the ancestral spirits of Nehanda and Kaguvi, who guided the nationalist struggle, and whose statues now stand in the Zimbabwe Parliament.

*The Association of Zimbabwe Traditional Ecologists

AZTREC, or the Association of Zimbabwe Traditional Ecologists, was founded, among others, by one such spirit medium, Lydia Chabata. The Association operates from Masvingo, some 300 km. south of Harare. The mainly ecological activities of the Association are the protection of the sacred mountains (especially the High God cult of the Matopo Hills, which Rhodes had profanely desecrated), preservation of *Rambakutemwa (sacred forests where spirits reside)*, the growing of indigenous trees (including fruit trees), and the protection of water resources, marshlands and wild life. Over the last two years, AZTREC has planted 700,000 seedlings of indigenous trees (such as baobab, mahogany, *muzeze, mukamba, muchecheni* and *mutondo*, as well as fruit trees such as oranges, mangoes, pawpaws and avocados), and distributed these to widely scattered rural communities.

Development, Chabata says, means empowerment of the people. But you cannot do so without restoring the wholeness of the community, and integrating the life of the people with their natural environment. In a situation where this environment has been either destroyed or profaned because of decades of colonial rule, you have to help restore it so that the spirits of the ancestors are at peace. Otherwise there can be no development. Development does not come with Western experts, nor does it come with foreign science and technology. These must be created by the people in the process of living in harmony with nature. This means interpreting traditional responsibility (stewardship) towards nature and ancestral spirits in the present context, and the mobilization of rural communities to develop self-reliant and self-resourced projects.

African intellectuals chart a new path for Africa

AAPS, or the African Association of Political Science, is a pan-African NGO founded by activist African scholars and social scientists at the University of Dar es Salaam in 1973. It was formed to challenge the dominant Western paradigms for analysing African and Third World societies, as well as the relations between the North and the South. It seeks to promote debate and discussion on issues of concern to African 'scholar-activists', and to promote solidarity with forces of liberation and democracy. At its 8th bi-annual conference held in Cairo in January 1990, it issued a statement – called the Cairo Statement – on the 'African Crisis'. We quote in *extenso* from this document. After having described the root causes of the crisis in Africa, the Statement goes on to offer a new vision for Africa:

> All these developments go to show that the present state of affairs existing on the continent cannot be sustained. Serious efforts must be made by all the African people to address this horrible situation. Fundamental changes are called for which alone can restore the continent's viability as a community. The large gap of confidence which

exists between the people and the leaders can only be removed if the continent's leadership becomes wholly accountable to its people. This is the crux of the matter. Accountability implies a new democratic system and style of life and method of political organisation. These have to be articulated in accordance with the demands of the people.

New economic programmes based on the people's own aspirations and needs have to be arrived at after a democratic restructuring based on the people's right to self-determination and independence. External pressures on the continent's resources which ignore the well-being of the people must be resisted. Africa must export its resources and import goods and services only for its needs and on a balance of net return to itself. No society can sustain itself without a major crisis if it operates on the principle of a net outflow of its resources. The present mega-crisis which the continent faces is in fact a reflection of this net outflow of resources which has been going on over the last 500 years of plunder and of our own role in allowing this plunder and exploitation to continue. This has to stop if Africa is to rediscover herself and find her new role as an equal and respected partner in the international community of peoples.

We call upon all members of the AAPS and all the continent's organisations to dedicate themselves to the task of the continent's revival and rediscovery in conditions of extreme marginalisation which currently prevail. We must not view the current crisis negatively, but also as presenting us with the opportunity to change course and move the continent on its own feet in a world of rapid change and inter-dependence. African scholars and activists are called upon to link themselves with the people's organisations at the grass-root and assist their survival efforts in order to find solutions with them.

No detached academic position will be adequate to cover-up for the lack of our social and political commitment. A truly new revolutionary political movement, based on *revolutionary pan-Africanism* will only arise out of people's own efforts at reorganisation and self-administration. African intellectuals have to find their role in this endeavour and not in a separate academic freedom for themselves. We must claim academic freedom as part and parcel of the general struggle for democracy and freedom for all the people.

In conditions of generalised dismemberment of civil society, new social and political values will only arise out of people's struggles. We must all join these struggles and help to create these new values for all of us and for the world's peoples in a new revolutionary way. The destiny of the African continent is in our hands, and instead of complaining about Africa being 'marginalised' by the developments of Eastern Europe, we must seize the opportunity which these developments and the generalised crisis on the continent presents us to change course and be ourselves with bravery. We must begin to emphasize our responsibility to ourselves and in this way unite to resist external and internal pressures which oppress our continent. Without such committed responsibility to ourselves, we cannot be truly liberated. But with such a determination, we can for a start say: AFRICA SHALL BE FREE AND SELF-DETERMINING.

Conclusions: resistance is today the main form of 'sustainable development'

As stated in the introduction, we shall try to analyse the foregoing rather disjointed accounts, but without claiming to fully comprehend their significance. The material was not drawn from books and secondary sources as in an academic exercise, but as a practitioner of 'development' we have drawn these from the living experiences of people. And therefore, being too close to events in the cases and episodes described above, we could be prone to exaggerated subjective assessments of their import which more objective minds might discount.

To start with, we think we are witnessing a renewed phenomenon of rejection and resistance in Africa. Historically, it has its precedent in the time when Africans were resisting colonial imposition some 80 to 100 years ago, and later, in the 1960s, at the time of the movement for political independence. When the first historical resistance had collapsed (finally around 1920s), Africa had settled down to adapting to the new situation forced upon it. Later, the independence movement, sparked off after the Second World War, culminated in the political independence of many African states. Ideologically, however, these states were divided between the 'radicals', led by Kwame Nkrumah, who were definitely in the rejection or resistance mould, and 'moderates' who were quite happy securing political independence whilst accepting to remain within the neo-colonial ambit of the West.

The latter part of the 1960s, the decade of the 1970s and the first part of 1980s were two 'lost decades' for Africa, and indeed for most of the Third World. Illusions of development built on two alternative models were shattered. The first model, based on growth through Western capital aid, only served to further deepen these countries' dependence on the West and to increase their impoverishment; Africa was thoroughly exploited by the USA, Japan and the EC countries. The second model, based on (or rather caricatured after) the bureaucratic socialist model of the Soviet Union, resulted in brutally authoritarian regimes with an even worse economic performance than those states wedded to the Western capitalist system. At the same time, the Cold War took a serious toll on African lives and African economies, as the situation in Mozambique continues to bear its horrid testimony to this day.

With the end of the Cold War, but especially because of the collapse of the Socialist world as we knew it, a new era has begun worldwide. Capitalism at present holds unchallenged monopoly; it is also at the same time thoroughly discredited as a world system. The benefits of the system (such as they are) have definitely not 'trickled down' to two-thirds of humanity. Indeed, their fate is worse than ever before. Ecologically, the system has almost reached its nadir. The whole notion of 'development' is open to serious question as humanity seems to move inexorably towards its own demise through ecocide. And the 'war system' is still intact, despite the end of the Cold War. America displayed calculated callousness in its handling of the Gulf crisis in utter disregard of wiser counsels for peace and justice. Eastern Europe is now a cauldron of seemingly insane violence as also are parts of Africa, Asia and Latin America.

In all this, is there then, perhaps, a glimmer of hope in the stories we have recounted showing the renewed spirit of resistance that seems to be arising from within the womb of pain? Long lost are the illusions of yesterday. Long lost also are the promises of the politicians, especially those in the Third World. A new spirit, we think, is arising from within the hearts of the downtrodden who now seek remedies out of their own resources, meagre as they are. The stories we have recounted may have little significance now, but they may contain a germ of the future: the story of women in the Dande Valley in Zimbabwe and of *Thusano Lefatsheng* in Botswana digging into their historical past to rediscover the knowledge of ancient food systems; of men in Dande Valley, defying authority to hunt at night and fish using the traditional methods; of the women in VDF in Zambia forming their own club to undertake practical research into the growing of potatoes and soya beans using local compost; of the peasants in the village of Ukwile and Msia in Tanzania fighting the EC and others against great odds to prove the sustainability of LEIA; of Lydia Chabata in AZTREC invoking the spirit of her ancestors to resurrect the ancient African culture based on the unity between nature and humanity spanning across generations; of the new kind of African intellectuals who no longer pretend they have answers to problems but are prepared to sit with people at the grassroots and learn from them.

We don't know. What we are seeing is only perhaps what we so desperately want to see. The forces of reaction and obscurantism are certainly quite formidable. The tendency to violence in practically every part of the world is only too painfully manifest. The callousness with which the powerful countries of the West treat the less powerful Third World countries is only too apparent. The blindness to the impending doom of the environment as a result of the excessive greed of barely 20 per cent of the world's population is acknowledged sadly by only a thin layer of eco-conscious humanity.

Above all, every good initiative on the part of the people seems to lend itself to manipulation by the existing global economic and political power structures. Thus, Western governments are working out rules to tie 'development aid' to environmental conditionalities, the so-called 'greening of aid'; this to be reinforced by the 'greening of trade' through unilateral trade embargoes to impose an environmental regime on the South; and the 'greening of debt' through debt-nature swapping tricks. All these amount to packaging aid, trade and debt into international conventions in order to enforce environmental discipline on the South. This will result in an erosion of the South's sovereignty over its national resources, its right to determine the use and conservation of these resources, and a corresponding increase in the control over them by the transnational corporations of industrialized countries.

All this notwithstanding, we reserve the right to be optimistic, to see the beginnings of mass resistance, worldwide, against oppression and injustice. True development is as a result of the struggles of the people from the ground, not something that can be 'delivered' to the people by policy-makers from on top. Struggle necessarily implies opposition, even confrontation. Resistance, therefore, is the main form of sustainable development today.

Acknowledgements: Whatever insights there are in this article, I owe to the many people in the various communities cited here who talked with me about their efforts. In addition, I would specifically like to thank my colleagues Ludwig Chizarura, Nick Dziva, Mary O. Chelvam, Ephraim Murendo, Paul Nyathi, Joshua Gwiitira and Ruvimbo Mujeni in Zimbabwe; Anthony Chishimba, Bandawe Banda and Alex Kwandu in Zambia; Gottfried Mwamanga and N. K. Murusuri in Tanzania: Florrie de Pater and David Sogge in the Netherlands; and the many comrades in the African Association of Political Science from all of whom I have learnt much.

16. No Nature Without Social Justice: A Plea For Cultural and Ecological Pluralism in India

Smitu Kothari and Pramod Parajuli

I wholeheartedly detest this mad desire to destroy distance and time, to increase animal appetites and go to the ends of the earth in search of their satisfaction. If modern civilisation stands for all this, and I have understood it to do so, I call it Satanic.
Mahatma Gandhi

If we talk only of singular Man and singular Nature, we can compose a general history, but at the cost of excluding the real and altering social relations. Indeed, the idea of nature contains an extraordinary amount of human history.
Raymond Williams

When any environmental problem is probed to its origin, it reveals an inescapable truth – that the real root cause is to be found in how men interact with each other; that the debt to nature ... cannot be paid person by person, in recycled bottles or ecologically sound habits, but in the ancient coin of social justice.
Barry Commoner

Why are struggles for cultural and ecological identity and autonomy being asserted militantly at a time when the wind of democracy is blowing all over the globe? These struggles, we argue, are not just utilizing democracy with a criticial edge; they are redefining it. We find these movements to be 'the most subversive field of social struggle' for democracy (Mouffe 1988). Ecological justice is the driving force in these struggles because they interrogate the distributional aspect of development as well as argue for a new ecological praxis.

The concept of ecological justice involves at least three shifts in the standard environmental narrative as it exists today. First, there has to be a shift from the assumption of 'poverty as the largest pollutant' to the achievement of social justice as the prerequisite to ecological sustainability.

Second, the primary focus of political praxis has to shift from the state to communities. Third, the concept of democracy has to be radically reconstructed to accommodate these survival, identity, and ecological claims from the grassroots. Through the notion of ecological justice, we thus redefine conventional political economy in ecological terms and ecology in political economic terms.

The Indian context

The issue of ecological and cultural pluralism looms large in the complex civilizational mosaic of India. India is endowed with one of the most diverse ecosystems of the planet. This diversity ranges from the temperate and subtemperate mountainous regions of the Himalayas to the deciduous and tropical hill ranges of the Aravalli in Western India to the Eastern and Western Ghats; from the cold deserts of Ladakh to the searing deserts of Gujarat and Rajasthan; from the high rainfall areas of the North-East to areas fed by grand rivers like the Narmada and the Ganga which have nurtured among the most fertile soils of the world; from the landlocked regions of central India to the thousands of islands in the Arabian Sea and the Indian Ocean.

The diversity of ecosystems has nurtured a staggering complexity of cultural systems that have evolved diverse ways of human–nature interactions, bringing into being remarkable traditions of socio-ecological wisdom. Ecologically speaking, people in each eco-cultural region have evolved their own systems of describing and interacting with the physical and natural world. In the past few decades, there has been a wider revival in appreciating and understanding the range and diversity of these systems. Madhav Gadgil, for instance, has documented systems of ecological 'prudence' among different groups of people. An ecologically prudent community 'exercises restraint in the exploitation of natural resources such that the yields realized from any resource are substantially increased in the long run even though restraint implies forgoing some benefit at the present (Gadgil 1985:1909).

The examples of the codes, rituals and practices that governed the relationship with the natural world are numerous. For example, tribals in the North-East and central India while practising shifting cultivation evolved sophisticated regulations for maintaining sacred groves. In other parts of the country, settled agricultural communities have restricted quotas of weekly harvest from communal groves. The *Orans* of Rajasthan impose restrictions on the kinds of metal instruments to be used in cutting wood from communal forests, while the *Phasepardhis* of Maharashtra have a complex system of sanctions in their relationship with natural systems. For instance, hunting a pregnant doe is forbidden.

These cultural systems also evolved remarkable institutions to withstand climatic stress. Where drought and epidemics led to drastic production failures, communities fell back on reserves of various forms (grains and livestock)(Shanmugaratnam 1989). Religious notions such as *Punya* (merit) and *Dharma* (righteousness) also led groups to sources and pathways for the benefit not just of local communities but also for visitors and travellers (Singh, 1991). Such ecological prudence was not limited to small communities but extended to watersheds and to regional networks. Minoti Kaul (1991) for example, shows how interdependent groups of pastoralists, nomads and agriculturalists used regional 'commons' in Punjab without degrading them.

We are not implying that these traditions of knowledge were/are perfect or in harmony among humans or between humans and the natural world. By invoking these diversities we do not intend to justify the discrimination and oppression that might be encoded within these systems. For example, such ecological prudence in the period of massive agrarian expansion in India during 800 to 1800 AD might have contributed to the rigid caste hierarchy which codified differential access to ecological resources. It is also true that the growing resource demands and political ambitions of the local chiefs and Rajas were often in conflict with forest dwellers and tribals (Grove 1990). Today, however, it is encouraging that cultural and ecological movements are increasingly conscious of addressing not just external but internal inequalities and discriminations. What we want to highlight here are debates and efforts on how to respect such immense cultural diversity in close relation to ecological diversity within the framework of democracy.

These ecological traditions were radically altered by resource exploitative regimes such as the British Empire from the late eighteenth century until India's Independence in 1947. The intensive resource-extractive British system not only compelled Indian farmers to reorient production to the priorities of Empire, it also heralded an urban-industrial sector (from the early nineteenth century onwards) which accelerated demands on rural and agrarian resources. Agricultural lands and commons were forcefully brought into private or state ownership and linked to the needs of national and global markets. In this process, ecological prudence, which was widely embedded in the reciprocity and complementarity between the users and defenders of environment, got a severe blow.[1] Much of the later controls imposed by the state were justified in the name of scientific resource management.

This process intensified after 1947. The post-Independence developmentalist state exacerbated the pressure on the natural systems of prudence and regulation. While the British could colonize other parts of the world to sustain industrial growth, India had no option but to colonize internally.

Thus, within India itself distinct peripheries were created to facilitate the regular supply of natural resources. In fact, in the early years, natural resources were sought in the name of nation-building. The elders in Jharkhand still narrate how Pandit Nehru, the late Prime Minister of India, would come to remote corners of Jharkhand and invoke nationalist sentiments in order for them to sacrifice their land, forest and rivers. These areas were labelled 'backward' and the local people were characterized as 'uncultivated' and 'underutilized' needing to be converted into 'human resources'. State subsidies were provided to 'develop' these areas. Major industrial establishments such as the Tata Iron and Steel Company, and big dams such as the Danodar Valley Corporation in the Jharkhand region, were built on such a sacrificial altar. Ecological and cultural democracy, as is being reasserted by the movements today, were thus subjugated within a developmentalist discourse bestowed with nationalist and progressivist metaphor.

It is the impacts and implications of this nationalist tryst that compels a fresh examination of the interface between nature, culture and democracy. In this chapter, we shall closely examine two specific movements to illustrate this: the ethno-regional and ecological movements in Jharkhand; and the movement to stop the dams on the Narmada river.

Cultural and ecological pluralism in a democracy: two case studies

Both the Narmada valley and Jharkhand are distinct ecological regions. Situated at an elevation of 500 to 1,000 metres above sea level, Jharkhand, in east-central India encompasses an unmistakable identity that separates it, geographically, ethnically and culturally from the surrounding plains of northern Bihar and West Bengal. Jharkhand's name itself suggests an ecological identity (*Jhar*, meaning forest and *Khand*, meaning area). The Narmada, one of the most sacred rivers in India, is the longest west-flowing river. It originates at Amarkantak in the Maikal range and passes through several districts in the three states of Madhya Pradesh, Maharashtra and Gujarat. The Narmada basin has supported a remarkable array of cultural and ecological diversity. It covers an area of about 10,000 square kms with a total population of 21.78 million (1981 estimate).

Ethno-regional and ecological movements in Jharkhand

For the past century, the hilly terrain of Jharkhand has been the site of numerous local protests against state and private control and management of land, forest and water resources. Ecological movements, which have recently intensified, are expanding the scope and political relevance of the 50-year-old movement demanding greater regional autonomy in the form of a separate state within the Indian union, which will include 21 districts spread among the four states of Bihar (12 districts), West Bengal (three), Orissa (three) and Madhya Pradesh (three). These movements challenge the Indian state in a fundamental way. While the ethno-regional movement seeks political autonomy on the basis of regional 'under-development' and ethnic discrimination, the ecological movements challenge the monopoly of the state and private capitalist interests over the use and management of natural resources such as water, forest and land. We recognize that among these movements, there continues to be a wide range of perceptions regarding political and economic priorities for the region – for instance, the conception of the Jharkhand state itself. Among the most important challenges that the ethno-regional movement for Jharkhand faces is to infuse ecology as a central theme of social justice – a fact that a growing number of representatives of these movements recognize.

This seems obvious in Jharkhand because this region has the most economically deprived people despite being the richest in natural resources (JCC Manifesto 1987). Jharkhand is a region where capitalism realizes its cruel law – regional and spatial inequalities in order to continue the motion of capital (Soja 1989). Stretching 450 km from the Raniganj coalfields in West Bengal to the Sundargarh iron ore and manganese deposits in Orissa, this zone contains the bulk of India's basic, heavy and metallurgic industries (Saha 1986). The first mining operation in Jharkhand began as early as 1775 in Raniganj, just a decade after the British occupation. This was followed by three huge coalfields in Jharia, Bokaro and Karanpur in 1856. In 1907, India's largest iron and steel company was established in Jamshedpur, irreversibly transforming the economy and ecology of the region.

The pattern of industrial capitalism played out its predictable game as it transformed the ecological and cultural milieu of Jharkhand. This transformation followed the double mandate of capitalism: the commodification of Jharkhandi tribals as labourers; and their forests, minerals and rivers as resources. Both the natural wealth of Jharkhand as well as the labour of Jharkhandis were brought into the orbit of capitalist production. Jharkhand thus became an important arena for planned resource management during both the colonial and post-colonial periods. As Vandana Shiva (1992: 206–7) has pointed out, 'since nature needed to be developed by humans, people also had to be developed from their primitive backward states of embeddedness in nature. Nature's transformation into natural resources needed to go hand in hand with the transformation of culturally diverse people into skilled human resources.'

The 60 million tribal people of India have faced similar processes of uneven development. For almost two centuries now, they have suffered from decline in access to and control over productive natural resources – land, forests and water. This has caused the deterioration of their multiple relationships with the land and forest (Sengupta 1982; Singh 1985; Sharma 1990). The intermittent encroachment by 'plains people' which some call the 'plainsmen's burden' (Sinha 1987) and by the British state was given legal status with the introduction of legislation such as the Indian Forest Act of 1865 and with the imposition of the concept of private property. Such laws delegitimized most of the customary rights on land and forest. Moreover, such legislation effectively made the tribals criminals by declaring them intruders in their own habitats.

The extent of displacement caused by development best illustrates the burden borne by the tribals. Several studies indicate that since Independence, over 20 million people have been displaced for one reason or another (Kothari 1988). Tribals comprise half of those displaced making up no less than 15% of the whole tribal populace (Sharma 1990: 27). Fernandes and Thukral (1989: 80–81) estimate that the percentage of those displaced in different activities of development were as follows: dams and canals (71%), coal and other mines (11%), industries (6%), sanctuaries and parks (4%) and others (8%). Do not these facts suggest that there is a basic incompatibility between resource-intensive development and the realization of the oft-repeated promises of distributive justice?

From passive consent to active resistance

A continuous series of ecologically motivated resistance movements in the tribal belt of India provide the best answer to the above question. Even before Independence in 1947, tribal communities did not acquiesce quietly in the face of external intervention. There were protests and rebellions against such colonial forest laws as the Forest Act of 1876. While the newly emergent colonial science of forestry had begun to blame the agrarian system of forest dwellers for decline in forest coverage (Grove 1990), tribal peasants in India were waging struggles against state intervention in forest resources based on their own moral economy. Guha and Gadgil (1989) have aptly described this conflict as between the political economy of profit and the moral economy of provision.

The Jainti hill tribes revolted in 1744, the Bhils in 1846. The Naikads revolted in 1858. The Koya tribals revolted successively in 1862, 1879 and 1880. The rebellions in Bastar in 1876 and the Rampa rebellion in the Godavari district were just the first glimmer of the successive forest *Satyagrahas* against the Indian forest department after 1878 (Guha and Gadgil 1989; Grove 1990). In Jharkhand, the recorded history of resistance movements dates back to as early as 1600 AD. The well documented ones among them such as *Tika Manjhi* (1780), *The Kol revolt* (1831), the *Santal Hul* (1855) and *Birsa revolt* (1900) are only landmarks in a continuous genealogy of dissent in Jharkhand (Guha 1983).

The ecological intent in these agrarian struggles continues today. The new forest policies have increasingly restricted shifting cultivation of tribal people from their land as a result of debt transactions and development projects. The *Dhan Katti Andolan* (forcible harvesting movement) in Jharkhand during 1968–75 was a direct effort to tackle these problems. During this movement, Jharkhandis also regained state-controlled forest which gave rise to resistance to the planting of teak during 1978–80. The main slogan '*Teak is Bihar, Sal is Jharkhand*' captured the ecological content in the demand for political autonomy from Bihar. During the same period, the Naxalite movement, which was widespread in northern West Bengal and the Jharkhand belt, mobilized peasants with grievances against official agricultural and forest policies. The evolution of the Bhil movement around Dhulia and the Warli revolt of 1946–48 and 1963–71 in the Thane region in Maharashtra have had similar ecological roots: access over forest, reclamation of alienated tribal land and cancellation of illegal debts. Recently, widespread resistances against alienation of land for the purpose of big dams, parks and sanctuaries continue the same logic of resistance.

There have been numerous anthropological studies of the area, but rarely have these studies highlighted these movements as ecological; they were instead cast as 'millenarian' or of a peasant type (Singh 1985). Today, we can no longer deny how deeply they are ecological in intent and content. Their ecological character is becoming even clearer when we look at how resistance movements to large development projects have also been sharpening a critique of the current patterns of economic development. In a study of protest against big dams in Jharkhand, Parajuli (1990) observed at least three phases in resistance. If the 1950s and 1960s were a period of passive consent to development, in the 1970s, Jharkhandis became increasingly militant in their struggle for proper compensation. However, starting in the 1980s, Jharkhandis have transcended the demand for compensation and are protesting outright against these projects. The struggle against the construction of Subarnarekha Multi Purpose Project is a case in point. Here, people of the Kolhan area of Singhbhum have resolved not to let the dam be built.

Movements in the Narmada valley and in Jharkhand are also formulating alternative strategies by reviving and updating indigenous systems of irrigation and water use. For example, in the Kolhan area, people resisting the Subarnerekha dam are seeking alternatives to big dams by reviving check dams, ponds, wells and pits which were abundant in the past. Their estimate shows that the cost of irrigation per hectare by big dams is six times more than by the smaller schemes (Ghanshyam 1992: 27). And this does not even include the external costs of big dams such as displacement, submergence of agricultural lands and forests and the cost of post-facto impacts of these dams, such as waterlogging and salinization. Baba Amte (1990), in the same vein, argues for a moratorium on large dams and the implementation of ecologically sound land and water technologies.

These alternatives are not merely a revival of traditional technologies but involve the whole matrix of democracy, governance and participation. The issue then is not merely choosing between small or large technology but involves deeper questions such as: What is the resource for? How should it be used? Who decides? In the case of water, this critical discourse then also interrogates how the distribution of water decides what kind of agriculture to practise.

Struggle to stop the Narmada Dam

In many respects, the movement in the Narmada valley, representing a significant proportion of those who will be affected by the Sardar Sarovar Dam Project (SSP hereafter) on the Narmada river has emerged as one of the most unusual popular struggles in the post-Independence period in India. The SSP is part of the massive Narmada Valley Development Project that plans the building of 30 large and 3,000 medium and small dams on a single river. If ever completed, the entire Project would displace over two million people, besides threatening complex cultural and religious processes in the Narmada valley. The reservoir of SSP alone, will cover the thin strip of territory nearly 125 miles long and submerge 254 villages.

While there have been sporadic protests since 1979, a major sustained mobilization since 1986 has grown into a popular movement that opposes the SSP as well as other large dams on the river. A *class-benefit* analysis of the SSP clearly reveals who will benefit from the harnessed waters of the Narmada. The landless, the marginal peasants, the tribals and the bonded labourers will be displaced and if not displaced, will have to wait for surpluses that will trickle down to them. The dominant narrative supporting big dams repeats the dictum that 'some will have to bear the cost of development'. Any talk of a fundamental alternative is seen as a throwback to a 'primitive' past. Dams, to paraphrase Nehru, are, after all, 'the temples of modern India'. They are seen as monuments of progress, as essential elements for achieving self-sufficiency and 'national security'. Small wonder that the movement opposing it has been labelled as being not simply anti-development and anti-progress but also anti-national.

Questions posed by this movement are far reaching. As B. D. Sharma (1990: 29) has also cogently asked: is the social identity of a people negotiable? Can a tribal community be forced to stand on a precipice knowing that disorganization as a community and destitution for its members are its destiny? In short, can there be a barter between the survival needs of a majority and more facilities and greater comforts for some?

The Narmada valley is, like most major river valley systems, one of the hubs of the Indian civilization. In fact, the river is widely regarded as being more sacred than the Ganga. Both banks of the river are dotted with thousands of temples which provide the base for the *Parikrama*, one of the most remarkable rituals practised in the country. The ritual includes a full circumambulation of the river (Paranjype 1991). Archaeological finds place the first human habitations in the valley at 5500 BC. Several of the towns on the river date back to 1600 BC and have been referred to in India's ancient texts, the *Puranas*. A diverse group of people now inhabit the basin – they range from landed farmers, many of whom migrated from the west, to seven main tribal sub-groups, from petty traders to modern professionals. The basin contains a wide range of ecosystems. Large tracts of the basin contain extremely fertile black, cotton soils that have thrived with minimal human intervention (Kothari 1991; *Lokayan Bulletin* 1992; Kalpavriksh 1988). In fact, a special commission appointed by a British Governor-General in 1901 opposed any major irrigation project in these soils as any introduction of a canal 'would do more harm than good'.[2] In the central portion of the basin, we can find some of the finest tracts of old forests. For instance, the only stand of *anjan (Hardwickia binata)* left in India is in this valley, as well as some remarkable forests of *sal (Shorea robusta)* and bamboo. Timber contractors and other commercial demands have ravaged most of the remaining forests and exacerbated the perennial problem of water availability.

The river, however, has been the subject of numerous studies since the beginning of this century aimed at 'harnessing' its waters. The Narmada Valley Project is the culmination of these studies in that it is meant to be a comprehensive development plan for the entire river basin. It is the loss of cultural, social and ecological diversity that the project entails that has generated widespread opposition. It is this resistance that has become more closely co-ordinated and militant around one of the proposed dams, the SSP.

Politically, the movement shares, in part, the legacy of the earlier rebellions against the British – particularly in our tribal areas – in that it represents a sustained response to centralized state control over local economies as well as the imposition of 'remote' administrative and political processes on local societies. At another level, however, its politics is singularly different – it is not, for instance, a class movement, neither is it an effort to redraw the internal boundaries of the country to achieve a more politically autonomous region, such as in Jharkhand discussed above.

In that respect, it articulates, more sharply and pungently, the critical legacy of Mahatma Gandhi, of the *Chipko* and *Appiko* movements,[3] of the struggles all over the country that continue to challenge both the growing centralization and authoritarianism of the state and the extractive character of the dominant economic process – a process which not only erodes and destroys the subsistence economies of these areas, but also the diversity of their systems. This diversity should not be misunderstood as romanticization of a glorious past that – for those on the margins – never was. It is rather a plea to respect and understand and, if one is so inclined, to celebrate the multiple traditions which have evolved in the uniqueness of the sub-continent's complex history and geography. The movement is therefore representative of growing assertions of marginal populations for greater economic and political control over their lives.[4]

Given the seriousness of the situation in the Narmada valley and the continuation of resistance, the response from the intellectuals and elites of India has been below expectation (Kothari 1991; *Lokayan Bulletin* 1992). The basic reason for the apathy might be because the *Narmada Bachao Andolan* (Movement to Save the Narmada) poses a challenge to the very model of economic development which still continues to shape the ideas, images and dreams of these élites. Are they scared of the fact that in its very essence, the movement contests the incorporation of communities, cultures, knowledge systems and the eco-systems they inhabit into an instrumental vision of modernization?

Despite this widespread resistance, destructive developmental programmes are still being implemented both in the Narmada valley and in Jharkhand. However, the struggling people are asserting new values, new indicators of social justice, governance and are seeking new solutions. We will highlight two such trends: First, how in a recent gathering, tribal activists formulated a programme for 'Our rule in our villages'. Secondly, how ethnicity combined with ecology has emerged as a new alliance confronting the developmentalist nation-state.

Our rule in our village: from 'opportunity' to 'autonomy'

Like Jharkhand, other tribal areas are witnessing an unprecedented range of collective assertions and grassroots mobilization – stimulated in part by the continuing conflicts over natural resources. Within the past two years alone (1990–92), in addition to numerous actions at the local levels, there have been several significant events at the national level – events which have not only challenged the 'destructive development' that generates social and economic insecurities but also the threats that this poses to tribals' social cohesion and identity. Both tribal and non-tribal groups have participated in these collective assertions, and have been seeking not only greater political autonomy but also control over productive natural resources that are the basis of their lives. In many cases, they are demanding a redefinition of the internal boundaries that were drawn on a linguistic basis in the years following Independence in 1947 – arguing that these boundaries discriminate and divide communities which belong to a common cultural and ecological zone.

For example, on 25 December 1990, over 400 representatives of nearly 100 tribal movements and groups, including those from Jharkhand and other areas of middle India, converged in New Delhi, the capital city of India. They had two goals: to speak to the President of India and announce before him a programme of collective action in response to continuing systemic and systematic violations of their constitutional rights; and secondly, to highlight this situation and their resolve before the country. Arguing that their plight called into question the very meaning of freedom, of equity, of participation and of progress, they announced a comprehensive programme towards establishing 'our rule in our villages' (Kothari 1990: 2).

What fascinates us is how such statements directly intervene in the discursive arena of development, democracy and governance. This crucial action shows a shift from the 'realm of opportunity' to the 'realm of autonomy'. We emphasize this shift from 'opportunity' to 'autonomy' because this expresses their acute realization that the nation-state was no longer either the guardian against local exploiters, or the liberator from subjugation, 'underdevelopment' and 'backwardness'. On the contrary, they found the state to be a cause of their insubordination, exploitation and deprivation (Kothari 1988). Whilst challenging the very nature of development itself, these movements are no longer pressing for a greater share in the pie of national development but for greater autonomy. It is true that the line between 'opportunity' and 'autonomy' is very thin and does criss-cross in multiple ways. Although claims to autonomy are still primarily constructed within the paradigm of the state (not the Indian state but state nonetheless), they have to be taken seriously because such claims contest the developmentalist nation-state as the guardian of subaltern groups.

Such contestation has challenged electoral democracy's ability to provide a resolution to ecological conflicts. Formal processes of representation (electoral politics) have threatened social cohesion and unity, as individuals in the communities have been compelled to align themselves with contending political parties. We need to reconsider the concept of majority and minority and re-demarcate communities in terms of ecological bio-regions, cultural boundaries and access and control over productive resources.

The modern nation-state inscribes its domination in the very constitution of the territorial and cultural domain of its subject citizens (Poulantzas

1980). The Jharkhand region, for example, is a product of the arbitrary creation of state boundaries in British India. The states of West Bengal, Bihar and Orissa are themselves very new. Bihar became a state only after 1912, when it was separated from the Bengal Presidency. Orissa became separated from Bihar after 1930. As officials redrew boundaries in the twentieth century, they deliberately erased the unique political and cultural character of Jharkhand by lumping most of Jharkhand within Bihar state and the remainder within the states of Orissa, West Bengal and Madhya Pradesh.

Electoral constituencies within Jharkhand and Narmada valley are divided among different states, governed by different political parties. For example, in the past two parliamentary elections, the people of the Narmada valley have voted for politicians (belonging to one party) who supported their stand. However, after elections, these politicians have fallen prey to the dictates of their party high command as it does not want to alienate its electoral base in the areas that are to receive the benefits of the project (in Gujarat state).[5]

These processes have generated tremendous frustration, and the resisting people have taken alternative stands. On the one hand, people in the movement have asserted greater autonomy from centralized governance, arguing that their livelihood and lives themselves are critically dependent on the productivity of the local resource base and that they must have primary control over those resources. To this end, they have launched a comprehensive programme of non-cooperation with governmental officials. Secondly, a significant local debate has been initiated that is primarily concerned with class and governance issues.

What are the alternatives to divisive representative democracy? We posit 'community' as a possible alternative arena of political praxis. Because as Partha Chatterjee (1990) has argued, while both the state and civil-social institutions have been enveloped within the narrative of capital, community continues to lead a subterranean, potentially subversive life within it. Communities still have eminent possibilities of being the site of resistance to capitalist recolonization.

Mahatma Gandhi's anti-colonial discourse created such a counter-hegemony by resurrecting the community beyond the civil society/state nexus. The Gandhian discourse shows deep ecological currents. His critique and the contemporary ecological critique converge because the logic of self-reliance is the logic of place, people and resources bound into locally sustaining ecological systems (Chowdhary 1989).[6] Ramchandra Guha (1990) has accurately characterized the deeply ecological and deliberately political agrarian environmentalism of Gandhiji. The political programme of Gandhian agrarianism was 'to resist the onslaught of commercialism and industrialism where they have not yet made inroads, and where they have, to resolutely turn one's back on modern society and go back to the land' (Guha 1990: 434).

Thus we argue for greater autonomy for each community. At the same time, we also see the necessity for building linkages among communities, watersheds, bio-regions and nations. We cannot construct ecological and cultural pluralism within the framework of a homogeneous national community. We need a framework in which each community can exercise enough autonomy to defend its internal solidarity and find some common definition of mutual rights, responsibilities and obligations. For example, a community which has access to forest but lacks access to water sources might create an alliance with an adjoining community for mutual sharing. Similarly, a community at one end of the watershed might have strategic alliance with the communities at the other end of the watershed. In such mutual recognition of identities, all communities can realize themselves.

Ethnicity and ecology: an emerging alliance?

Contrary to the conventional wisdom of isolation, ethnicities do relate to larger society in inherently conflictual ways. They are not only concerned with distributional politics but also with qualitative issues – issues of identity, ideology, and so on. An ecological perspective best highlights this proposition, because ethnicity is constituted and reconstituted in contemporary times through its uneasy interaction with the developmentalist nation-state. Ecology is central to this interface. Regrettably, however, most of the prevailing nationalist as well as colonialist discourses on Jharkhandi ethnicity do not capture this dynamic.

On the other hand, the tribals and peasants of various castes involved in the Jharkhandi and Narmada valley movements have broken rigid caste/tribe barriers and facilitated new kinds of alliances, which we argue are based on ecological identity. In fact, these alliances are giving a fresh social content and ideological body to ecology. And this redefinition is giving a new life-force to ethnicity as a historical agent of the struggle for social justice. For example, a Jharkhandi now is defined not in terms of tribal identity alone but in terms of those who share common territory and a common history of exploitation by the *dikus*.[7] Thus, besides tribal groups, *sadans* (non-tribals but original to Jharkhand) who comprise at least 55% of the population are considered Jharkhandi. Only those 10–15% who have migrated from outside and are in exploitative relations with native Jharkhandis are considered non-Jharkhandis (JCC Manifesto 1987). A new Jharkhandi identity is in the making by revitalizing cultural rituals (for example, *Sarhul, Soharae*), by observing such rituals collectively and by mobilizing people in the protection of the commons, pastures and *Sarnas*.

Remarkable new alliances are also emerging between historically conflicting groups in the Narmada valley. Tribes who were in subservient relationships with landed farmers have for several years now been marching together in their opposition to the dam. While the dam became the 'primary contradiction', debates have been sustained among the various communities to find ways of reducing social inequities. Undoubtedly, some scepticism remains among tribal populations, and the years to come will show the extent to which justice can be realized. At the moment, however, an at times uneasy, and at other times comradely, peace prevails.[8]

This new alliance cross-cutting tribal and caste identity subverts the colonial and nationalist categories and creates an ecological terrain of struggle. Jharkhand was constructed and sought to be 'developed' as a tribal society by the Indian state both in colonial and post-colonial times. Today, via a new ecological identity, many Jharkhandis are posing identity and autonomy as the locus of struggle against integration into the national mainstream.

Conclusion: no nature without social justice

The two new trends mentioned above encourage us to look at the nature-society equation in a different light. Struggles in Jharkhand and the movements opposing the Narmada dams transcend the prevailing idea that development is inevitable and that conservation is the answer to ecological problems. Instead, these movements show that ecological problems are largely the product of uneven patterns of development both between and within more industrialized and less industrialized countries. Thus, we contend that ecological problems in India require political-ecological solutions. In short, *there will be little nature without justice and little justice without nature.*

We characterize these movements as ones for 'ecology' with justice'. Following the analysis of Hecht and Cockburn (1989) on the Amazon, Martinez-Alier (1990) on Latin America and Guha (1989) and Gadgil and Guha (1992) on India, we argue that in a highly stratified society like India, the appropriation of ecology and culture is a contested terrain between competing social actors: have *vs* have-nots, men *vs* women, city dwellers *vs* rural peasants, marginalized groups *vs* dominant groups. Since we take ecology, like culture, as always 'constituted by conflict', both are also the battle ground for competing hegemonies. Both dominant and subordinate groups try to articulate and exercise hegemony around culture and ecology.

It is thus pertinent to recognize, as does Martinez-Alier (1990), that some social struggles by poor people (and some national struggles by poor countries) can be understood as ecological struggles. This approach challenges dominant environmental narratives such as *Our Common Future*. This report points out that poverty is a cause of environmental degradation and proposes a growth plan so that poverty can be eradicated and environment can be saved (Sachs 1992).

The 'ecology with justice' perspective not only raises the issues of natural resource and labour exploitation by uneven capitalist development but a whole range of related concerns. While some ecological movements for justice defend traditional methods of resource use and diverse traditions of knowledge associated with it (for example, the Chipko movement in India and the rubber tappers' movement in Amazonia), others protest against mega projects like dams, road-building or industries that cause massive displacement and pollution.

Unlike the conservationists, who primarily propose national parks and sanctuaries as sites of protection and survival, ecological struggles combined with social justice defend 'social nature'. As Hecht and Cockburn (1989) have powerfully shown in the case of Amazonia, ecology is about land and people where the practice of justice restructures the concept of nature. The forest must be visualized as the dynamic outcome of human as well as biological history. For the people struggling for identity and autonomy, the territory of Jharkhand and Narmada valley are not merely biological entities – a repository of forest, minerals and water; they are cultural entities. Jharkhandis and those who protest in the Narmada valley could be called the 'true defenders' of their respective environments. Their position as defenders derives not from the concept of 'nature under threat' as does that of the conservationists, but rather from a relationship with the land, water and forest as the fundamental basis for 'their own elemental struggle to survive' (Haraway 1992: 310).

The struggles in Narmada valley and Jharkhand are symptomatic of this elemental struggle to survive. That is why the crude economic indicators of who gets what at what cost do not do justice to the depth of the issues involved here. Concern for survival is not also the end in itself. The salience of these movements is that the struggle for survival has grown into a struggle for regional autonomy as well as the formation of ethnic and gender identities. Increasingly, these 'cultures of dissent' are diverging into a common ecological identity. While the struggles find their initial impetus in the concrete problems of diminishing livelihood, they have evolved into searches for alternatives to the process of maldevelopment (Parajuli 1991, 1992). Should not this new multi-diversity become the basis for the New Ecology?

Devising alternatives to the pervasive knowledge empire of development is a challenging task indeed. The whole orientation of the development industry for the last 50 years has been to de-legitimate such possibilities. But when we recognize that resistance movements are themselves not a readymade product but a historical process, such tensions between the 'realm of opportunity' and that of 'autonomy' become the site of cultural critique and invention of possibilities.

Notes

1. Again, this is not to argue that all relationships between humans and the natural system were symbiotic and sustainable, or that wars, conflicts or greed did not erode or destroy sustainable relationships. However, the survival and continuing practice of a diversity of knowledge systems that are also ecologically prudent are an indication of the range and depth of traditions that had evolved in the Indian sub-continent.
2. First Irrigation Commission Report, 1901.
3. The Chipko movement evolved in the lower Himalayan belt of India, primarily on the Tehri-Garhwal region of the state of Uttar Pradesh. Spearheaded by women, the movement has resisted the extractive processes of economic development which had devastating effects on the livelihoods and lifestyles of the hill people. The Appiko movement, active in the Western Ghats of the southern state of Karnataka, opposes monoculture forestry and clear-felling of forests for industrial purposes.
4. It is indeed ironical that, today, many leading Gandhians in Gujarat are supporters of the dams on the river Narmada. For them, narrow political considerations have sidelined the very essence of the Gandhian legacy that we spoke of earlier.
5. Similarly, the demand for Jharkhand becomes dissipated when it is differentially mediated by the different parties that rule the four different states: the Communist Party of India (Marxist) in West Bengal; the centre-left Janata Dal (People's Party) in Bihar and Orissa; and the right-wing Bhartiya Janata Party (India People's Party) in Madhya Pradesh.
6. The complex debates on the state and civil society are beyond the scope of this chapter. Please see the longer version in *Capitalism, Nature, Socialism* (forthcoming 1993).
7. A common term in daily use in the Jharkhand area which means 'outsider'. This is usually equated with exploiters comprised of the troika of *zamindari* (landlords), *sarkari* (persons related to government) and *sahukari* (merchants).
8. For a sceptical view of the tensions between resident tribals and non-tribals of the Narmada valley, see Amita Baviskar (1991).

References

Agarwal, Bina (1991) *Engendering the Environmental Debate: lessons from the Indian subcontinent*, Michigan State University, Center for Advanced Study of International Development Distinguished Speaker Series No. 8.
Amte, Baba (1990) 'Narmada Project: case against and alternative perspective', *Economic and Political Weekly*, 21 April, pp. 811–18.

Baviskar, Amita (1991) 'The Researcher as Pilgrim', *Lokayan Bulletin*, Vol. 9, No. 3/4, pp. 91–7.

Beuchler, et al. (1992) *New World Order of the Global Community*, Boston, South End Press.

Chatterjee, Partha (1986) *Nationalist Thought in the Colonial World: a derivative discourse*, London, Zed Books.

—— (1990) 'A Response to Taylor's Modes of Civil Society', *Public Culture*, Vol. 3 No. 1, pp. 119–32.

Chowdhary, Kamla (1989) 'Poverty, Environment, Development', *Daedalus*, Winter, pp. 141–58.

Devanathan (1988) 'Factors in the Jharkhand Movement', *Economic and Political Weekly*, January, pp. 185–7.

Esteva, Gustavo (1992) 'Development', in Sachs (ed.) (1992a), pp. 6–25.

Fernandes, W. and E. G. Thukral (eds) (1989) *Development, Displacement and Rehabilitation*, New Delhi, Indian Social Institute.

Gadgil, Madhav (1985) 'Towards an Ecological History of India', *Economic and Political Weekly*, Special Number, pp. 1909–18.

Gadgil, Madhav and Ramchandra Guha (1992) *This Fissured Land: an ecological history of India*, New Delhi, Oxford University Press.

Ghanshyam (1992) 'Sustainable Development: going back to the roots', Madhupur, Bihar, Lok Jagriti Kendra (mimeo).

Grossberg, L. et al. (1992) *Cultural Studies*, New York, Routledge.

Grove, Richard (1990) 'Colonial Conservation, Ecological Hegemony and Popular Resistance: Towards a Global Synthesis', in John MacKenzie (ed.), *Imperialism and the Natural World*, Manchester, Manchester University Press, pp. 15–50.

Guha, Ranajit (1983) *Elementary Aspects of Peasant Insurgency in Colonial India*, New Delhi, Oxford University Press.

Guha, Ramachandra and Gadgil Madhav, 'State Forestry Policy and Social Conflict in British India', *Past and Present*, 1989, no. 123, pp. 141–77.

Guha, Ramchandra (1989) *The Unquiet Woods: a century of protest in the Indian Himalaya*, New Delhi and Berkeley.

—— (1990) 'Towards a Cross-Cultural Environmental Ethics', *Alternatives*, 15, pp. 431–47.

Haraway, Donna (1992) 'The Promises of Monsters: a regenerative politics for inappropriate/d others', in L. Grossberg et al. (1992), pp. 295–337.

Hecht, Susanna and Cockburn, Alexander (1989) *The Fate of the Forest: developers, destroyers and defenders of the Amazon*, New York, Harper Collins.

Jharkhand Co-ordination Committee (JCC) (1987) *Manifesto*, Ranchi.

Kalpavriksh, *The Narurada Valley Project: A Critique*. New Delhi, 1988.

Kaul, Minoti (1991) 'Self-organizing Communities: the institutional roots of colonial rural Punjab', paper presented at the Conference on Common Property, Collective Action and Ecology, Bangalore, 19–21 August.

Kothari, Rajni (1988) *Rethinking Development*, Delhi, Ajanta Publications.

Kothari, Smitu (1988) 'Vikas Aur Visthapan', *Udvasit*, Lokayan.

—— (1990) 'Redefining Tribal Politics', *Lokayan Bulletin*, Vol. 8, No. 6, pp. 1–7.

—— (1991) 'Cry Our Beloved Narmada', *India Magazine*, April.

Lokayan Bulletin (1990) special issue on tribal India, Vol. 8, No. 6.
―― (1991) special issue on the Narmada Dam, Vol. 9, No. 3/4.
MacKenzie, John (ed.) (1990) *Imperialism and the Natural World*, Manchester, Manchester University Press.
Martinez-Alier, Joan (1990) 'Ecology and the Poor: a neglected dimension of Latin American history', *Journal of Latin American Studies*, Vol. 23, No. 3, pp. 621–39.
Mouffe, Chantal (1988) 'Hegemony and New Political Subjects: toward a new concept of democracy', in Nelson and Grossberg (1988), pp. 89–104.
Nelson, C. and L. Grossberg (eds) (1988) *Marxism and the Interpretation of Cultures*, University of Illinois.
Parajuli, Pramod (1990) 'Grassroots Movements and Popular Education in Jharkhand India', PhD thesis, Stanford University.
―― (1991) 'Power and Knowledge in Development Discourse: new social movements and the state in India', *International Social Science Journal*, 127, pp. 173–90.
―― (1992) 'Communities of Resistance: space, identity and autonomy in the margins of the New Global Order', in Beuchler (1992).
Paranjype, Vijay (1991) 'Narmada Valley: the cultural ethos', *Lokayan Bulletin*, Vol. 9, No. 3/4, pp. 21–31.
Poulantzas, Nicos (1980) *State, Power, Socialism*, London, New Left Books, Verso edition.
Sachs, Wolfgang (ed.) (1992a) *The Development Dictionary: a guide to knowledge as power*, London, Zed Books.
―― (1992b) 'Environment' in Sachs (1992a), pp. 26–37.
Saha, Surajit Kumar (1986) 'Historical Premises of India's Tribal Problem', *Journal of Contemporary Asia*, Vol. 16, No. 3, pp. 294–321.
Sengupta, Nirmal (ed.) (1982) *Fourth World Dynamics. Jharkhand*, New Delhi, Authors Guild.
Sharma, B. D. (1990) 'Scheduled Castes and Tribes: a status report', *Lokayan Bulletin*, Vol. 8, No. 6, pp. 27–38.
Sheth, D. L. (1989) 'State, Nation and Ethnicity in the Third World', *Economic and Political Weekly*, Vol. 24, No. 12, pp. 619–26.
Shiva, Vandana (1988) *Staying Alive: women, ecology and development*, Delhi and London, Kali for Women and Zed Books.
―― (1992) 'Resources', in Wolfgang Sachs (1992a) pp. 206–18.
Singh, Chattrapati (1991) 'The Legal Economies of Natural Resource Management and Sustainable Development'. Paper presented at the Conference on Common Property, Collective Action and Ecology, Bangalore, 19–21 August.
Singh, Kumar Suresh (1985) *Tribal Society in India*, New Delhi, Manohar.
Sinha, Arun (1987) 'The Plainsmen's Burden', *Economic and Political Weekly*, Vol. 22, No. 48, pp. 2051–53.
Soja, Edward (1989) *Postmodern Geographies*, London, Pluto Press.
Taylor, Charles (1990) 'Modes of Civil Society', *Public Culture*, Vol. 3, No. 1, pp. 95–118.
White, Robert A. (1990) 'Cultural Analysis in Communication for Development – the Role of Cultural Dramaturgy in the Creation of a Public Sphere', *Development: seeds of change*, No. 2, pp. 23–30.

17. Towards Green Villages

Anil Agarwal and Sunita Narain

India faces an extraordinary challenge over the next two decades. The Indian population today is about 800 million. By the end of the century it will be about 1,000 million. Every million hectares of India's land today supports about 2.5 million people and by the end of the century this figure will reach three million.

Studies conducted by Indian environmentalists over the last decade have clearly shown that the majority of the people survive within a biomass-based subsistence economy, that is, on products obtained from plants and animals. Over the coming years, India's demand for food, firewood, fodder, building materials like timber and thatch, industrial raw materials and various such products will grow by leaps and bounds. In the next 10 to 12 years, food-grain production must increase from about 170 million tonnes to about 240 million tonnes. Similarly, production of milk, cotton, rubber, fish and various other sources of food and industrial raw materials must grow rapidly. Almost half the industrial output comes from biomass-based industry and so even industrial output will be seriously affected if biomass production cannot keep pace with the population growth. At the same time, to meet basic survival needs, firewood production must increase from a current production of 100 million tonnes to about 300 million tonnes and green fodder production from about 230 million tonnes to 780 million tonnes.

India's land area is not going to increase and, therefore, these growing demands can be met only if we can find highly productive systems for growing all forms of biomass, from food-grains to grasses and trees, which will be at the same time ecologically-sound and sustainable – not technical systems that give bumper yield today but discount the future. The limited land and water resources will come under increasing pressure to meet these diverse biomass needs. India has to find a strategy to optimize the use of its natural resources in such a way that it can get high productivity as well as sustainability.

This will pose a major scientific, social and political challenge; and in this,

India can learn precious little from the countries of the so-called developed world. As the economies and the populations of the Western world grew, they began to extract resources from other parts of the world. First there was the stage of colonialism. Today, resource extraction is facilitated through the world market system. Western countries are net importers of biomass products from the Third World, not net exporters to the Third World.

An interesting study in the Netherlands has tried to calculate how much land every Dutch person uses on average within the Netherlands and outside it. For every one hectare of land that a Dutch person uses in the Netherlands, he/she uses about five hectares outside, mostly in the Third World. Given the fact that an average Indian is unlikely to pick up the kind of purchasing power achieved by Europeans and North Americans, Indians can hardly import much biomass from abroad for their needs, thus using others' resources. They can mainly consume that biomass which they can grow within their own limited land mass.

Contrary to what the need is, the overall biomass production in India seems to be declining rapidly, despite the so-called Green Revolution, and nearly one-third to one-half of the country can be called a wasteland.

- Production from the forest lands has been steadily decreasing because of the ongoing erosion in the forest cover.
- The productivity of the country's grasslands is today a mere fraction of their biological potential – in most cases less than 20%.
- And in the croplands sector, productivity has increased mainly in the irrigated areas. Many experts believe that it may not be possible to sustain the increased productivity in some of the irrigated croplands over a long period because of growing problems of waterlogging and salinity, micro-nutrient depletion and excessive withdrawal of groundwater. In most non-irrigated areas, productivity continues to be abysmal and subject to the vagaries of the weather.

Thus, of the approximately 260 million hectares of India's land used for biomass production, there has been increased production on only a very small fraction, that is on irrigated croplands. Elsewhere, productivity is still very low or even declining.

To reverse this situation, every inch of land must produce grains, grasses or trees and all hands must be put to this task in a scientific and highly productive manner. But this 21st century problem cannot be solved with 19th century administrative systems and laws and 20th century concepts of economic and social development borrowed from the West.

Economists will have to redefine poverty not as a shortage of cash but as a shortage of biomass resources to meet basic survival needs. This definition will far more accurately measure the acute poverty and drudgery that the poor of India face today. In other words, a concept like the *Gross Nature Product* will be more relevant to measure the survival economy of the rural poor than the prevalent concepts of *Gross National Product* and per capita incomes, all of which have been borrowed from the market economies of the West. If enough biomass was available, poverty as defined by modern economists would not disappear. But the rigours of poverty and increasing susceptibility to natural emergencies like floods and drought will certainly be arrested. Economic growth and rural development programmes must, therefore, focus on one major aim: to increase biomass in an equitable and sustainable manner.

The current political discussion and steps to achieve democratic decentralization and devolution of powers to village communities can be extremely important for this objective. We cannot think of a more important objective for this decentralization process than to mobilize the power and labour of millions of people to regenerate India's land and bring it to its maximum levels of productivity. If its people can do this, the country's land resource base is such that India can feed not only its own growing population but also many other countries of Asia. India has an extremely rich natural resource base, but it is not a fixed asset. It can grow and it can be depleted. India can have a very rich and green future, or become a vast desert. It is for Indians to choose.

Village ecosystem planning

If we were to accept the growth of biomass as a vital objective of India's planned economic programmes, then we must also recognize that India is a country with extremely diverse ecosystems. Within the same country, we can move:

- from the hot desert of Rajasthan to the cold desert of Ladakh;
- from areas with extremely low rainfall, usually less than 200 mm per annum, to areas with extremely high rainfall in the North-East and Kerala, where the average levels can be over 4,000 mm;
- from the sub-temperate high mountains of the Himalayas to the tropical high mountains of the Nilgiris and Palnis in Tamil Nadu.

Between all these systems are numerous plateaux, hill ranges, riverine deltas, extraordinary wetlands like those of the Sundarbans, and, above all, the massive, alluvial Indo-Gangetic Plains whose potential productivity is probably unmatched in the world.

The same kind of biomass cannot be grown on a sustainable basis, in all these ecosystems in the same way. If high biomass productivity is to be obtained in all these ecosystems, every effort must be made to understand the social and ecological dynamics of each ecosystem and to develop biomass production programmes in harmony with the inherent dynamics of these ecosystems. High productivity on a sustainable basis is possible only by observing the laws of nature, not by contravening them. In other words, we will have to develop ecosystem-specific development plans.

The basic precept for ecosystem-specific development is that ecologically sound land use must differ from one ecosystem to another. The landmass within any ecosystem can, for the sake of simplicity, be divided into three basic functional components: croplands; grazing lands; and forest or treelands. The balance between these three components is crucial for ecologically sound land use within any ecosystem.

To understand this, let us look at three of India's different ecosystems: the Indo-Gangetic Plains; the Thar Desert; and the Himalaya. The major component of land use within the Indo-Gangetic Plains can easily be croplands, with forest and grazing lands in a minor and supportive role. In the Himalaya, the major component will have to be forest lands, with grazing and croplands playing a minor role. But in the Thar Desert, the main component will have to be grazing lands with croplands and forest lands in a minor role.

This means that development programmes in each of these ecosystems must be built upon what is ecologically sound land use for that particular ecosystem. The occupational structure will also reflect the ecosystem-specific land use. For instance, in the Indo-Gangetic Plains, people can be mainly farmers. But in the Thar Desert, they will have to adopt a mixed enterprise system in which farming is strongly backed by animal husbandry. And in the Himalaya, farming will have to be combined with forest and tree-based occupations. Thus, India's planning systems must devolve to the level of India's ecosystems so that a framework for ecosystem-specific development can be prepared.

As the action level will be the human settlement – in other words, the hamlet – what needs to be developed at the level of the ecosystem are not detailed plans and programmes, but ecosystem-specific action guidelines which will inform and guide the village-level planning process and action. Any effort to develop ecosystem-level plans will again leave the action with the bureaucracy, making it top-heavy, and maintaining the alienation of the people towards common property resources like ponds, tanks, grazing and forest lands. For instance, a macro-level decision that particular lands be brought under a protected forest cover to maintain ecological balance by declaring them sanctuaries or national parks will immediately lead to tensions with local villagers who will see their basic survival interests being neglected. In other words, the idea of ecosystem-specific development must not translate itself into the establishment of ecosystem-level development authorities like a Thar Development Authority or a Himalaya Development Authority, unless the very purpose of such an agency is to promote grassroots planning and action. To sum up, while an eco-development strategy for the Himalaya as a whole can be envisaged in conceptual terms, the Himalaya will have to be seen as a huge mosaic of several thousands of village ecosystems for the purpose of village level action and planning.

Indian villages are highly integrated agro-sylvo-pastoral systems: each village has its own croplands, grazing lands, and tree or forest lands, and each of these land-use components interacts with each other. What happens in one component invariably impacts on the others.

The entire village ecosystem is often held in fine ecological balance. Trees or forest lands provide firewood. This helps villagers avoid burning cowdung, which in turn helps them maintain the productivity of their croplands where this dung is applied as manure. Simultaneously, trees and crops help complement the grasslands in the supply of fodder for domestic animals. The grasslands generally provide grass during the monsoon period. As grass availability declines with the onset of the dry months, crop residues from croplands and leaf fodder from trees help to tide over the animals in periods of scarcity.

This finely-tuned system can be easily split apart. If too many trees were cut for commercial or other reasons, or growing population pressures forced local people to expand their croplands, thereby reducing the area of adjoining forest and grazing lands, there would be a growing shortage of firewood leading to the use of cowdung as cooking fuel, leaving little manure to fertilize the croplands, thus in the long run reducing their productivity. Moreover, as fodder sources decline, animals will starve and produce little dung anyway. Overall biomass production in the village ecosystem will steadily decline, the system will become increasingly susceptible to the vagaries of the weather (floods and droughts) and the land soon resemble a pseudo-desert. Nearly half of India is, today, a pseudo-desert.

Not only do the various components of the land sub-system interact with each other. The land sub-system itself in turn interacts with the animal, water and energy sub-systems of the overall village ecosystem, and all these sub-systems interact with each other to sustain overall productivity and extend economic and ecological stability. Animals, for instance, not only provide the critical energy input into croplands that is required for ploughing, threshing and other farm operations, they also lend stability to the village economy during a drought period when cropland production is most likely to fail. Similarly, the land sub-system interacts with the water sub-system. When digging ponds and tanks for harvesting water to tide over the dry period, it is equally important to change the land-use of the village ecosystem in order to ensure that the catchment of the tank is protected by trees. Otherwise soil erosion will be excessive and the village community would have to de-silt the tank from time to time.

Indian peasants have always understood these interrelationships and not surprisingly Indian farmers are not just simply agriculturalists but also practised in animal husbandry and sylviculture which require the intensive use of croplands as well as grazing and forest lands adjoining the village. Indian village communities have also been great water harvesters, possibly the best in the world.

What India desperately needs today is the holistic enrichment of its village ecosystems. By holistic we mean an approach which attempts to increase the productivity of all the components of the village ecosystem – from grazing and forest lands to croplands, water systems and animals – and in such a way that this enrichment is sustainable. Current rural development efforts are extremely fragmented, they focus mostly on agriculture, and often the efforts are contradictory and counter-productive. For instance, those who build ponds and tanks do not concern themselves with the implementation of appropriate land use to protect the catchment of these water systems. Those engaged in animal husbandry or in promoting dairying operations pay little attention to increasing fodder supply. The only way to end these fragmented approaches is to promote integrated village ecosystem planning.

This type of planning can be attempted only at the village level, village by village, and not at the level of a district, an ecosystem or a state. There are two important reasons for this. Firstly, there is an enormous diversity in Indian village ecosystems. No entity, even if at the level of a district, can plan for each village. Even within one overall ecosystem, village agro-ecosystems can vary greatly from one another. Within the narrow confines of the high Himalaya, village ecosystems have considerable similarities but also considerable differences.

For example, a village at the bottom of a mountain valley and one situated on the same mountain slope will have widely differing land-use systems. Plans for the ecologically sound development of each of these village ecosystems will necessarily differ and the planning process must be appropriate for the accommodation of these differences. This can be achieved only if the planning was undertaken at the micro-level of a village and not at any macro-level.

Secondly, this complex task of planning for every village can be achieved, and judiciously, only if it is participatory. It can be assisted by government bureaucracies but not done by them. Despite the fact that migration to towns has led to an erosion of villagers' interest in their immediate environment, experience shows that they still relate well to their immediate village ecosystem. And it is at this level they can act most easily and readily, given the appropriate framework for action.

Villagers also relate to their overall ecosystem. A *pahadi* is culturally conscious of the fact that he or she belongs to the Himalaya. A person from the desert also is culturally conscious and proud of the desert culture. But villagers cannot get together to participate effectively in the planning of the entire Thar or the entire Himalaya. We have not found any successful case where even a few villages situated in one micro-watershed have got together to plan for the ecosystem of their watershed. Participatory planning is most feasible and effective at village level. District or any other level planning must support and encourage this village-level, grassroots planning process, not supplant it. Otherwise, participation cannot be assured and biomass regeneration plans will remain ineffective.

The alienated commons

The biggest problem lies in the alienation created by the modern state amongst village communities towards their commons. Before the advent of the modern state, grazing lands, forest lands and water bodies were mostly common property and village communities played an important role in their use and management. The British were the first to nationalize these resources and bring them under the management of government bureaucracies. In other words, the British initiated the policy of converting common property resources into government property resources.

This expropriation has alienated the people from their commons and has started a free-for-all. Today even tribals, who have lived in harmony with forests for centuries, are so alienated that they feel little regret in felling a green tree to sell off for a pittance. Repeatedly, we have been asked by tribal groups, what is the point in saving the forests, because if they don't take them first, the forest contractors would take them away. The desperate economic condition of the poor, made worse by the ecological destruction, has often left them with no other option but to survive by cutting trees. Unless people's alienation from their commons can be arrested and reversed, there cannot be any regeneration of common lands.

Why is people's participation in the regeneration of common lands so crucial?

To answer this question it is important to understand the key obstacle to environmental regeneration. *India's ecology is such that any piece of land, left to itself, will soon get converted into a forest except in a few desert districts of Western Rajasthan and in the upper reaches of the Himalayan mountains.*

The birds and the wind are excellent and extremely powerful disseminators of seeds, which human beings can never hope to match. Unfortunately, the natural regeneration taking place is constantly suppressed. The main agent for this suppression is India's vast stock of domestic animals.

Therefore, all new plantations and grasslands have to be protected from animals, especially if the biomass that is sought to be grown is browsable, that is, biomass capable of meeting the crucial need of fodder. But since all common lands have intense users, any attempt to enclose a patch of degraded land will be strongly resented, however underproductive it may be, for fear of loss of grazing land and sources of firewood. And all such attempts will be subverted by the poor unless – and this is crucial – they are fully assured that the biomass grown inside those enclosures will meet their felt needs on the basis of priority and equity.

Without people's support, then either the survival rates will be extremely poor, or non-browsable plants like eucalyptus will continue to be planted – a technical fix for a social problem. In fact, both the above things are happening today. Over 90% of all the tree seedlings planted today under official programmes are non-browsable. The major species are eucalyptus, pine, teak, *Prosopis juliflora*, *Acacia auriculiformis* (Australian acacia or akashmoni) and casuarina – all non-browsable. Despite this the survival rates are extremely poor.

Between 1980 and 1988, India's state forest departments claim that together they distributed over 2,000 crore seedlings. Given that India has about 570,000 villages, there should be over 35,000 new trees per village today, but rarely can this large number of new trees be found in any Indian village.

In any case, of what benefit are such plantations in periods of drought? During the acute 1987 drought, the vast social forestry plantations of Gujarat, mainly eucalyptus, could do nothing to meet the fodder crisis. Fodder had to come all the way from Punjab.

In fact, India's afforestation programmes have become a travesty for employment creation. It was probably Keynes, the famous economist, who once said that unproductive employment can easily be created. Simply dig a hole, fill it up, dig it up again and keep doing this. Afforestation is exactly such an exercise today. Dig a hole in the ground, put a seedling in the middle and fill it up with earth. The seedling will soon die and we will start digging up the earth again. *Official figures show huge forests emerging while the earth remains barren and degraded.*

The same will happen to any major programme to dig ponds and tanks until the villagers are prepared to protect their catchments. They will soon silt up and new programmes will be needed to dig them again.

The upshot of all this is that *ecologically vital but fragile rural resources like trees, grasses, ponds and tanks cannot be created and maintained by any bureaucracy, it can be done only by the rural people.* Every year nearly half of India is planted with wheat, rice, maize and other crops, which are equally fragile rural resources, but they do survive because of the rural people's extraordinary effort to ensure their survival. If all farms in India were to be

managed by the Central and State Krishi Bhawans, there can be no doubt
that Indians would starve. Then why should forests and grasslands be
managed by the bureaucracy?

That people must be involved in afforestation is now widely accepted. But
how is this to be done?

Privatization or the community way?

There are two basic ways of dealing with this problem. The first would be to
take a cue from the successes that have taken place in promoting biomass
production on private croplands. Let us also privatize the common lands
and then provide the beneficiaries with a technical and financial package
which promises them a good income and we can be sure they will come
forward.

The best government programmes we have seen are based on the principle
of privatizing the commons. Various state governments have developed
programmes to lease revenue as well as forest land for afforestation. In all
these schemes, the basic approach is to give ownership rights to a few
families, either to the land itself or to the produce from the land. These
families then have a vested interest in protecting the trees.

There are several such afforestation schemes in the country, like the Tree
Patta Scheme in different states in which a family is leased the trees but not
the land. Some states like Maharashtra, Madhya Pradesh and Rajasthan
have adopted a scheme called the Social Security Scheme, in which
government forest land is leased to a poor family for afforestation. The
family is then given a monthly stipend for five years for afforesting and
protecting the land. And every year the family gets an additional one or two
hectares to plant and protect, taking the total leased area to 15 to 20 hectares
over time. The beneficiary family has full rights over the grass and all other
produce from the trees, except timber, which it shares with the forest
department.

The state of West Bengal, which has a successful social forestry
programme, has combined its afforestation programme with its ongoing
programme of land distribution. Poor, landless families are granted pattas
for plots of government land, but as these lands are usually highly laterized
and degraded, afforestation agencies encourage them to plant trees instead
of growing crops, which is usually impossible. These poor families have
carefully protected the afforested land and ensured the survival of trees.

This approach has major problems. In a densely populated country like
India the privatization approach effectively reduces access to the commons
for a large number of village people while giving control to a few members of
the community. There is not enough land to benefit all the poor on a private

basis. There will always be some poor people left out. Given that these lands are vital for the survival of the poor landless and marginal farmers who use them for fodder, fuel, grazing and other subsistence needs, they will be adversely affected by the reduction of common lands.

In Rajasthan, we found that a beneficiary family of the government's Social Security Scheme had become a target for those in the community who could no longer benefit from the privatized commons. Under the Social Security Scheme, the forest department had given forest land to a landless family for afforestation. The family had protected the area, which was extremely degraded, and in the height of the 1986 drought had even harvested grass from the plot. But they faced intense antagonism from the rest of the villagers who could no longer use this land for grazing. The family had been cut off by the village community and could not participate in community functions like marriages or festivals. We can expect similar resentment wherever the commons are already under heavy pressure and scarce, and further privatization is permitted to undertake ecological regeneration.

In the plateau region of West Bengal, which covers Midnapore, Purulia and Bankura, the people face an acute energy and fodder crisis. Women take brooms to sweep the forest floor to collect leaves and twigs for burning. Land is mostly privatized but there are many marginal and landless farmers whose only source of energy is from the common lands. The state has very little revenue land left. This intensifies the use of forest land by the villagers and their animals. The state government, enthused by the response to the farm forestry programme, was even considering leasing degraded forest land to private families to protect. The degraded forest area in West Bengal is around 0.65 million hectares and even if two hectares of forest land was allotted to each family to grow trees, only four per cent of the total rural families would benefit while the remaining people, all dependent on these lands, would lose out. This situation would obviously create immense conflicts.

The second, and admittedly more difficult, option is to retain the commons as commons and manage them by organizing and mobilizing village communities to develop the commons as a community enterprise. This is socially and ecologically the best option but obviously difficult. This, however, is not to say that it cannot be done. The best efforts in the country to manage the environment show it is indeed possible but provided the three principles of control, co-operation and equity are observed.

1. *The commons must be brought under the control of the village communities.* This will mean divesting government agencies of their control over the common lands through changes in legislation. But this does not necessarily mean transfer of ownership.

2. *The entire community must be involved in the protection of the commons under its control.* If only a section of the community is involved in the protection of a patch of the commons, then that section of the community must have clear control over a definite patch of the commons. In other words, the legal situation must be clear and whichever group controls a portion of the commons, it must control it completely and protect it jointly. If only a few members of a group are left to protect a common resource against the wishes of the rest, they will fail. It does not matter whose goat enters the protected patch, the damage will be the same. All have to keep their animals away.

3. *All the members of a group will protect a common resource only if all of them know that they will benefit from the resource equally.*

These principles of *control*, *co-operation* and *equity* may sound difficult to implement in practice. But the experiences of voluntary groups across the country show that given the right leadership and the suitable legal framework for community action, villagers will come together to protect and manage village resources. This chapter sets out the institutional, legal and financial framework in which this may become possible – the chance for India to become green, improve the standard of living for its people, and revive the dying community spirit.

Lessons from traditional knowledge

Every Indian schoolchild is taught about the unity in India's diverse cultures. But few are taught why we have such diverse cultures. Cultural diversity is not an historical accident, it is the direct outcome of the country's extraordinary biological diversity. Until the global 'multinational culture' fuelled by the Industrial Revolution hit the world, each culture – in India, as much as in the rest of the world – was the result of the people trying to survive within their immediate environment and indeed of an attempt to optimize the resources of their environment. The people of Rajasthan developed nomadism and animal care-based occupations because the land was fragile and could not be used intensively. The people of Miziram and Nagaland developed shifting cultivation as their system of survival, because they had to live on slopes and this was the best way to maintain their fertility. Lifestyles and production systems like these developed steadily through experimentation and observation over centuries till they became so culturally imbibed that they became almost like genetic knowledge – knowledge that is coded into each one of us and which we practise every day, but of which we rarely know the basis.

Traditional land use and occupational structures have invariably been locale-specific and also invariably ecologically sound. Today, however, all these systems are either being negated or directly destroyed by modern development programmes, often in the name of scientific progress. Modern science is usually logical and rational but its application has become the 'new superstition' – 'it has to be applied' is the refrain and it is done without much thought being given to its social and ecological context.

Traditional knowledge is vital because of its ecological rationality – its inspiration being the sustainable use of the ecosystem in which it has developed. Over the years, we have come to see several outstanding examples of traditional systems – in land use, in water use and water harvesting, in agriculture and animal care, in food preservation, herbal medicine, and so on. For example, Indians have traditionally been great water harvesters – possibly the best in the world. All across the country there are numerous traditional technologies to collect and store rain water. But probably the most fascinating traditional water harvesting system is that of Jodhpur – a major city of the dry Thar Desert. During the 1980s, the city repeatedly faced acute water shortages – as indeed most desert cities do nowadays. But most desert cities like Jodhpur, Bikaner and Jaisalmer are old. How did they ensure water for their citizens when there were no pipelines, tankers, tubewells and power stations? Drought was not an unusual phenomenon in the desert even then. And there is no recorded instance in history when these cities had to be depopulated because of lack of water.

What we have discovered is that Jodhpur once had an outstanding system of water harvesting which has been mercilessly destroyed over the years. The city is situated at the end of a rocky plateau, which constituted the main catchment for its water supply. Long canals were built, running over kilometres, all along the catchment area which transported the rain water to the city where it was stored in numerous tanks. The most important tank in the city is Ranisar, which was built by Maharani Jodha in 1500, and is situated inside the ramparts of the Jodhpur fort because of its strategic importance.

The fort is on a high hill, and the canals draining water from the hilly region near the city feed Ranisar. The overflow runs into another tank, called Padamsar, which was traditionally used by the public. As both Ranisar and Padamsar are situated at a high elevation, the seepage from these tanks was further collected through an extensive system of wells and step wells in the city, thus ensuring that both surface and ground waters were fully utilized. Each locality in the city had its own well or *bawdi* (step well), often with steps going down three to four storeys underground so that people could collect the water. Each *bawdi* was elaborately carved and beautifully decorated. In addition to Ranisar and Padamsar, there were many other tanks in the city similarly fed by canals draining large upland areas surrounding the city. At the start of the century, the city of Jodhpur had nearly 200 water sources – about 50 tanks, 50 step wells and 70 wells. Inside the houses, people collected the rain water from roof-tops through devices called 'tankas'. These were underground storage tanks within the house, and the rain water from the roof was carefully channelled into them. Today there is little left of these systems.

Yet another area of traditional knowledge, full of ingenious innovations, is agroforestry.The Thar Desert farmer has several conservationist practices to preserve all possible sources of fodder. Rainfall levels fluctuate drastically from one year to another and so does agricultural production. People, therefore, rely heavily on animal care-based occupations for their survival. This in turn demands that sources of fodder be well-protected.

Bhanwarlal Kothari of the Rajasthan Go Sewa Sangh in Bikaner says that people survive in the Thar Desert because of three things – the sewan grass, the khejari tree and its excellent breeds of cattle. The Thar Desert has three excellent sources of fodder – sewan grass (*Lasirius sindicus*), a bush called 'jharberi' (*Zizyphus mummularia*), and a tree called 'khejari' (*Prosopis cineraria*). Sewan is extremely nutritious, it grows in clumps and can grow fast even with little rainfall. The dried leaves of the jharberi bush provide excellent fodder during the dry months when no fresh fodder is available. The farmers cut the bush, let the leaves dry and then just shake them on to the ground. Similarly, the khejari provides excellent top feed for livestock during dry periods.

These trees and plants were purposefully maintained even on farm lands. The density of the khejari tree in the 300 mm to 500 mm rainfall zone of the Thar Desert is about 40 to 100 trees per hectare, thus giving agricultural areas the appearance of an open woodland. Khejari was rarely planted, but grew mainly through natural regeneration. Farmers cared for and rarely cut or uprooted it. Similarly, while ploughing the Thar Desert farmers never uprooted the clumps of jharberi or sewan. Thus, the grassland character of the desert was maintained and when the rains were inadequate and crops withered the fodder was still assured from these grasses and bushes.

But in the last 40 years this has changed. The cultivated area in West Rajasthan has grown from 36 per cent of the total area in 1956–57 to 46 per cent in 1977–78. The use of tractors has also increased rapidly from about 698 in 1956 to nearly 20,000 now. Tractors have become popular because large areas can be ploughed and sowed quickly during the short period of moisture availability in the top soil. But while the desert farmer would take his plough around the clumps of sewan and jharberi and the young khejari trees, the tractors recognize no such thing. Thus, repeated use of tractors has eliminated sewan clumps and roots of jharberi over vast areas of the desert; and trees have had to be cut to facilitate easy movement of tractors. The permanent sources of fodder have therefore been largely lost. And now, when the drought comes, the people of Rajasthan wait for trucks from Punjab to bring rice straw for their cattle.

The sewan pastures now remain only in the most inhospitable and dry parts of the desert. In 1986, ironically, it was these distant and remote pastures of the Jaisalmer district that gave 8,000 tonnes of grass fodder to nine western districts of Rajasthan. Elsewhere, in the desert, the picture is of severe ecological degradation.

What do these examples show? Firstly, that traditional systems are extremely important even in this so-called world of modern science and technology. Their ecological rationality remains valid even in the modern context. The Khonoma example shows that people are innovating even today in response to the challenges they face. Wherever modern technology has been introduced, without testing it for its ecological rationality, societies have suffered – often gravely. Because productivity is also important in a world where population, and consequently human demands are growing, modern science and technology is needed. But it must build upon traditional systems keeping intact their ecological rationality. This is the true challenge before modern science.

If the country's biomass production is to be increased on a sustainable basis, India will have to adopt an ecosystem-specific strategy for development which takes into account the specific strengths and weaknesses of the local natural resource base. If it were to do that, traditional knowledge would have to be the starting point, especially in the areas of land use, water use and agroforestry systems.

Where all decide

The village of Seed near Udaipur provides an excellent example of how the village ecosystem can be managed by an executive gram sabha. The village is registered under the Rajasthan Gramdan Act of 1971 – a unique act in the country which gives executive and legal powers to the village gram sabha. The Act, inspired by Vinoba Bhave, permits a village to declare itself a Gramdan village. And once it is so accepted, the Act allows the village gram sabha to manage all the natural resources within the village boundary; it also has powers to judge, penalize and prosecute.

As a Gramdan village, the gram sabha of Seed has full control over all the land within the village boundary, including erstwhile government lands, and exercises full control over their use. The gram sabha of the village consists of all adults in the village. It has devised clear rules for the protection of the village common lands. It is the only village in the country that we have seen which has a clear land-use plan and rules to enforce that plan. The common lands have been divided into two categories – one consists of lands on which both grazing and leaf collection are banned; and the second consists of lands on which grazing is permitted but leaf collection or harming trees is banned. The first category of land is lush green and full of grass which villagers cut only once a year. In the denuded Aravalis, this area looks like an oasis of green. Even during the unprecedented drought of 1987, Seed was able to harvest 80 bullock-cartloads of grass, worth about Rs. 50,000 on the market. The grass was distributed equitably amongst all the households.

Seed's gram sabha does not allow even trees on private lands to be cut. Prior permission from the gram sabha is required and granted only if the owner needs the wood for domestic reasons but not for sale. The gram sabha also has a system of penalties to enforce disciplined use of the village trees and grasslands. Seed became a Gramdan village only in the early 1980s yet in the first few years, the gram sabha had levied and collected fines worth nearly Rs. 5,000 – an enormous sum for a poor tribal village – for cutting trees, grazing in prohibited areas and for even breaking leaves. Often, the fines were levied on people from neighbouring villages who strongly resented the fact that Seed's commons were now closed to them.

The experience of Seed shows clearly how Gandhiji's concept of village republics can work for ecological regeneration: each village with an active community forum and an ecosystem of its own to control, manage and share, in which common resources are developed and improved and all get their due benefits. We are absolutely convinced – after observing the environmental scene in India for over 15 years – that there is no alternative to this concept. Increasingly we are convinced that the most sophisticated decision-making will begin only when village people start sitting under banyan trees as a group to discuss their problems and find common solutions. Only this form of decentralized decision-making can match the enormous cultural and biological diversity of Indian villages. People sitting in closed rooms in distant Central and State capitals or even district headquarters can only produce monolithic nonsense which will have little relevance on the ground.

This chapter is an adapted extract from the report 'Towards Green Villages. A Strategy for Environmentally Sound and Participatory Rural Development'. The complete and illustrated edition is available from the Centre for Science and Environment, F-6, Kailash Colony, New Delhi 110 048, India.

Index

patent laws, 126, 127
patriarchy, 211
Pearce Report, 91
people depletion, 136
permafrost, 77
Phasepardhi peoples, 225
Philippines, 52
planetary brain, 188
Plato, 160
poaching, 209
pollen, examination of, 139
'polluter pays' principle, 82
pollution, 73, 135; of water, 33;
    pesticides, 34
Popper, Karl, 183
population, growth of, 53, 135, 153, 246;
    control of, 33
poverty, 8, 53; as pollutant, 224;
    elimination of, 10; redefinition of, 243
Prakriti, 200
Prigogine, Ilya, 183, 185, 190
privatization, 250-2
productivism, 5
progress: concept of, 105; motivation of,
    114
Progressive Conservation, 197
property rights, 62
punya concept of, 226

Rajasthan Gramdan Act (1971) (India),
    255
Ratzel, Friedrich, 50
Raubwirtschaft, 50, 52
Reagan, Ronald, 107
refugees, environmental, 84
religion, African, 218
resistance, forms of, 158
resistance movements, ecological, 229
resources: constraints of, 54; efficiency of,
    16; limits of, 27; natural, 50, 55
Rhodes, Cecil, 107
Rifkin, 185
Rio Declaration, 3, 37
rivers, sacred nature of, 232
roads, building of, 8, 24
robotics, 184
rubber tappers' movement (Amazonia),
    238
Rufin, Jean-Christophe, 186, 187
Rural Development Bank (Mexico), 27
Russel, Peter, 184, 188, 190
Russia, 75

sacred groves, 197-207; maintaining of,
    225
Sagan, Dorion, 190
Sahu, Raghaba, 203

sal, growing of, 232
salinity, 243
Sandbrook, Richard, 133
Santal Hul revolt, 230
sardine industry, 141
satellites, observation by, 18, 19, 30
satyagrahas, 229
Saudi Arabia, 3
scarcity, 104-16; as social construction,
    109-10
schistosomiasis, 76
Schmidheiny, Stephan, 47, 92
Schneider, Bertrand, 97-8
scientists, 40, 172
sea ice, as animal habitat, 70
sea levels, effect of rise of, 71 *see also*
    flooding
Seattle, Chief, 110
El Serafy, Salah, 94
Serres, Michel, 184
service sector, 15; limits of, 16
sewan grass, 254, 255
Sharma, B.D., 231
Shell company, 151
shifting cultivation, 212, 252
Shiva, Vandana, 228
Shona culture, 218
Singapore, 56, 58, 65
Singer, Isaac Bashevis, 62
Smith, Adam, 108
snow cover, changes in, 77
Social Security Scheme (India), 250, 251
soil: compaction of, 27; depletion of, 136
solidarity, international, 86
South Commission, Report of, 97
South, distorted images of, 171
space, travel in, 18
Spirit Medium, invocation of, 218
Stockholm Conference, 36, 40
Strong, Maurice, 36-7, 38, 42, 46, 47
Subarnarekha Multi Purpose Project, 230
sustainability, physiological, 135
sustainable development *see* development
Sweden, 51
Szasz, Andrew, 26

tanks, water, construction of, 253
Tanzania, 213-15, 222
Tata Iron and Steel Company, 227
techno-nature, 184
technology, 123, 158, 255; challenge of,
    100; clean, 14; transfer of, 4, 9, 16,
    100, 153
temperature, increases of, 73
Thailand, 55, 56, 57
Thar Desert, 254
Thienemann, A.F., 124

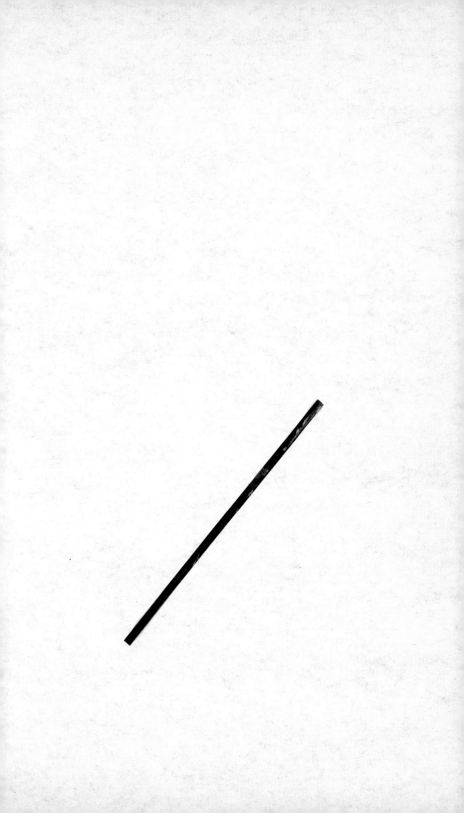